NEVER GIVE UP!
The Life of Pearl Carter Scott

▼▼▼

By PAUL F. LAMBERT

The Chickasaw Press

*This book is dedicated to the family
of Pearl Carter Scott, to the people of Pearl's hometown,
Marlow, and to the citizens of the Chickasaw Nation.*
▼▼▼

CONTENTS

▼▼▼

PREFACE AND ACKNOWLEDGEMENTS

▼▼▼

When I visited with Bill Anoatubby, Governor of the Chickasaw Nation, about the possibility of writing a book for the Chickasaw Press, he immediately began telling me about Pearl Scott. As he related the story of a Chickasaw girl who drove her own car to school at age eleven and who was taught to fly by Wiley Post at age twelve, he captured my interest immediately. When he related some of the other details of her remarkable life, I knew I wanted to be her biographer. Governor Anoatubby and the Chickasaw Nation made that possible, and I appreciate that opportunity.

When I began this project, I had no way of knowing that I would have only about three months to work with Pearl. Fortunately, I was able to have several long interview sessions with her, and her memory and sense of humor remained strong to the end. In addition, my research was augmented significantly by interviews with Pearl's son Bill and her daughter Louise. Other members of the Scott family, including Pearl's brother George Carter, Jr. provided important information and perspective. Many of Pearl's long-time friends, both in Marlow and in Ada, were interviewed, and I am grateful to all of those individuals. Pearl also wrote about her life on several occasions and I was fortunate to have access to all of her personal materials and photographs. All of this information helped me piece together the life of an amazing woman who went from "riches to rags to riches" during the course of her eventful life.

I also want to acknowledge the outstanding editorial work of Dr. Tim Zwink and Dr. Bob Blackburn. Their review of my manuscript greatly improved its readability and significantly reduced the number of errors of various types. Gary Childers of the Chickasaw Nation also read the manuscript at an early stage and offered helpful suggestions and information. Any remaining mistakes that may remain are, of course, strictly the responsibility of the author.

Late in life Pearl's aviation exploits were recognized by her induction into the Oklahoma Aviation and Space Hall of Fame, and her outstanding service to her people was honored by her induction into the Chickasaw Nation Hall of Fame. In conjunction with the Wiley Post Commission, the Chickasaw Nation continued to recognize Pearl posthumously by establishing an annual scholarship for a Chickasaw student interested in pursuing a career in aviation. In addition, in recognition of a generous contribution by the Chickasaw Nation, the pilots' lounge in the Curtiss-Wright Wiley Post Hangar in Oklahoma City will be named in Pearl's honor when the hangar restoration project is completed.

An aviation pioneer, a devoted mother, and a dedicated public servant, Pearl Scott of Marlow, Oklahoma, lived a life worth remembering. She was a paragon of courage, love of family, and devotion to helping others. This is her story.

Paul F. Lambert,
Oklahoma City

NEVER GIVE UP!
The Life of Pearl Carter Scott

▼▼▼

Chapter One
▼▼▼

GEORGE
AND LUCY

O ne morning in 1928 near Marlow, Oklahoma, flying in a Curtis
Robin monoplane equipped with dual controls, Slim Marshall decided to test the nerve of the young, student pilot who was with him that
day. She was a twelve-year-old Chickasaw girl named Eula Pearl Carter.
Marshall had Eula Pearl put the plane in a spin, headed straight for the
ground. Just three-hundred feet from impact, Marshall took control of
the plane and pulled out of the dive while his diminutive student laughed
at him! When they landed, Marshall told Eula Pearl that he would never
try to scare her or test her nerve again because she had more nerve than
anyone he had ever seen. When her aviation mentor, a one-eyed flyer
who was destined to become internationally renowned, heard about this
incident, he scolded the girl sternly for being too much of a daredevil. Her
mentor was Wiley Post.[1]

Pearl, as she preferred to be called, would prove to be unique in many
ways throughout her life. Her aviation exploits eventually would earn
her a place in the Oklahoma Aviation Hall of Fame, and her lifetime accomplishments would be recognized by induction into the Chickasaw Nation Hall of Fame. Her story could be described as a "riches to rags to
riches" story, with the "riches" of her later years consisting of the love of
her family and the overwhelming satisfaction she received from helping
others. Her motto, "Never give up!" was inspired by Post and her remark-

George Carter and Lucy Gibson at the time of their wedding in 1910. It ap-
pears that Lucy may have acquired a new hat for the occasion. (Courtesy Joseph
Carter Brooks)

▼▼▼

able family. But her amazing father, supported by her devoted mother, had the most impact in shaping Pearl's character and values.

Pearl's maternal grandparents both were full-blood Indians. Her grandfather, Silas Gibson, was an enrolled Choctaw while her grandmother, Minnie Gibson, was an enrolled Chickasaw. Pearl's Choctaw and Chickasaw ancestors had arrived in Indian Territory because they were forced by the federal government to abandon their ancestral homes in the Southeastern United States. Although the Chickasaws' removal experience was not as severe as that of some other tribes, the Chickasaw Nation certainly endured its own "Trail of Tears" in being uprooted from its ancestral homelands.[2]

Silas Gibson was born near Pauls Valley, Indian Territory. His parents, Issac and Lucinda Gibson, had migrated there from Mississippi, and it was there that he met and married Minnie Mike in 1876. Minnie was born in Indian Territory between 1859 and 1862. Her mother, She-Min-Tah or She-Minth-A, apparently was a widow when she arrived in Indian Territory, and it is believed that her husband died en route to the new homeland. Minnie never knew her father. Minnie and Silas Gibson had eight children, seven of whom survived. They were Mitchell, Josiah, Robert, Lucinda, Jane, Mississippi, and Rhodie. Lucinda, named after her mother, was born in 1894 in Tishomingo, capital of the Chickasaw Nation. The Gibsons called their daughter "Lucy" to distinguish her from her mother, and the nickname remained with her throughout her life.[3]

By the early 1900s, Lucy had moved with her family to what would become Stephens County, settling near the Foster community. Lucy and her siblings attended the one-room Sand Hill School, located east of Marlow. While in school, Lucy met a Marlow businessman named George Washington Carter, who operated a livery stable and rented pasture for his horses from Lucy's father. Also, when the family would travel by wagon to Marlow, usually on a Saturday, they would leave their horse and wagon at George's livery stable. A white resident of the area, George was born at Booneville, Arkansas, in 1886 and had moved to the Marlow area in 1906 from the Choctaw Nation. [4]

George's mother, Amanda Lominick Carter, was from a southern family with roots in Alabama and Georgia, as was his father, James

Pearl's maternal grandparents were Minnie and Silas Gibson. Minnie was Chickasaw and Silas was Choctaw. The couple had eight children, one of whom was Lucinda "Lucy" Gibson, who became Pearl's mother. (Courtesy Marlow Chamber of Commerce)

Madison Carter. Several ancestors of James Carter fought for the Confederate States of America during the Civil War. Like the Gibson family, and typical of the era, the Carter family was large, consisting of five daughters and three sons.[5]

George's life was altered dramatically at age sixteen. He and his brothers, Arthur and Charles, were helping with the broomcorn harvest on the family farm. During the course of the harvest, the boys' eyes became irritated by broomcorn chaff. The irritation perhaps changed into an infection as it was determined that they had "pink eye." A doctor was summoned to treat their sore eyes. He decided to put drops in their eyes. For some reason, Charlie decided that he did not want to be treated by the doctor, and he hid until the doctor departed. Arthur and George, however, did have drops put into their eyes. Their mother, Amanda, was horrified when blood began to pour from the boys' eyes! Both boys were blinded by the drops. Charlie recovered from the "pink eye" without benefit of the doctor's services. As a result of this family tragedy, Pearl would have a lifelong fear of having drops put in her eyes for any purpose.[6]

After recovering from their initial shock and grief, James and Amanda realized that Arthur and George had to receive specialized training to enable them to lead as normal and productive lives as possible. Consequently, the boys became students at the Arkansas School for the Blind, located at Little Rock, Arkansas. There George learned to read and write in Braille, to use a typewriter, and to write his name. Among his teachers was Emile Trebing, a partially-sighted instructor of music described by students as a "big, jolly, lovable teddy bear" who could play numerous instruments. George learned how to play and to tune a piano and developed a lifelong love of music. At the school, George also gained the confidence he needed to move ahead with his life, determined to achieve all the success that a sighted person could obtain.[7]

By 1906 the Carter family had moved to the Marlow area, and George Carter married a Chickasaw woman named Sarah Brown, who died before they could have children. George inherited the land that had been allotted to his first wife. He established a livery stable in Marlow and operated it with the help of his brother-in-law, Mike Harbour, and a secretary. George was a short man who "walked tall" with his head up. He walked straight, with confidence, and never used a cane. He was never heard to complain about his blindness, and he never considered himself handicapped.[8]

Pearl's paternal grandmother was Amanda Lominick Carter, shown here with her two oldest grandchildren, Ovid Bayliss and Opaletta Carter in 1912. Opaletta was the first of George and Lucy Carter's children. (Courtesy Art Williamson)

Lucy Gibson was impressed by the confident, young businessman when she met him at his livery stable. And George was intrigued by the friendly, young lady. The fact that they both loved music—Lucy also played piano—and that they enjoyed talking to each other allowed their relationship to blossom into love. They were married on June 12, 1910, and established residence at George's home northwest of Marlow. George was twenty-five years old and Lucy was fifteen when they were married.[9]

After his marriage to Lucy, George continued to operate his livery stable. He had a black horse named Coley that he rode unaccompanied to work each day. The horse knew the way to the livery stable and took George there every morning without fail. At the end of the day, George would mount Coley, and the horse carried his master home. When the

Marlow was a typical rural Oklahoma community when the Carter family moved there in 1906. This is view of the Hodnett store in 1909, which sold agricultural implements and other items. (Courtesy Oklahoma Historical Society)

Carters moved to town, the amazing Coley was sold to the United States Cavalry at Fort Sill, located at Lawton, Oklahoma.[10]

George and Lucy began their family with the birth of a daughter, Opaletta, on June 19, 1912. Subsequent children were born at approximate three-year intervals: Eula Pearl, December 9, 1915; Jewell Arnetta, April 22, 1918; and George, Jr., August 31, 1921. The Carters later adopted a Choctaw boy named Willie Wilson, who would become an equally loved member of the family. Willie was born in 1910, so he became the older brother to the Carter children.[11]

While still operating his livery stable, George, Sr., began acquiring land either by leasing or purchasing and having it farmed by share croppers. By the time Pearl was born in 1915, the Carters had moved to town. George had transitioned into being a "land man" because the livery stable business was quickly being killed by the increased use of automobiles and pickup trucks. For a time, during the transition he sold Oakland automobiles.[12]

The Oakland Motor Car Company had been founded by Edward M. Murphy in 1907 in Pontiac, Michigan. Previously, he had operated the

Oakland Buggy Company, and he quickly realized that automobiles were the technology of the future. By 1909 General Motors had acquired a 50 percent interest in the company and upon Murphy's death in 1910 obtained complete control of the company. General Motors marked cars with the Oakland brand until 1932, when the Oakland Division was merged into Pontiac. As a dealer, George kept promotional literature on hand, and as needed he hired drivers to deliver cars from Michigan to Marlow.[13]

The livery stable at 115 ½ West Main Street was remodeled to serve as George's office for his automobile business and for his real estate business. He transitioned out of the automobile business as his real estate and agricultural ventures grew. As he acquired property, he would mortgage it and use the proceeds to purchase more land. He also leased a great deal of land, often from Indians who did not wish to farm the land themselves. Crops such as broomcorn, cotton, watermelons, and other vegetables were grown by share croppers, who received houses in which to live and "shares" of the proceeds from the sale of the crops at harvest time. He also acquired business buildings and rent houses in town.[14]

As George's business grew, he became known for his bright yellow houses both in town and in the countryside in Stephens and Grady counties. Some speculated that he painted them such a bright yellow because even he could see them! Others theorized that he simply got a good deal on a large quantity of yellow paint. Whatever the reason, as one Marlow resident noted, "Any time you were out in the country riding around on a horse and you saw a yellow house, you would say 'that belongs to George Carter.'" To maintain his rent houses and other buildings, George purchased two trucks and employed two men full time. He also had a carpenter on duty full time to work on his properties. For efficiency, all of his rent houses were built on the same floor plan.[15]

Perhaps because of his marriage to Lucy and the fact that he treated them fairly, he was trusted by the Indian families in the area. In many instances, he leased their land and did not take advantage of them. Pearl recalled that, "He could speak the Indian language as well as he could English," which likely meant that he was conversant in both Chickasaw and Choctaw, as the languages are closely related. Consequently, Indians in the area often came to him for advice on various matters. His relationship with the Indians in the area and his ability to speak the language caused at least some Marlow residents to assume that he was at least part Choctaw or Chickasaw.[16]

George was known for his fair treatment of his tenants and share croppers and thus was liked and respected by his tenants. During the Great Depression of the 1930s, he helped many families in the area by purchasing food and clothing for them. Some he helped with cash. Pearl recalled that she and her brothers and sisters were encouraged to give some of their excess clothing to those in need. The compassion that George and his family exhibited made a lasting impression on many. Years later, in 1998, Pearl met an "old man" at a church function in Marlow. When he heard that Pearl's maiden name was Carter, he indicated that his parents used to rent from a blind man named Carter. After Pearl informed him that he was speaking about her father, the man exclaimed, "That was the best man I have ever seen in my life!" He said that his father had repaired the rent house in which they were living, and when it came time to pay the annual rent, George told his father that, "You don't owe me a penny of rent" because of the improvements that had been made. Farmers and tenants frequently brought sweet potatoes, pumpkins, watermelons, peas, and corn to George because they liked and respected him.[17]

George became highly influential in community affairs in Marlow, serving for a time as justice of the peace, playing a major role in getting one of his best friends elected sheriff, helping his brother-in-law Bill Bayliss get elected mayor, and assisting in the selection of the town's law enforcement officers. He had his office set up to function as a court room in which, as a justice of the peace, he held court and conducted civil marriage ceremonies.[18]

While George was a serious businessman and town leader, he did like to relax on occasion. In later years, Pearl recalled that "about once a year" he and his friends Horace Dyer and Walter Blalock got drunk. They would lock the door to the stairs leading up to George's office and get loud, talking and laughing.[19]

Carter operated his business with the assistance of a secretary. Over the years, both Gladys and Lelia Gandy worked as his secretary at different times.

People often were amazed by George because he often greeted them by name when they entered his office and would recognize them by the unique sound of their footfalls on the steps leading to his second floor office. He knew by memory the legal descriptions of all the land that he owned or leased. Moreover, he knew where everything in his office was located. His secretary maintained the office carefully and informed him if anything of significance in the office had to be moved. Consequently, he knew how many steps were required to go to any point in his office, and he walked confidently without a cane. Visitors who did not know in advance that George was blind often did not realize that he had such a handicap.[20]

After the couple purchased a car, Lucy would drive George to his office in the morning and park in the same place in front of his office door. George knew how many steps it was to his office door. He would walk into his building, go up the steps to his desk, and get his work day started without any guidance. In the evening, Lucy again would park on the curb in front of his office door and honk the car horn. Soon George would exit the building, walk to the car, and get into the passenger seat for the ride home.[21]

While George was becoming a widely respected and admired man in the Marlow community, he was loved as a husband and father at home. Lucy Carter and the children were careful to keep the furniture and other items in their home in the same place and to inform George if anything was moved. He knew his way around the house and could easily move from room to room without assistance. Moreover, he was independent in many other ways. For example, he kept a pocket watch which had a lid over its face. The crystal of the watch, however, had been removed. He could open his watch, feel the hands, and know by touch the time immediately. George also handled money without difficulty. He knew that pennies and dimes were about the same size, but dimes had ridges while pennies are smooth on their edges. He kept his paper money separated, with ones in one pocket, fives in another.[22]

When George and Lucy first moved to town, they lived in a large, two-story house on North Second Street. Soon, George began building a larger, two-story home at 411 North Second Street. While the house was under

One of the crops grown on land controlled by George Carter was broomcorn, a crop that was used, as its name implies, to make brooms. Approximately one ton of the panicles from the plant were required to make 1,000 brooms. Until synthetic materials became available for use in making brooms, broomcorn was a major crop in the United States and was grown widely, along with cotton, in much of Oklahoma. Here harvested broomcorn is being brought to Marlow in horse-drawn wagons in 1919. (Courtesy Oklahoma Historical Society)

construction, a tornado roared through that part of Marlow and demolished the structure. The devastation made quite an impression on George and the entire family, causing him to modify his plans for the house. It became a one-story structure with extraordinarily thick walls.[23]

The home had a large basement room with a washing machine and a "mangle" for ironing sheets. A large, two-room cellar was connected to the basement by a forty-foot tunnel. The cellar rooms were equipped with beds, electric lights, and kerosene lanterns. The cellar also featured an escape hatch in the event that a tornado might cause the house to collapse and otherwise trap them. Anytime a storm blew in, the Carters retreated to their cellar and often would just retire for the night. Pearl was about five years old when the tornado struck, and for the remainder of her life she was terrified of storms.[24]

The new Carter home was a joy for Lucy and her children. Facing east, the front of the home featured a porch and porte-cochere over the driveway, which ran along the south side of the home to a two-car garage. It had four bedrooms, large living and dining rooms, a breakfast room, a bathroom, a long hall, a sewing room, and a fish pond in the back yard. And the organizer of the household who devoted her life to the well being of her husband and children was Lucy Carter.[25]

Shortly after George and Lucy were married, George hired a driver to teach Lucy how to drive. Because George had tenants over several counties in the Marlow area and in eastern Oklahoma, Lucy served as his chauffeur and had to be able to drop what she might happen to be doing on a moment's notice so she could drive her husband. Consequently, the Carters employed a housekeeper so the children would have supervision when

The newly constructed First Methodist Church of Marlow. Here Lucy took her children to worship on Sundays and Wednesdays. Pearl was a lifelong member of the church. (Courtesy Marlow Chamber of Commerce)

Lucy was away with George. With five children at home, there was plenty of work to be done for both Lucy and her housekeeper.[26]

Each year in the fall it was necessary for Lucy and George to make a trip to southeastern Oklahoma to collect rent from his tenants in that area. In the years before they owned an automobile, they would make the trip in a buggy pulled by George's faithful horse Coley with Lucy at the reins. The trip would take several days, so they usually ate supper and spent the night with a farm family along the way. One evening it began to get dark before they could find a place to spend the night. Their concerns were compounded when some sort of large cat, perhaps a mountain lion, began stalking them. The creature would howl, adding to the tension. Whenever the cat would get too close, Lucy would throw something at it to scare it away. When she ran out of ammunition she threw her shoes! They finally found a friendly farm family, but Lucy had to borrow or buy some shoes from the family the next day to continue the trip. Years later, in recounting the story, Pearl would marvel at the courage displayed by her mother and blind father in making such trips by themselves.[27]

In Marlow, Lucy was noted for her devotion to George and her family. A religious woman, she "always had her kids in Sunday school at the Methodist Church." In addition, they routinely returned to the church every Wednesday night for prayer meeting and choir practice. Another ritual that the girls enjoyed was Saturday visits to the beauty parlor where they would get a "Marcel," a method of curling hair. Pearl later recalled that, "A Marcel was given with a curling iron that looked like the ones today—only hair would be fired in the waver." On occasion, Lucy would take the children to the Chisholm Studio to have their pictures made. The photographer would get the children posed and "then put the black cloth over his head and hold up that big flash."[28]

George acquired what was perhaps the first electric refrigerator in Marlow. Prior to obtaining this new marvel, the family had an ice box which was filled by Frank Dawson, who delivered blocks of ice by horse and cart and later by truck. Lucy had a square card that she would put in the window to tell Frank whether she wanted a five, ten, twenty-five, or fifty-pound block of ice that day. Frank would put the requested size block of ice in the ice box, which was accessible to him from the outside of the house. A pan was kept under the ice box to collect water as the ice melted. Pearl and other neighborhood kids would follow Frank up the street, and he would chip some ice off a block for the youngsters to eat.[29]

When the new electric ice box was installed in the Carter home, numerous people came to see it and eat the ice that it made to see if it tasted like the ice Frank Dawson provided. The people who sold the device to the Carters told Lucy that when the ice froze she could take it out and put more water in to make more ice. Lucy understood this to mean that she was required to remove the ice and put more water in to make new ice. As a result, she soon had the refrigerator filled with pans and bowls of ice; there was no room for anything else! Finally, Lucy asked the people who sold the machine what to do, and they told her she could leave the trays of ice in the machine until she needed to use the ice. She did not have to empty them every time they froze. In later years, Pearl and her brothers and sisters enjoyed kidding Lucy about her ice-making exploits.[30]

▼▼▼

Lucy also loved to fish, and she frequently would go fishing with Mrs. Tom O'Quinn, who was her "fishing buddy." One hot summer day the two ladies had a highly successful fishing outing, returning home with a large catch. To cool down and slake their thirst, they decided to drink some cold beer. By then it was getting late in the day, so Lucy hurriedly cleaned her fish, breaded them, and fried them for the family's dinner. After the family gathered around the dinner table and the blessing was delivered, the fish were passed. Opaletta was the first to take a bite of the entrée. Suddenly she began spitting the fish out and declared, "Momma, you forgot to scale these fish!" Everybody at the table looked at their plate and saw that all the scales indeed remained on the fish. Lucy for years was teased about how many beers she had before preparing the fish.[31]

Lucy enjoyed treating her children in the evenings to popcorn, homemade candy, or, on rare occasions, snow ice cream. Once the children had their treats, she would read interesting stories to them from the newspaper or tales about "Little Black Sambo" or "Brer Rabbit." Lucy orchestrated birthday parties for the children, and the Halloween parties she arranged were especially memorable. "The tunnel and cellar would be filled with all kinds of scary things," Pearl later remembered. Lucy also hosted Thanksgiving dinners for the Marlow High School football team, as they used to play archrival Duncan High School on that holiday, and she enjoyed entertaining neighbors, relatives, and special guests of her husband.[32]

Lucy always decorated the home extensively for Christmas. The Carter family Christmas tree was there, with relatives congregating at the large home during the holidays. Each year George hired a man to play Santa Claus. He would come by the home at the appointed time and distribute gifts to the children. Before the children were allowed to receive their presents, however, each of them had to sing a song or recite a poem. After the gifts were opened, the adults would play games such as "musical chairs" or "spin the bottle," while the children would play with their new toys. For Pearl, Christmas was a "wonderful time." In later years George, Jr., would play Santa Claus.[33]

Although Lucy usually left corporal punishment of the children to George, she was not reluctant to discipline them as needed. Pearl remembers that

George Carter's brothers and sisters posed with his mother for this photo ca. 1922. Seated left to right: Ella Carter Bayliss, Lulu Carter Loudermilk, Amanda Lominick Carter, Hattie Carter Stanford, and Maude Carter Harbour. Standing, left to right: George W. Carter, Arthur T. Carter, and Charlie Carter. (Courtesy Marlow Chamber of Commerce)

among the punishments Lucy would prescribe were washing the dishes and ironing sheets and pillowcases. At age seventy-five, Pearl would declare, "To this day, I hate to wash dishes and iron."[34]

Lucy's devotion to George and her children was well known in the community, especially after an incident that occurred when George was campaigning for election to the Oklahoma House of Representatives in the 1930s. A pie supper was held at the Oak Grove School, and George was introduced to speak. As he spoke, a woman rose, called George a crook, and asserted that he "would steal a penny off a dead man's eyes!" Lucy rushed over to the woman and asked, "What did you say?" The woman, noting the look in Lucy's eyes, denied saying anything. "Yes you did!" Lucy exclaimed, and then Lucy "knocked her down and whipped her good." The wide-eyed Pearl witnessed the incident and recalled someone shouting, "Give her a good one, Mrs. Carter!" And she did. [35]

Chapter Two
▼▼▼

PREPARING
FOR ADVENTURE

W hen Pearl was three or four years old, the family traveled to Valiant, Oklahoma, and picked up Willie Wilson, a young, full-blood Choctaw boy whose parents had died. George and Lucy knew the boy from previous trips to the area to collect rent from tenants and had grown to like the youngster. He was eight or nine years old at the time and spoke only Choctaw. Pearl recalled that when he first came into their home he would sit by himself, sing Indian songs, and sometimes cry. "He was so lonesome, and I would cry with him," Pearl recalled. Bill, as the family called him, and Pearl quickly bonded as brother and sister. She taught him some English words, and he taught her "a lot of Indian words." They became "buddies" and it was Bill who later taught Pearl how to drive.[1]

Bill soon learned to speak English and enjoyed school. He played football, learned to play saxophone, was loved, and was given every advantage that his brothers and sisters received. As a young married man, Bill learned that his sister-in-law was being abused by her husband. One evening in October of 1929, Bill's sister-in-law and her mother got involved in an argument with his brother-in-law over whether to drive or walk a short distance to a party. The volatile brother-in-law scuffled with the two women and pulled a gun on them. When Bill attempted to assist

Pearl's Uncle Josiah "Joe" Gibson was one of several talented musicians on the Gibson side of Pearl's family. Joe along with her Uncle Bud Gibson and Grandfather Silas Gibson played at many of the country dances Pearl and her family attended when she was a child. (Courtesy Marlow Chamber of Commerce)

▼▼▼
17

them, he was shot to death by his brother-in-law. He was only twenty-three-years old and had one child at the time of his death. This tragedy had a major impact on fourteen-year-old Pearl and her family.[2]

Pearl's other brother, George, Jr., was the baby of the family and thus was "spoiled." He was a typically adventuresome youngster who enjoyed his dog Sarge, his Shetland pony Patsy, and playing and getting into mischief with his friends. On one occasion, he was dared by his friends to eat some earthworms, so he did. On yet another occasion, George found a shotgun shell and, while playing with his friends, decided to take the powder out of the shell. Using a pocket knife, he cut the shell and emptied the powder into a pile on the sidewalk. By this time it was getting dark, so to take a better look at it, George lit a match for some light. As he eyed the gunpowder, he got the match too close and ignited the powder—"Whoosh, burned my eyelashes, my eyebrows, my hair, and my face!"[3]

George, Jr., and his buddies secretly used to swim at night in the water tank at the railroad depot. This was an elevated tank that stored water for the steam locomotives that passed through Marlow. On one occasion, while he was swimming in the water tank with his friends, a train stopped so the locomotive's boiler could be filled with water from the tank. This lowered the water in the tank so the boys could not get out. But the water remained sufficiently deep that they could not touch the bottom. George, Jr., later recalled that, "We were in trouble. We swam and swam and swam and were just about to give up when they filled the water tank back up and we got out." Their parents did not learn about this incident until the boys were adults.[4]

Although George, Jr., enjoyed playing tricks on his older sisters, occasionally the girls would get their revenge. One evening he went to see the movie "Frankenstein" starring Boris Karloff at one of the two movie theaters in town. The impressionable youngster was frightened by the movie and was on edge during the walk home in the dark. Pearl and her sisters knew the route George, Jr., likely would take and they knew when the movie was scheduled to end. Consequently, they hid in a culvert by the side of the street and waited for him: "Just as I walked by, they jumped out of there and hollered and it scared me to death! I ran all the way home."[5]

To earn money for the movies and other treats, George, Jr., would go to his father's office and do chores, such as taking the spittoons across the street to a lumber yard, cleaning them, and bringing them back to the office. He would sweep the office and do other odd jobs. His usual pay was fifteen cents, which was sufficient to pay for admission to a movie and purchase a sack of popcorn.[6]

George, Jr., learned how to play drums but gave that up when he discovered high school football. A popular leader in school, he played quarterback and was an effective field general for the Marlow Outlaws. Although George, Jr., had a sweetheart, Alta Sparks, in junior high, he eventually married Catherine Parker, and they had one child, Beverly. George, Jr., was eighteen when the Japanese attacked Pearl Harbor, thrusting the United States into World War II. He served his country with distinction and was recognized as a hero who saved a buddy from drowning during the D-Day invasion of France. He again served during the Korean War, surviving serious wounds.[7]

Willie Wilson as he appeared shortly before he was killed at age twenty-three by his brother-in-law. Adopted by George and Lucy Carter when he was eight or nine years old, his untimely death was devastating to Pearl and her family. (Courtesy Joseph Carter Brooks)

Pearl was the "middle" sister between Opaletta, the oldest, and Arnetta, the youngest. Although they shared many of the secrets and activities that are typically enjoyed by sisters in a close, loving family, Pearl was different in that she was more of a "tomboy" and a "daddy's girl." Pearl's inclination to be interested in her father's activities and interests ultimately would impact her childhood dramatically.[8]

As a toddler and pre-school child, Pearl was energetic and outgoing. She was just a few days short of her third birthday when World War I ended in Europe, triggering exuberant celebrations throughout the United States. Marlow was no exception. At 11 a.m. on November 11, 1918, in Marlow, sirens were sounding, people were honking car horns, and others were yelling and beating on pots and pans, anything to make noise and express their jubilation. One of the Carters' neighbors, a Mrs. Buzzard,

The Marlow grade school building as it appeared in the early 1920s when Pearl was an elementary student. The handsome brick structure replaced the "little red school house" in which Pearl started the first grade. (Courtesy Marlow Chamber of Commerce)

had a son named Glen in the war. Pearl grabbed a pan and a spoon and marched up and down the street with Mrs. Buzzard, beating her pan and yelling with her neighbor.[9]

On another occasion, Pearl, Opaletta, and Arnetta were pretending to be swimming on the floor of their living room. While her sisters continued "swimming" on the floor, Pearl stood on the piano bench, shouted, "Hey, look at me! Look at me!" and then executed a backward "dive" into the "swimming pool." On the way down, she hit her nose on the piano bench and started crying with blood flowing profusely. This quickly ended the swimming session.[10]

Pearl was eager to learn at an early age. Before she started to school, her father taught her how to count and to recite the alphabet. About the time she began the first grade he started teaching her how to add, subtract, and divide. Being blind, George could not teach basic math using pencil and paper. Instead, he used coins and paper money, and he was patient. "If I made a mistake we would start over," Pearl recalled. Usually, when these lessons were completed, Lucy would have popcorn ready and have a story in hand to read.[11]

Pearl pleaded with her parents to send her to the first grade the fall when she was still five years old. One of her favorite cousins, Tony Bayliss, was six years old and she wanted to start to school with him. Her sixth birthday would not take place until the following December. Lucy and George knew that Pearl was eager to learn, so they relented and sent her to school with Tony. When the teacher, Ruth Barnes, asked Pearl her name and age, she replied, "Eula Pearl Carter. I'm five but Daddy said to tell you that I'm six!" Tony exclaimed, "Why Eula Pearl!" To her great embarrassment, Pearl was sent home and had to wait until the following year to start school.[12]

When Pearl finally got to go to school, it was held in a little red school house just off West Main Street in Marlow. A few years later, the students were moved over to a nearby, three-story building. An adjacent water tower periodically would get too full, causing water to spill out. Pearl and her friends had a great time running through the resultant waterfall, getting "sopping wet." The first bell in the morning rang at 8 a.m. At 8:30 a.m. Snoots Kreiger would beat a triangle and the youngsters would line up and march into the building to that sound. The school day ended at 4 p.m.[13]

One lesson that Pearl learned early was that she was to respect the authority of her teachers. Miss Henry McMurry caught Pearl chewing gum, which was against the rules. She made Pearl select the switch that would be used for her punishment from the hedge that grew around the school yard. "Miss Henry" then proceeded to give Pearl the only whipping she ever received in school. After school, she told her father about it, expecting him to be upset with the teacher. To Pearl's surprise, "He gave me another whipping for getting the one in school!" George explained that if Pearl did anything she should not do in school, she would have to face the consequences and not sniffle about it to anyone else. Almost seventy years later, Pearl thanked "Miss Henry" "for that whipping and lesson. I learned from you, and it has stayed with me all of my life."[14]

On one other occasion, Pearl "sassed" a teacher, "so she slapped me." Pearl went directly to her father's office after school to get some sympathy, hoping he would "really get the teacher." Instead, her father informed her that she had been in the wrong and observed that "anytime a person does wrong in life they will get slapped one way or another. . . ." He then told Pearl to quit crying and take her medicine because she had it coming to her. [15]

Pearl also was impressed by Miss Mattie Kincannon and her ruler. When students in her grade school classes misbehaved, she had them expose the palm of one of their hands in front of them so she could smack it with the ruler. Decades later Pearl could still feel that sting when she thought about it, but "we learned our lessons and we respected them."

Pearl's children also were students of "Miss Henry," "Miss Mattie," and Mr. Schrock, the principal of the grade school, all of whom were beloved figures in the Marlow schools for decades.[16]

The Carter children learned that their parents expected them to live up to high standards of behavior. Their father was "stern and strict," and if the children "didn't mind, we would get a whipping. . . . When he said jump, we didn't ask where, but how far," Pearl asserted. Yet Pearl's father "was so good and kind to us and loved us so much. We minded him not because of fear but because of respect and love. . . ."[17]

The Carter children knew that there were three things that their father absolutely would not tolerate. One of these was to say "I can't." George Carter believed that a sufficiently motivated person with a reasonably realistic goal would find a way to achieve it. Undoubtedly, his own experience of overcoming blindness to lead such a productive and "normal" life caused him to believe in the power of self discipline and in focusing on an objective. "I can't" were words that George Carter never used, and Pearl knew that you just did not say those words within earshot of her father.[18]

Pearl's father also emphasized to his children that they must never make fun of another person. He told them that it was "a sin to laugh at someone who could not help what or how they were." Pearl knew that if she teased or mocked a person with any sort of handicap or someone who had some physical abnormality, she would be punished severely. "I don't care if they were rich or if they didn't have a penny," Pearl remembered, "you didn't make fun of them."[19]

Pearl also was trained never to be a "snob" just because the family had money. Pearl's father emphasized to her that money did not "make or break" a person, and they were just fortunate to have more than many others in the community. He wanted Pearl to understand that, "It was what a person was inside that counted." He admonished Pearl to always be herself "and to be friends with everyone." People who were down and out had a "heart, soul and feelings too," and her father stressed that to assist others, people should "lend a helping hand if they needed it."[20]

Pearl had a chance to apply her father's teaching in school when a boy was subjected to taunting by other students. He was from a poor family and the Ku Klux Klan had dragged his father from his home and had severely whipped him for being a drunk and a wife beater, an incident that was common knowledge in the community. Pearl knew the boy was not responsible for his father's actions, and she was incensed by the students teasing him. She "tore into them tooth and toe nail" and made it very clear that it was not right for them to torment the boy. As a result they "let him alone from then on, for they knew I was his friend." Thirty-eight years later, the "boy" made a point to contact Pearl in person to express his gratitude to her. Because of her support, he had stayed in school, graduated and left Marlow, was happily married, had a good job, and enjoyed a nice family. If it had not been for Pearl's help, he said he would have dropped out of school. Pearl had been taught "to help whoever needed a helping hand," and it became her "way of life."[21]

For the most part, Indian and white students got along well together, Pearl recalled in later years. Of course, most Indian children in Marlow, including Pearl and her siblings, at this time were raised "strictly white." Pearl's parents believed strongly that their children must be prepared to succeed in the predominant white culture. Nonetheless, Pearl had some early reminders of her Indian heritage. When she was small, her Grandpa Silas Gibson lived with the family. He developed what was believed to be a skin cancer. Lucy took him and the children to Beaver Creek, west of Marlow, to search for a certain kind of mud. Silas found what he was looking for and brought a bucket full of it home. He kept a mud pack on the cancer spot for a period of time, and the cancer ultimately was cured.[22]

Pearl also was exposed to Indian and share cropper families throughout Stephens County and sometimes beyond because George and Lucy took their children to revivals, both at the First Methodist Church in town and to brush arbor revivals at country churches. They would attend every night of the revival, and on Sunday they would have "dinner on the ground" at noon, visit during the afternoon, and attend the revival service that evening. George usually would leave a significant donation for each church. Many of those attending were George's tenants and he enjoyed interacting with them. Pearl had a great time playing with the other children who were there with their families. She especially enjoyed attending revivals at the St. York Indian Church southeast of Marlow.[23]

On many occasions in the evening, George would tell Lucy that they were going to visit a particular tenant family in the country and have supper with them. The entire family would go visit, eat supper, and then visit some more before returning home. The relationship between George and these families went beyond that of landlord and tenant; they were friends. [24]

Country dances, often hosted by one of George's tenant families, also brought the Carter family in contact with county residents. Most of the married couples who attended brought their families, and it was a wonderful time for the children to play together. The host couple generally would clear their living room of furniture, and a few musicians, usually a guitarist and a fiddle player, would play. The adults would dance and the children would learn to dance, as well. The youngsters could play outside using lanterns for light, or they could come inside and dance. As the evening progressed, younger children would get sleepy and use their family's wagon or one of the bedrooms in the house as a place to sleep. Pearl's uncle, Robert "Bud" Gibson, and her grandfather, Silas Gibson, both played fiddle at many of these dances. [25]

Like her father, Pearl loved music and enjoyed the dances. Among the dances that were performed were the waltz, the two-step, and the square dance. Approximately sixty-five-years later, Pearl would observe that the square dancing they did then "was a lot prettier then than what they call square dancing now because they did it by the rhythm." However, to Pearl the waltz was the prettiest. She loved to dance with her waltz partner, Jess Gann. He was older, but they were "just friends." [26]

George and Lucy wanted their children to develop an appreciation for music. Consequently, George had acquired a baby grand piano and a "large, square" piano that was one of only one hundred of that particular type, Pearl recalled. He also converted the front bedroom in the house to become a music room. All the children took music lessons from Mrs. Bob Anderson. Bill learned to play saxophone, Opaletta played piano, Arnetta played cello and clarinet, George, Jr., played drums, and Pearl played violin and saxophone. [27]

The children had talent and began playing together, eventually forming the Carter Family Band. They began to provide entertainment for

Broomcorn was one of the primary crops grown in the Marlow area and on farms operated by George Carter, Sr. Here is a crop of broomcorn that was growing near Marlow in June of 1955. As a child, Pearl enjoyed the broomcorn harvest because she loved helping "Broomcorn Johnnies" devour the huge meals that were prepared for them. (Courtesy Roger Harris Collection, Oklahoma Historical Society)

pie suppers, plays, Christmas parties, and other events at country schools such as West Ward, Oak Grove, Stover, and many others. They also played at various country churches. Many of those in attendance at the school or church functions were George's tenants, and he enjoyed the opportunities to visit and to provide entertainment for them. Moreover, he believed that his children were benefiting from the experience. Pearl enjoyed playing violin and practiced diligently. She made her parents especially proud when she won gold medals for violin at the Stephens County Fine Arts Festival at age twelve in 1927 and at thirteen the following year. For the contests, Pearl played "Barcelona" and "Tales of the Vienna Woods." [28]

Pearl always enjoyed her family's excursions into the countryside, but she especially looked forward to when the family would visit one of their tenants during broomcorn harvest time. The hands, called "Broomcorn Johnnies," worked hard all day cutting the corn, and then the crop would be thrashed at night to remove the chaff. A huge meal would be pre-

Cotton was another important crop grown on many of the farms operated by George Carter, Sr. The magnitude of the crop is illustrated by this partial view of the Harbour Cotton Yard in Marlow in the early 1920s. Marlow's school building and water tower can be seen in the background. (Courtesy Marlow Chamber of Commerce)

pared for the workers, and Pearl loved to sit and eat at a long "Broomcorn Johnny" table. "Such good food," she remembered, "later in life I cooked for them." [29]

Harvest time in the fall was an exciting time at the Carter household. George hired additional men to haul his "rent," his portion of the crops produced by his share croppers. Corn, grain, and hay would be hauled to his storage barns, while his share of cotton and broomcorn crops would be sold immediately. The hired hands ate at the Carter home and sometimes would spend the night until the rush was ended. George would get up early during this time and say, "Get up kids, it's a pretty day and I hear the [cotton] gins already humming." During harvest time, especially when he was taking his cotton crop to the gins, George often would come home in the evening with $2,000 or $3,000 in cash. He had a special

▼▼▼

The Carter family enjoyed going to the movies at both the White Way and Alamo theaters. Even though he was blind, George also was able to enjoy the shows because Lucy would describe the action to him. In this photo, people are waiting to enter the Alamo Theater to see "Gone with the Wind" in 1939. (Courtesy Marlow Chamber of Commerce)

hiding place for the cash under the house, where he would put it for safe keeping until he could deposit it in the bank the following morning.[30]

George and Lucy found many other activities in which the entire family could participate. Most Saturday nights the family would go to the movies, either at the Alamo Theater or the White Way. At that time they could enjoy the movie and have a soft drink, popcorn, and candy for about twenty-five cents each. It the early years, the movies were silent. George still enjoyed going, however, because Lucy described the action on the screen and read the dialogue line to him. He also enjoyed music of Irene Todd, who would play piano throughout the movie. When "talking" movies became available, the entire family drove to Chickasha to see Al Jolson in "The Singing Fool." Pearl and her family were amazed by the new technology: "That was really something—talking movies!"[31]

One of Pearl's fondest childhood memories involved the entire family going hunting at night. Her father and his friend Bill Williams of Marlow each owned "wolfhounds," and they would chase wolves, or more likely coyotes, almost all night. The Williams children, Joella, Quinton, and H. B., would sit around the camp fire with the Carter children and their parents. The youngsters would listen to the adults spin yarns, and they were allowed to drink coffee. Their mothers brought blankets for when the children would get sleepy, although they made their best efforts to stay awake as long as possible.[32]

The Carter family also enjoyed circuses, carnivals, tent shows, and medicine shows. Pearl recalled that if a circus came within one-hundred miles of Marlow, the entire family would go see it. There were virtually no paved roads at that time, so some of these trips were challenging, but the children loved the entertainment and being with their parents. When circuses or carnivals came to Marlow, city officials blocked Main Street from Second to Broadway, and the circus or carnival was staged there. A tent show also came to Marlow each summer during Pearl's youth. Their tent was set up on West Main, where the Calloway-Smith-Cobb Funeral home later would be located. A local musician, Tommy Cato, and his wife were in the show's band. A different show was staged each night for a week, and then the show would move on.[33]

Medicine shows also came to town. These would feature entertainment, often a banjo player, to draw crowds so the show operator could "hawk" his tonics and soap. Many of the medicine shows were held on the northwest corner of Main and Second streets, in front of the State National Bank. One of the medicine shows that visited Marlow annually was owned by a distant relative of George, who stayed at the Carter home while he was in town. He used a motorized covered wagon to keep the look of the traditional shows that had used horse-drawn wagons. Pearl was impressed by one "trick" the showman used to sell soap. Before the crowd would gather, he would lather his hands and arms with soap and let it dry. Then "when he added some more water and soap for his demonstration, his hands and arms would really lather up."[34]

George and Lucy enjoyed taking the children with them to as many events as possible, but occasionally this would lead to adventures that they did not anticipate. Once, the family traveled to Lawton to view a large parade. It was a hot, summer day, so Pearl and Arnetta pulled off their shoes and eventually wandered away from their car and their parents. Soon they were lost in the crowd, with the hot sidewalk burning their feet. They walked in what little shade they could find next to the buildings and cried. Some Lawton policemen found them and eventually reunited them with their anxious parents.[35]

Along with other citizens of Marlow, the Carter family enjoyed watching the drilling of one of the first, if not *the* first, oil wells in the Marlow area. The Carters and others found it fascinating to go out in the evening to watch the drilling crew at work and hopefully to see a "gusher." The activity also provided another opportunity to socialize with neighbors and friends.[36]

Sports provided another family activity. George liked a variety of sports and believed that young men benefited from the competition and teamwork required to be successful. Before Marlow had a football or baseball field, he let the school use some of his pasture land on the north edge of town. The competitors used the part of the pasture that had been mowed and braved the "grass burrs and cockle burrs" that were "everywhere on the field." There were no bleachers, so spectators simply stood on the sidelines or sat in their cars to view the action. The Carter family "went to all the games," and Lucy served as George's personal play-by-play announcer.[37]

The Carter family also shared the excitement of acquiring one of the first radios in Marlow. The new contraption was a source of wonderment for the family and many of their friends who came to their house to experience the marvel of wireless transmission of sound. The radio came equipped with headphones, so only one person at a time could listen to it, leaving others eagerly awaiting their turn. In later years, Pearl would remember listening to the funeral of former President Calvin Coolidge on the radio. By the time the "Grand Ole Opry" radio show, broadcast live from Nashville, Tennessee, could be heard in Marlow, the family radio had a speaker so everyone could listen. The Carter family "never missed a week of it."[38]

Another first experience the Carter children enjoyed together was a ride on a passenger train. Because the family had a car, they had never had a reason to take a train for any of their various trips or vacations. Consequently, the children became curious to learn what riding a train would be like. George's brother Charlie, who drove a cab, lived in Chickasha. George called him and arranged for the children to ride the train from Marlow to Chickasha to visit with their aunt and uncle for a day and then ride the train back to Marlow that evening.[39]

Some of Pearl's best childhood experiences involved traveling with her family. Vacations were adventures featuring road trips to Alabama, Mississippi, Tennessee, and Georgia to visit George's relatives. Lucy had the responsibility of driving and keeping George informed as to where they were and what they were seeing, as well as keeping an eye on the children. One of the early highlights of these trips for Pearl was crossing the Blue River in southeastern Oklahoma. This was accomplished by ferry, because there were no bridges on the river in the area where the family needed to cross.[40]

The ferry that the Carters used was a large one that could accommodate four to six cars or wagons at a time. The ferry had a railing around it, a gate at each end that could be lowered for vehicles to enter and exit, and a little "building" in the middle. There the ferry operator kept ropes and other supplies and had a small office. Once the vehicles were loaded for the transit across the stream, the family would get out of the car and walk about the deck during the crossing. "We always looked forward to crossing Blue River," Pearl remembered. The beautiful, spring-fed river featured clear water and always provided a scenic highlight of their trips as well as the fun of the ferry crossing. Later in their trips the Carters also would cross the Arkansas River via ferry.[41]

These vacation adventures also featured camping out each night until the Carters reached their destination. The "roads" for the most part were rough, narrow trails, and there were no motels or hotels to provide accommodations. Consequently, Lucy packed quilts, and the family simply slept by the side of the road, usually near a creek. Lucy also brought pots and pans for cooking, since there were no cafes either. She also had to pack groceries, plates, and silverware. Their touring car had running boards to which luggage carriers were attached. Packing clothing for seven people, along with the other supplies needed for the trip, into one automobile must have been a major challenge for Lucy.[42]

Usually, toward the end of the day, they would find a grocery store where they could purchase some eggs and meat for dinner and breakfast.

Dinner was prepared over an open fire and the food always tasted wonderful. Breakfast was prepared the same way early in the morning, and the children would awaken to the smell of coffee freshly brewed and of bacon or sausage and eggs frying. Then the pots, pans, and dishes were washed and packed into the car along with the quilts, and a new day of traveling would begin.[43]

The trips usually took about a week. In 1990, Pearl would observe that she then could make the same trip in her car in about twelve hours. However, Pearl remembered those family vacations fondly as highlights of her childhood. She also would observe that Lucy "was sure brave, doing all the driving with daddy blind and five kids" through what was largely "wilderness then."[44]

A highlight of these trips was visiting Pearl's Uncle Jim Lominick, who lived at Iuka, Mississippi, as did other Lominicks and Carters. Uncle Jim was a Confederate veteran who had served as a cavalryman under the command of the renowned General Nathan Bedford Forrest. An aggressive officer, Forrest became famous North and South for his daring raids, often deep into enemy territory. Lominick loved to wear his cavalryman's hat and tell stories of the action he saw in the war, mesmerizing children and adults in the process. He then taught the children to sing "Dixie" while he accompanied them on the fiddle.[45]

Pearl had an unanticipated adventure on one of these vacation trips. Accompanying the Carters on the trip was Juanita Harbour, one of Pearl's cousins. The family traveled to Chattanooga, Tennessee, to visit relatives and to see the sights. George's Aunt Mary Middleton had a summer home "on top of" Lookout Mountain. The children wanted to see the cable cars of the famous incline railroad on the mountain once again, so the adults took them to do that. The four girls, Juanita, Opaletta, Arnetta, and Pearl, somehow wandered away from the adults and became lost on the mountain. They "walked and walked 'till we were so tired and so scared," because, except for the summit, the mountain featured "just trees and rocks and no paths." Finally, the girls found the incline railway tracks and began climbing up them. Their presence on the tracks caused the operators to have to halt operation of the cable cars until the children reached the top.[46]

Pearl also had two unsettling experiences involving the local klavern of the Ku Klux Klan, a nefarious organization that was powerful in Oklahoma and much of the nation in the 1920s. Pearl recalled that during this period of segregation there were signs on the north and south boundaries of Marlow warning "Niggers do not let the sun set on you in Marlow." In addition to their hatred of blacks, their intolerance toward Jews, and, in some instances their prejudice against Catholics, the Klan professed to support Protestant denominations and to revile gamblers, drunks, irresponsible fathers, and others who did not meet the Klan's standards of conduct. With their identities hidden under white sheets and pointed hoods that covered their faces, in many communities the Klan counted ministers and lawmen among their ranks.[47]

During one of the annual tent revivals sponsored by two traveling evangelists each summer, the proceedings were interrupted one evening when members of the Klan "came marching in from the back in their white hoods and robes." Pearl and her family, along with the others in attendance, were scared by the dramatic appearance of the Klansmen, who proceeded to the front, "gave the preacher some money, and marched out" without bothering anyone.[48]

Another brush with the Klan occurred one evening when Pearl and her brothers and sisters were playing with other neighborhood kids under the street light near her home. Three or four cars "with KKKs" in them and standing on the running boards passed by them heading north, stopping just a few blocks from where the children were playing. The Klansmen had stopped at the home of a poor family whose father was known for frequently getting drunk and spending most of his money on drinking and gambling, thereby not providing for his wife and children as he should. He also was known to "beat on his wife and kids." Soon Pearl and the other children who had retreated to the porch of her house, heard screaming and crying, sufficiently loud to be heard "all over town." The Klansmen had entered the man's house, dragged him outside, tied him to a tree, and were giving him a severe beating. Pearl and the children were "so scared because that is when the KKK was so active." Fortunately for Marlow and the rest of the state, the power and pervasiveness of the Klan would decline dramatically in the 1930s and the following decades.[49]

Pearl's childhood experiences, however, were overwhelmingly positive, featuring good times with her family and friends. One such family experience was visiting with her paternal grandmother, Amanda Lominick, who lived on a nearby farm. Just about every two weeks during the summer, the entire family would "go to Grandma's to make ice cream and have cake." Some of Pearl's fondest childhood memories involved "staying all night with my Grandma and snuggling down in her big feather bed by her and hearing the clock ticking." Pearl and the other children "had a lot of fun sitting on those ice cream freezers while" the adults "turned them." After eating ice cream and cake, the adults "would put ice down each other's back and have water fights and things like that. We were all a real close family."[50]

Pearl enjoyed a childhood filled with adventure, friendship, learning, and love. She had a nurturing family life with doting parents, who were determined to give her and her brothers and sisters every advantage possible. Their parents' love was leavened with discipline, ethical and religious principles, and a passion for music and learning. Yet, no one could have anticipated that as Pearl entered her second decade of life, she soon would be driving a car and flying into the pages of history.

Chapter Three
▼▼▼

DADDY'S GIRL

P earl was "not very old" when she realized that she was her "daddy's pet and substitute son." Her older, adopted brother, Willie Wilson, had been married a short time and then had been killed, while her other brother, George, Jr., was "the baby of the family." Pearl was a "tomboy," and she loved her father "almost to the point of worship."[1]

Unlike her sisters, Pearl would sit in her father's lap and "pet him and kiss him." She would "cut his fingernails, comb his hair and do everything" she could for him. Whenever he needed something, Pearl would fetch it for him.[2]

When she started school, Pearl quickly learned how to read, and she became more proficient because she read the newspaper to her father. Every day, Pearl would get the newspaper and read the headlines to George. If the headline indicated a story in which he had interest, he would have Pearl read it. Most of the "big headlines" on the front page were stories that he wanted to hear. He was more selective with regard to the stories "on the inside" of the paper. George used this daily exercise to keep up with the news and to improve Pearl's reading skills. When she came to a word she could not pronounce, George would have her spell the word. He helped her divide the word into syllables and then had her pronounce each syllable until she could say the word easily. He later had her find each new word in the dictionary to learn its meaning.[3]

Pearl posed proudly with her Curtiss Robin airplane ca. 1930. Note that she is wearing her aviator's outfit, including the fine leather boots that were given to her by her parents one Christmas. Pearl quickly became a celebrity and frequent guest of honor at air circuses, airport dedications, and other events in southwestern Oklahoma. (Courtesy Pearl Scott Collection)

Pearl knew that someone had to be with her father whenever he was in an unfamiliar location outside their home or his office. Moreover, she understood that he did not want to appear to be handicapped. Conse-

Pearl was a stylish young lady at age twelve or thirteen. Here she was wearing a sailor's suit outfit and sporting short or "bobbed" hair, both of which were popular in the 1920s. Her family's affluence also is reflected by the two strands of pearls that she was wearing as she confidently gazed into the camera. (Courtesy Marlow Chamber of Commerce)

quently, she learned quickly that she did not lead him anywhere; instead, they walked "side by side" and hooked their little fingers. If Pearl needed him to turn left or right, she simply turned her hand in the appropriate direction. Other subtle signals indicated an approaching step up or down. In this manner Pearl and George could stroll Marlow's sidewalks or attend various events without his blindness being obvious.[4]

In addition to her music lessons, Pearl's father also had her taking lessons in art and in "expression." He attempted to give Pearl "all the advantages he could, so I would know a little about everything. . . ." He even taught her about legal land descriptions.[5]

George used Pearl's musical ability to teach her how to do basic banking and to save for the future. When Marlow's present Methodist Church was built, the pastor established a church orchestra. Pearl played violin and sometimes saxophone in the orchestra both for Sunday services and for prayer meetings on Wednesday evenings. Soon after she started playing for the church, George called her to his office and told her that he had forgotten to tell her that the church was going to pay her five dollars a week for her services. He then gave Pearl her first payment, instructing her to take it to the bank, tell them that she wanted to establish an account, and make her first deposit. She went directly to the bank from her father's office, established her personal account, and made her first deposit. Of course, George had alerted the bank's personnel by phone and they were ready to help Pearl when she arrived.[6]

Every Monday morning, Pearl would receive her five-dollar payment from her father and would deposit the money in her account. After some time had passed, he had her make a small withdrawal. She also had to maintain her "bank book" in which she kept track of deposits and withdrawals and calculated the current balance of her account. Thus, George taught Pearl about banking. She later learned that her father was the source of her payment, not the church.[7]

George enjoyed Pearl's music and believed she had significant potential as a violinist. Decades later, Pearl had vivid memories of how "mad he got one time, when he came home and I was washing dishes." George wanted Pearl's hands to be soft and to "look nice" for her violin playing. He did not want her doing manual labor of any kind that might cause her hands to be less supple or pretty. Nevertheless, Lucy continued to have Pearl wash dishes when she believed such punishment was required.[8]

The special bond between Pearl and her father would make it possible for Pearl to make history as a teenager. Decades later she would "realize the difference he made in the other kids" and her, for she "became my daddy's eyes and a part of him and he became a part of me. I did the things he wanted to do and couldn't, so he lived it through me." Although he punished her when she "needed it," Pearl acknowledged that, "I had anything I wanted and did almost anything he thought I could do . . . and he trusted my judgment of what I could do." George's confidence in Pearl would enable her to own and drive her own automobile prior to becoming a teenager. Soon this would lead to even more remarkable accomplishments.[9]

By the time Pearl was eleven years old, her father had purchased a Ford roadster for her brother Bill, who was six years older than Pearl. Bill began dating a young woman named Billie Hefley from Loco, Oklahoma, located in southeastern Stephens County about forty miles from Marlow. Pearl and Bill were "buddies," and Bill let Pearl ride along with him on his excursions to Loco. Billie had a younger sister about Pearl's age, and the two girls enjoyed visiting and playing together. Unknown to her parents, Bill taught Pearl how to drive during these trips between Marlow and Loco.[10]

While she was still eleven, Pearl announced that she knew how to drive and began lobbying her father for a car of her own. Bill confirmed that she not only could drive, but she also was good at it! By this time, her father already had a great deal of confidence in Pearl. She was intelligent and seemingly mature for her age, so he agreed to give the matter serious consideration. One day her father called home and told Pearl to come to his office. To her surprise and delight, when she arrived she found a new, 1927 Durant convertible sports roadster "with a little jump seat and it was red and black." Her father handed her the keys and said, "This is yours. . . whoever you want to drive it drives it and if you don't want them to why don't let them."[11]

When school started that fall, Pearl drove the car to school each day and she sometimes drove her father to work. She was proud of her car and her father. With him sitting beside her, she "wanted to shout to the world 'look everybody, this is my daddy.' Oh, how proud of him I was."[12]

Durant automobiles were high quality cars built by a company founded in 1921 and operated by William A. Durant. Durant earlier had founded General Motors in 1908 and managed to lose control of the company twice, the second time in 1920. His new company manufactured automobiles until it failed during the depths of the Great Depression in 1933. Durant autos were fairly rare, and it is likely that Pearl had the only one in Marlow and perhaps in Stephens County.[13]

Pearl generally was a responsible driver, but she had a few adventures in her car that she likely did not share with her parents. On one occasion, when Pearl was twelve or thirteen, she was cruising Main Street with her two sisters and her little brother George, Jr., who was about six at the time. George was seated in the open "rumble seat" in the rear of the car, enjoying a sack of popcorn and the wind in his hair. Pearl was heading west on Main Street in Marlow and then made a "pretty sharp" U-turn near the present post office, throwing George, Jr., out of the rumble seat onto the pavement! Pearl and her sisters came to a quick halt and looked at each other. One of them said, "Oh, we've killed George!" They scrambled out of the car, ran back to George, and found him sitting on the pavement eating his popcorn![14]

Pearl and her friends also used her car and that of J. W. Steele for a unique style of rabbit hunting. J. W. had an electric car, and he and Pearl had the only two cars among the youngsters in Marlow at that time. J. W. was handicapped, but his car was equipped with hand controls in place of the usual foot pedals. On Saturday evenings, Pearl, J. W., and their friends would gather at the drug store or some other popular location,

At age eleven, Pearl drove a 1927 Durant Roadster, similar to this one. The sporty convertible featured a "jump" or "rumble" seat in the back. (Courtesy clubs.hemmings.com)

pile into the two vehicles, stand on the fenders and running boards, go to one of the pastures that belonged to Pearl's father, and literally chase rabbits. The kids on the running boards and fenders had long sticks that they would use to strike the rabbits. "It's a wonder some of them didn't fall off and get run over," Pearl recalled in later years, "but we thought it was fun."[15]

Pearl did have a wreck in her car when she was fourteen. A cousin, Ruby Loudermilk, and George, Jr., were with her at the time. Pearl cut one of her fingers and lost the ability to bend that finger down. This caused her to have to stop taking piano lessons and stick with playing the violin and saxophone. By this time, however, Pearl was involved in an activity that took precedence over playing the piano and almost every thing else in her life.[16]

One day in 1927, when Pearl was eleven, an airplane flew over Marlow, circled the community several times and landed in a pasture on the edge of town belonging to George Carter. Airplanes were a rare sight in rural Oklahoma at that time, so a large crowd of curious townspeople converged on the pasture to see the airplane and its pilot. The Carter

▼▼▼

family was among the throng, and, like most of those present, Pearl saw an airplane up close for the first time.[17]

As it happened, the pilot was the brother of Joe Post, one of the Carter's neighbors. Wiley Post, Joe's brother, had just completed his first solo flight and had flown to Marlow to visit Joe, who lived across the street from the Carters. Wiley introduced himself to George. Pearl was at George's side, as usual, and George introduced her to the fledgling aviator. Pearl did not realize it at that moment, but this would prove to be one of the most important days of her life.[18]

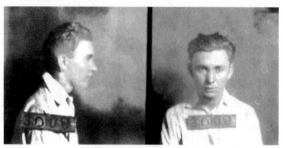

Wiley Post's mug shots taken shortly after he was convicted of robbery and sentenced to serve ten years at the State Reformatory at Granite. Post fortunately was paroled after a short time and would begin a transformation in his life that, despite the loss of an eye in an oilfield accident, would result in him becoming acknowledged as the greatest aviator in the world. (Courtesy Oklahoma Historical Society)

Wiley Post had traveled a difficult road in life to arrive in Marlow that day as a full-fledged pilot. Born in 1898, Post dreamed during his youth about being an aviator. Impoverished, possessing only a sixth-grade education, unemployed, and bored, he made a major mistake in 1921 when he began "hijacking" cars in Grady County. He eventually was caught, convicted of robbery, and sentenced to serve ten years at the State Reformatory at Granite. Although a "model prisoner," Wiley suffered from what later would be recognized as clinical depression. He was said to be in a "melancholic" state that likely would only deepen. Fortunately for Wiley, he was paroled by Governor J. B. A. Robertson in 1922 after serving a little more than one year of his sentence. Among the many terms he accepted in order to obtain his release was the avoidance of "improper places of amusement" and "all pool and billiard halls."[19]

Wiley spent several years working in the oil fields and then got involved with Burrell Tibbs as a parachutist in an air show, which fed his desire to be an aviator. Determined to acquire an airplane, Post began working on a drilling rig near Seminole, Oklahoma, hoping to save a sufficient amount of money to realize his dream. But the experience soon turned into a nightmare when a freak accident at work cost him his left eye.[20]

Wiley spent several months training himself to have depth perception with just one eye and then used his insurance settlement to buy an airplane. He was a convicted felon with one eye, but he was determined to become an aviator. His face, with his trademark eye patch, was destined to become known internationally for two flights around the world (one of them solo), for discovering the jet stream, and for inventing the pressure suit for flying at high altitudes. Post's pressure suit was the forerunner of pressure suits that astronauts and cosmonauts would wear in space. But Wiley's remarkable accomplishments were in his future when the short, stocky, dark-haired, one-eyed aviator stood before George and Pearl Carter in 1927.[21]

That afternoon, Wiley asked George if he would like to have the distinction of being the first person ever to fly with him. Always ready for new experiences, George accepted Wiley's invitation and became Wiley's first passenger. Although blind, George found the experience to be exhilarating and likely immediately saw how flying could help him conduct his business more efficiently. After Wiley and George landed, Pearl bombarded them with "a million questions . . . about the airplane and how he flew it." She then told them that she wanted to go up. With George's permission, Pearl became Wiley's next passenger that day. Wiley could see that Pearl was fearless and eager to learn. The plane had dual controls, so Wiley decided to give her a basic flying lesson. First he had her put her feet on the pedals that controlled the ailerons so she could feel how they moved and how the plane responded when Wiley manipulated them. He also told her to hold her stick "real light." Pearl was enthralled. She knew immediately that she wanted to learn all about flying.[22]

When they landed, Pearl was "thrilled to death" and continued asking questions. Later that same day, Wiley took Pearl up and gave her another lesson. That evening she went over to Joe Post's home where Wiley was staying and continued to ask questions. Impressed by her intelligence and her obvious fascination with aviation, Wiley patiently answered every one of her questions. By the end of the evening, he had promised Pearl that during his next visit to Marlow, he would take her up again and give her another lesson. Pearl could hardly wait until Wiley's return.[23]

Pearl was on pins and needles while she anticipated Wiley's return to Marlow. In a few weeks he came to visit his brother and he was as good as his word. He reviewed with Pearl the various controls on the plane, and then they went up for another lesson. For a while, Post returned to Marlow frequently to see Joe, visit with George, and give Pearl her flying lessons.[24]

During his visits to Marlow, Wiley liked to visit with George about aviation and "about different things that grown people talk about." Although the Carters had a wonderful yard with benches, lights, and a croquette set that attracted neighbors and their children, Pearl preferred to stay in the house and absorb the conversations between George and Wiley. "All the kids would be outside playing under the street light but me," Pearl recalled; "I wanted to learn. . . . Daddy and Wiley thought alike and they had a bond because Wiley lost that eye."[25]

Pearl was especially fascinated when Wiley and George would talk about the future. Her father suggested that "someday when you are talking on the phone you will be able to see who you are talking to." At the time that sounded like a flight of fancy to Pearl. She also was captivated by Wiley's discussion of an idea he had for a pressurized flying suit that would allow aviators to fly to unprecedented altitudes in the unpressurized airplanes of the day. Within a few years, Post built the first such suit and tested it at Bartlesville, Oklahoma. It was on this flight that Post got caught in the jet stream and eventually landed at Muskogee, Oklahoma.[26]

The prediction that impressed Pearl the most, however, came from Wiley when he talked about the ultimate use of his pressure suit. Using one of his nicknames for Pearl (the other was "Half Pint"), Post said, "Shorty, one of these days, man is going to walk on the moon. It won't be in George's or my lifetime, and it may not be in your lifetime, but man is going to walk on that moon." Predictions such as this one, with which George strongly concurred, caused Pearl's imagination to race and her en-

Wiley Post's first airplane, a Curtiss Cannuck, was an object of great curiosity to the people of Marlow when he landed in George Carter's pasture. Wiley came to Marlow to visit his brother Joe, and George became Wiley's first passenger. That same day Pearl became his second passenger, and both George and Pearl became instantly enamored with flying. (Marlow Chamber of Commerce)

thusiasm for learning, especially for flying, to continue to grow. Evenings spent listening to George and Wiley converse and asking questions of them would prove to be among her most pleasant childhood memories.[27]

For some time Pearl had been dropping hints about wanting an airplane of her own to fly. Finally, Post asked her one day when she was twelve if she was truly serious about wanting to be an aviator. Pearl responded that she was. Wiley asked if she was certain and again Pearl said yes. Post told her that she had the temperament and the determination to be successful. He urged her not to let "anything deter you from what you want to do. You may fall down once in a while," he continued, "but don't give up, get mad, and get up and show 'em that you can do what you can." They continued talking, and Wiley agreed to visit that evening with George about the idea of Pearl getting a plane of her own in which she could receive intensive training.[28]

That evening Wiley told George that Pearl was "just a born flyer" and was quite capable of becoming a pilot, even at her age. George asked

Pearl if she was really serious about flying, and she assured him that she was. George reflected for a moment and then asked Pearl, "Well, do you think you can do it?" Pearl replied, "I know I can." Wiley assured George that, "She has that feeling; she has that knack for it." After a few seconds, George said to Pearl, "Well, you've had that car for a year and you've been real careful and you've taken good care of it." He turned to Wiley and continued, "Well, all right, then. I'll build her an airport and I'll build her a hangar and . . . I'll let you pick out a plane and get it to her." Pearl was euphoric.[29]

Motivated by his own burgeoning interest in aviation, George moved quickly to develop the airfield and hangar. He enlisted the aid and advice of Ralph Eubanks of the Marlow Chamber of Commerce; Don Clayton, an aviator from Oklahoma City; and Bill Jones, a student aviator. Luther Wagnon, secretary-manager of the Marlow Chamber of Commerce, also wrote a letter to the United States Chamber of Commerce asking that organization to send an airport expert to Marlow as soon as possible. Whether an expert was sent to Marlow is not known, but work commenced to fill in prairie dog holes and to level and build up a large block of land on the north edge of town. Construction of a han-

Wiley Post in the pressure suit he invented for high altitude flying. Aided by his sponsor, Post flew his airplane the Winnie Mae above 50,000 feet on at least 8 different occasions. Pearl had listened to Post and her father discuss the aviator's idea for the pressure suit years earlier during one of their many conversations about the future of aviation. Post's pressurized suit was the forerunner of the space suit used decades later by astronauts and cosmonauts. (Courtesy Oklahoma Historical Society)

gar to be thirty-two feet by fifty feet was the next step.[30]

While the work was underway, Post had recommended a particular airplane for Pearl, a Curtiss Robin monoplane, which would cost more than $4,000–the exact cost depending on how the plane was equipped–a considerable sum in 1929. The plane was ordered so it could be delivered soon after completion of the airport and hangar.[31]

George telephoned Wiley to let him know that everything was ready for the arrival of Pearl's airplane. He then told Pearl the delivery schedule, so she had several days to anticipate the arrival of the Curtiss Robin. On the day the plane was due to appear, Pearl "couldn't sit still in school to save my neck, and when I heard those planes, oh man! And everybody in my school knew that plane was coming." Pearl heard two planes because Wiley was flying Pearl's new Curtiss Robin while Burrell Tibbs was flying Post's plane. After what seemed like hours to Pearl but in reality was only a few minutes, George called Pearl and told her to come to the airport. The supremely confident, twelve-year-old student aviator jumped into her sports car and raced to the airport where she found her new aircraft and a smiling Wiley Post waiting for her. The plane was equipped with dual controls, so Wiley and Pearl got in and went flying.[32]

Pearl's new airplane had been built in October of 1928 at a newly constructed factory in St. Louis, Missouri, that had been established by the Curtiss-Robertson Airplane Manufacturing Company specifically to produce the new Curtiss Robin. Pearl's plane featured a burnt orange fuselage and yellow wings. A strut-braced monoplane, its design was strongly influenced by Charles Lindbergh's famous "Spirit of St. Louis" aircraft in which the legendary aviator flew across the Atlantic Ocean from New York to Paris, France, in May of 1927. Anticipating that many of the Robins would be operating from pastures or poorly prepared fields, the aircraft was ruggedly built. Prototypes of the plane were test flown by several well-known pilots, including Lindbergh himself.[33]

The Curtiss Robin was "Built for Durability" and was powered by the venerable OX-5 engine. Described as "marvelous, often cantankerous but mostly reliable," the OX-5 engines were manufactured by the Curtiss Aeroplane and Motor Company, as the company was called prior to World War I. It was the engine of choice for barnstorming aviators of the 1920s

and early 1930s, and many remained in service until after World War II. A few OX-5s continued to power restored, vintage aircraft in the twenty-first century.[34]

Pearl's Curtiss Robin was just under twenty-six-feet long and its wing span was forty-one feet. The aircraft weighed 1,480 pounds when empty and was rated to carry a load of up to 737 pounds. Its maximum speed was 99 mph, its cruising speed was 84 mph, and its landing speed was 44 mph. The Robin had a range of up to 590 miles on a fifty-gallon tank of fuel, averaging more than eleven miles to the gallon. Equipped with dual controls and a "completely upholstered and pleasingly finished" interior, Pearl's airplane cost approximately $4,800. Of course, George also spent an unknown sum of money to prepare the airfield and build a hangar.[35]

George hired Slim Marshall of Duncan as a full-time pilot to teach Pearl how to fly and to fly George on business trips. Smitten by aviation fever, George soon purchased another airplane for his son-in-law Arthur Williamson to use in learning how to fly. It was an Eaglerock biplane,

equipped with an OX-5 engine and manufactured by the Alexander Aircraft Company in Colorado Springs, Colorado. It was a favorite aircraft of
barnstorming pilots in the 1920s and 1930s because of its maneuverabili-
ty and ability to land in pastures. Marshall gave Pearl lessons in both the
Curtiss Robin and the Eaglerock. Pearl enjoyed flying both planes but
preferred her Curtiss Robin because it had an enclosed cabin. Regardless
of which plane she flew, Pearl was thrilled that her aviation training was
underway.[36]

Chapter Four
▼▼▼

FLYING HIGH

P earl began flying and learning with Marshall virtually every day, and she "loved every minute of it." Pearl and Slim usually would meet at the airport by sunrise, fly until school time, and fly after school. Often George would fly with them since the Robin had room for two passengers in addition to the pilot.[1]

It was during one of these flying lessons that Pearl impressed Slim with her fearlessness. Slim decided to see if Pearl would panic under emergency conditions and he wanted to test her "nerve." He had Pearl put the plane in a spin headed toward the ground. At three hundred feet, Slim took control and pulled out of the spin and dive while Pearl laughed at him. On the ground he told Pearl that she had more nerve than anyone he had ever seen and that he would never again try to scare her.[2]

Pearl quickly discovered that she loved stunt flying. Barrel rolls, spins, and dives were exhilarating to her. "Looping and rolling" her plane gave Pearl her "greatest thrill." Moreover, she loved to take friends up and then "scare them to death. I'd go into those rolls and everything. Some of them liked it but most of them didn't." George, Jr., perhaps remembering how Pearl had flipped him out of the rumble seat of her car, absolutely refused to fly with her. Lucy and Arnetta would not fly with Pearl either. Lucy actually took a few flying lessons herself, but had to

Pearl, standing next to her mother Lucy, was a stylish young lady when this photo was taken, ca. 1930. Directly in front of Lucy was Pearl's younger sister Jewell Arnetta. George, Jr. is in the right foreground. Others in the photo are unidentified. (Pearl Scott Papers)

▼▼▼

make a forced landing and decided henceforth to remain on the ground. Opaletta did fly with Pearl, got scared, and refused to do it again. Her father, however, loved flying with Pearl; perhaps being blind in this instance was an advantage![3]

One memorable morning, September 12, 1929, Pearl and Slim were flying before school, as usual. When they landed, Slim said, "Pearl, you know all I know, so take it up!" Pearl immediately climbed back into her plane and took off. Years later, thinking about her first solo flight, Pearl asserted, "I wasn't a bit scared. I looked around and there was just me—just me!" For Pearl, flying solo was "just about as close to heaven as anyone can get." Just as Pearl took off, someone "ran to the phone" and called George. By the time Pearl landed, both George and Lucy were there to witness the end of Pearl's first solo flight. Pearl was convinced that she could have soloed much earlier, but she was so young her parents had been reluctant to let her. Still, at thirteen-years old, Pearl became the first Chickasaw aviator and the youngest flier in the United States.[4]

Pearl's older sister Opaletta married at age sixteen and her husband, Arthur Williamson, became interested in aviation and took flying lessons courtesy of Pearl's father. In this photo, Arthur and Opaletta posed in front of the Curtiss Robin with their first child, Bobby. Arthur had written on the photo, "Opaletta and me and baby makes three". (Courtesy Bob Williamson)

At age thirteen Pearl was granted her "Student Pilot's Permit" by the Aeronautics Branch of the United States Department of Commerce in June of 1930. The minimum age for individuals to receive such permits was sixteen, so George and Pearl had to lie about her age to receive the permit. On the permit her height was listed at five feet, so she apparently took the opportunity to add an inch to her height as well.[5]

Among the conditions outlined in the permit was one that limited solo flights "to the immediate vicinity of the airport or landing field upon which the instruction is based, and such flights shall not extend beyond a safe gliding distance thereof." The permit also stipulated that, "At no time shall persons or property be carried in a licensed aircraft piloted by the holder hereof, except a bona fide instructor assigned by the person or company with whom the student is enrolled." If Pearl bothered to read the fine print, she must have laughed. By the time she had obtained the permit, Pearl had made numerous solo flights far from her home airport! And she had flown many passengers other than Slim Marshall.[6]

Pearl soon interested Tony Bayliss, one of her cousins, in flying. He and Pearl had spent a great deal of time together and were great pals. "There wasn't a tree he climbed that I didn't too . . . . He looked after me as if I were his sister," Pearl later recalled. After flying a few times with Pearl, he was hooked, and George began paying for him to take flying lessons as well. Soon Tony was accompanying Pearl to many of the special events and flying circuses.[7]

Pearl's fame as an aviator spread quickly, and she was a guest of honor on many occasions. Organizers of special events, such as dedications of new roads or airports, flying circuses, and other occasions frequently invited Pearl to bring her Curtiss Robin and be a guest of honor. Photos of Pearl and her airplane, along with stories, often appeared in local newspapers, and her presence at an event enhanced attendance. One of her early appearances as a guest of honor was for the dedication of a new airport at Frederick, Oklahoma. Luther Wagnon, a former president of the Marlow Chamber of Commerce, had moved to Frederick and was responsible for the invitation. Pearl, who had "Marlow" painted in block letters under one of the wings of her plane, was a big hit at this and other events.[8]

Pearl became a popular figure on the air circus circuit in southwestern Oklahoma. She was quite a curiosity because of her age and diminutive stature. At most of these events, she would take passengers on flights for a fee, and, as taught by her father, faithfully deposited her earnings into her bank account. She got to know a man who entertained audiences by parachuting out of airplanes, an unusual and thrilling sight for people who had never experienced flight. The jumper hired Pearl to transport him to different towns to make his jumps. On the last day of a show, Pearl talked the man into letting her don the parachute, "my cousin to fly the plane and me to jump. Of course, we didn't tell my dad. . . ." Someone did call George, however, and before Pearl could get airborne, George and Lucy arrived and Pearl was not allowed to jump, much to her disappointment.[9]

George and Lucy were quite proud of Pearl, although Lucy did worry some about their daughter's aerial exploits. One Christmas, after Pearl had started making her appearances at special dedications and air shows, George and Lucy gave Pearl a new flying outfit. She received the "whole works—helmet, goggles, scarf, red leather jacket, and boots." The outfit was of the finest quality, and Pearl was "so proud" of it, especially the boots, which were "high lace-ups made of soft, gray, elk hide." One day, George, Jr., needed a piece of leather for a sling shot he was making, so he found Pearl's boots in her closet and "cut a big hunk out of one of the tongues. Made me a pretty good sling shot," George recalled seventy-five years later, "but I caught hell over it!" George was about six years old at the time. "Needless to say from then on he left my things alone," Pearl wryly remembered.[10]

Even as his aviation exploits made Wiley Post an internationally famous personality, he did not forget about "Shorty" Carter. Whenever he had occasion to be in Oklahoma City or southwest Oklahoma, he would call George and have Pearl meet him. Wiley enjoyed visiting with Pearl. He viewed her as his protégé and was proud of her. Several of these meetings would prove to be especially memorable.[11]

After Wiley and Australian navigator Harold Gatty had circumnavigated the globe in Wiley's beloved *Winnie Mae* in just eight days, completing the circuit on July 1, 1931, Wiley became an internationally-renowned celebrity. After enduring a tickertape parade in New York City and a visit to the White House, Wiley and Gatty headed to Oklahoma, where their first stop on July 9 was Chickasha, home of oilman F. C. Hall, owner of Post's Lockheed Electra aircraft. Despite his hectic schedule, Wiley had called George and asked him to have Pearl meet him at Chickasha. When Pearl arrived, Wiley and Gatty were on a platform and a large, enthusiastic crowd already had formed. Wiley spotted Pearl and motioned

Wiley Post, left, was photographed visiting with Harold Gatty, who was Post's navigator during his first 'round the world flight, which the duo completed in eight days in 1931. They are standing in front of the Winnie Mae, the airplane in which they accomplished their feat. Despite his fame, Post never forgot his protégé Pearl, and he arranged for her to meet Gatty at Chickasha, shortly after Post and Gatty had been honored by a tickertape parade in New York City and a visit to the White House. (Courtesy Oklahoma Historical Society)

for her to join him on the platform. She did so, and Wiley introduced her to his wife, Mae, and to Gatty. Just as Wiley began introducing Pearl to Gatty's wife, Vera, the navigator's wife fainted. When that happened, Pearl returned to her place in the audience. Nonetheless, meeting Harold Gatty and seeing Wiley again was a special treat for Pearl.[12]

Wiley's aviation exploits caught the attention of humorist Will Rogers, who by 1931 had become one of the nation's most beloved actors and newspaper columnists. The Oklahoma native, who was part Cherokee, had begun his career in vaudeville and had an amazing talent for performing trick roping. An early advocate of aviation, Rogers was proud of Wiley's accomplishments, especially his circumnavigation of the globe

▼▼▼

Around the World Solo Flight
7 days 18 hours 49 mins
Wiley Post
7/22/33

Post's international fame continued to soar after he completed his solo flight around the world in 1933. Shortly after this milestone achievement, Post allowed Pearl to fly the Winnie Mae. She became only one of three people ever to pilot the legendary aircraft. (Courtesy Oklahoma Historical Society)

with Gatty. Shortly thereafter, Post and Rogers met and became close friends. Their friendship would lead to another memorable experience for Pearl. [13]

George received a call from Wiley one day, telling him that he would be in Duncan on February 4, 1931, and asking Pearl to fly her airplane there to meet him. Wiley indicated that he had "a surprise" in store for Pearl. Pearl arrived at the Duncan airport before Wiley, so she waited patiently for the *Winnie Mae* to appear. "When Wiley landed," Pearl recalled, "the door opened and out stepped Will Rogers!" Rogers saw Pearl and said to Wiley, "Is this the little girl you've been telling me about?" Rogers then gave Pearl a big hug. At Wiley's invitation, Pearl flew alongside Wiley and Will to Lawton and from there returned to Marlow. For Pearl, meeting Will Rogers "was quite a thrill." [14]

▼▼▼

Pearl had another meeting with Wiley that would prove to be even more momentous for Pearl than her rendezvous had been with him at Chickasha and Duncan. Two prominent French aviators were going to be in Oklahoma City as was Wiley, who called George to make some special arrangements for the day. Wiley asked George to have Pearl fly her airplane to Oklahoma City's municipal airport, which was located between S.W. 29th and S.W. 44th streets, with an entrance at S.W. 36th Street at G Street (present May Avenue). In addition, Lucy and George were to drive to Oklahoma City, meet Pearl at that airport, and drive her to the Curtiss-Wright Field, located at the southeast corner of Britton Road and G Street in northwest Oklahoma City. George agreed to do this, and, as a result, Pearl and her family met Wiley at the Curtiss-Wright Field as planned.[15]

Wiley introduced Pearl to the French aviators, and a ceremony in their honor was held. After the festivities ended, Wiley told George and Lucy that they could start their trip home to Marlow and that he would take Pearl back to her Curtiss Robin. Pearl was thrilled by the prospect of getting to be Wiley's passenger in the world-famous aircraft. Wiley and Pearl got into the *Winnie Mae,* and Wiley talked about the plane and showed Pearl the various instruments. He then asked Pearl if she would like to fly the *Winnie Mae* to the airport at S.W. 36th Street! Pearl must have been momentarily stunned but recovered to indicate that she would love to fly Wiley's world-famous *Winnie Mae.* Wiley taxied the plane to the spot on the runway where they were ready to take off and then told Pearl, "Now you take it off and you do the flying." "It wasn't very far," Pearl recalled, "but I flew the Winnie Mae!"[16]

At the time she flew the *Winnie Mae*, Pearl could not have anticipated that she eventually would become known as only the third person ever to have flown the legendary aircraft. Other than Pearl, Wiley and his trusted chief mechanic are the only individuals known to have piloted Wiley's airplane. He loved the *Winnie Mae* second only to his wife, Mae. For Wiley to have trusted Pearl to fly the *Winnie Mae*, he had to have had tremendous respect for her flying skills. Although the flight was a short one, the most dangerous aspects of it were taking off and landing—flying was the easy part of the flight. Wiley's *Winnie Mae* did not have dual controls; the cockpit had room for one pilot only. Consequently, Wiley was in no position to assist Pearl if she encountered any problems. Wiley placed his fate, and that of the *Winnie Mae*, in Pearl's hands. In later years, Pearl was justifiably proud of the fact that Wiley had invited her to fly his beloved *Winnie Mae*.[17]

George Carter, Sr.'s enthusiasm for aviation was remarkable. His interest in the new technology and his confidence in Pearl enabled her to become one of the youngest pilots in aviation history.

After the ceremony, during the brief flight, and after they had landed, Wiley and Pearl talked about Wiley's solo flight around the world. They also talked about Pearl's flying experiences and reminisced about the first time Wiley took Pearl up and how she had responded to that experience. She had been Wiley's second passenger, and now, for that short flight, Wiley was her passenger. Fate would determine that this would be their last time to fly together, and Pearl later would be "so thankful that it was in the *Winnie Mae*."[18]

Pearl immensely enjoyed flying during her high school years. In addition to her appearances at special events and air circuses, she flew her father to various locations so he could conduct business. And she flew for the "fun, the thrills, and the danger of it!" Pearl and her compatriots "could land and take off wherever and whenever we wanted to, the skies were clear of planes, and there were very few regulations which no one paid any attention to." The only instruments in her Curtiss Robin were oil pressure and fuel-level gauges, an altimeter, and a compass. These early aviators flew by "the seat of their pants," and it was exhilarating. Six decades later, Pearl would "feel sorry for the pilots today, under so much stress, crowded skies, so many regulations, and so many instruments."[19]

Pearl benefited by her father's growing infatuation with aviation. By 1929, George was flying frequently and using his aviation facilities for the benefit of the Marlow community. For Easter in 1929, one of the eggs in the town's Easter egg hunt had a number on it that would entitle the owner to a free ride in the Curtiss Robin airplane. Unfortunately, the egg (number 411) must have been well hidden because no one found it! In July of 1929, George provided his airport facilities and his two airplanes for use during a three-day air circus that would take place July 3-5. Stunt flyer Don Clayton was featured, and he performed "wing-overs, nose dives, banks and virtually every other stunt that experienced aviators" had conquered to date.[20]

Don Clayton also served as George's pilot because Pearl's school obligations often prevented her from being available when George needed to travel. However, Pearl still flew her father on weekends and when she was out of school. One such trip must have been particularly memorable. She flew her father, with Clayton as a passenger, from Marlow to Ada, Oklahoma, and back. Because aviation was still a novelty, many of George's trips, including this one, were reported in the Marlow newspaper, which referred to Pearl as a "youthful aviatrix." The flight to Ada was routine and was accomplished in forty-five minutes, but they encountered "rough flying conditions" on the return trip, which required ninety minutes and a landing after dark.[21]

Pearl and her father had another aviation adventure on a trip to Tennessee, Alabama, and Georgia to see relatives in 1929. On this trip, George's pilot at the time, Norman Powell, flew the plane. They first went to Little Rock, Arkansas, so George could visit the Arkansas School for the Blind. While there, he was able to visit one of his old teachers who still remained on the faculty. Because the teacher was still using the same room as before, George was able to walk unguided from the main office to the teacher's room. Visiting his old school, which had done so much for him, was meaningful to George, and Pearl enjoyed seeing the school that her daddy had talked about.[22]

When they departed Little Rock, they encountered snow, and by the time they reached Memphis, Tennessee, the snow was getting heavy. Fearing the possibility of ice forming on the wings of their plane, they decided to land at Memphis. The airport had one hangar, a second one under construction, and a little house that served as an office. The secretary in the office served them coffee and doughnuts, and George made arrangements to store the airplane there. The travelers caught a train to continue their trip.[23]

George Carter, Sr.'s Eaglerock Biplane as it appeared after mechanical problems caused Arthur Williamson to force land the craft in a wheat field, during which the plane flipped. Fortunately, Arthur was not injured, and the Eaglerock was repaired and returned to service. (Courtesy Bob Williamson)

George enjoyed flying so much that he sometimes offered his plane and pilot to others for trips, especially if he could go along for the ride. One such trip was reported in the Marlow newspaper with the headline, "And the Speed Cops Couldn't Do Anything." R. H. Morgan, an attorney who lived in Anadarko, Oklahoma, departed that community at 11 a.m. on a business trip. "He first went to Lawton, then to Marlow, Muskogee, McAlester and up to Tulsa, transacting business in all those places," the paper reported. On the return trip, he stopped in Oklahoma City for fuel and arrived in Anadarko at 6 p.m. "on the same day, making the trip in exactly seven hours." The trip was undertaken in the Curtiss Robin with Norman Powell serving as pilot. George was a passenger for the trip which covered between five and six hundred miles. "All landings were made without mishap," the newspaper reported, and "the plane traveled at an altitude between 2,000 and 4,000 feet."[24]

▼▼▼

Pearl played violin in the Marlow School Orchestra when it was formed during the 1925-26 school year. She would have been ten years old at the time. In this photograph of the orchestra, she is on the far right in the front row. (Courtesy Marlow Chamber of Commerce)

Interestingly, George was not satisfied to be a mere passenger; from time to time he actually flew both the Curtiss Robin and the Eaglerock. Accompanied by his pilot, George could fly his planes, "and fly them well." He was able to "take off and maneuver ships in the air without difficulty and calls on [pilot Don] Clayton to take the controls when he wants to land." George asserted that he could feel his way off the ground and around in the air, but "feeling out a landing is something that simply can't be done." George would have loved to have been a full-fledged aviator, although he must have vicariously become one through his precocious daughter and her unbridled joy of flight.[25]

Pearl was a unique student in school because of her sports car and airplane. She managed to integrate her flying with school activities. As a member of the Marlow High School pep squad, the Marlow newspaper reported the young aviator would "be at the Marlow-Duncan football game at the county fairgrounds Thursday doing her share of the pep leading." Pearl flew to this and other Marlow away games in her Curtiss Robin.[26]

Flying remained a priority activity for Pearl during her school years, but other activities, especially her music, also were important to her. Pearl had been playing violin and saxophone for a number of years when the Marlow school orchestra was formed during the 1925-26 school year.

Lucy, left, Pearl, and George, Sr., proudly posed in front of Pearl's Curtiss Robin airplane in the pasture that George converted into an "airport." The photo appears to have been taken ca. 1931.

Tina Mae Gaylord, one of the teachers, asked all students who could play an instrument to report to her. Nineteen students reported and the Marlow school orchestra had its first players. Pearl was among them, playing violin. Most of the musicians had been taught by Mrs. Bob Anderson, the same lady who had taught Pearl.[27]

In 1927, to give the group a more uniform look, they acquired blue sweaters with a white lyre "that had a big blue 'M' on it." With that sweater, the girls wore blue skirts and the boys wore dark slacks. Later the group had white sweaters featuring a blue lyre with a white "M" on it. The youngsters were "so proud to wear" these first band uniforms. The orchestra played at school assemblies, graduations, and other functions. In 1928, the school formed a band in which Pearl played saxophone. For a while, the school had both an orchestra and a band, but the orchestra was discontinued in 1929, leaving only the band from then on.[28]

The new school band began playing at Marlow High School football games. At first there were no bleachers, so the band sat to play in chairs on the sideline. Fairly often, members of the band would have to grab their chairs and scramble to keep from getting run over by the football players. The band did not perform at half time, as it would in later years. The pep squad did perform at half time, however, so those band members who wanted to be in the pep squad were allowed to do both, and Pearl and many of her friends did that. While Pearl was in the band, she witnessed a huge fight that broke out during a football game between Marlow and Duncan. By then, the Marlow field had a stadium, and Pearl was shocked to see many townspeople from both Marlow and Duncan run onto the field to participate in the fracas. This led to the end of the football rivalry between Marlow and Duncan.[29]

The bandstand located on West Main Street in downtown Marlow was a popular gathering place for such varied events as band concerts, radio broadcast of election results, and championship boxing matches. Pearl played there with the Rush Springs band on several occasions. (Courtesy Marlow Chamber of Commerce)

Marlow also had a town band for a number of years as did nearby Rush Springs. Charlie Kreiger was the director of both bands. Pearl wanted to play her saxophone in the Marlow band, but it was full. Consequently, she played in the Rush Springs town band. Marlow had a bandstand located on West Main Street, where the post office later was built, and a band concert was held there almost every Friday night. The bandstand also was a gathering place where election results were announced over a loudspeaker. People gathered on the grass or sat in their cars to hear the election returns. Fights sometimes broke out among those with opposite political views. Radio broadcasts of championship boxing matches also were played through the sound system for the assembled crowds to hear. Band concerts, elections, boxing matches, and major radio events provided a good reason for a "big town get together." "It was so good then," Pearl recalled years later.[30]

A favorite gathering place for Pearl and her friends was called "End of Pavement." Highway 29 was paved for only two miles heading east from Marlow. Where the pavement ended was the location of many skating and dance parties. The students used the pavement as a skating rink, "It was the only place large enough around Marlow, and of course there was hardly a car to come by in those days." Parents would pack lunches for their children, take them and their skates to "End of Pavement," and then retrieve them at an agreed upon time.[31]

In high school, Pearl got to work as an "office girl," but the job must not have been too demanding. Sometimes "kids would play hooky from Rush Springs or Duncan and come around," and Pearl "would slip out of the office and run around with them until time to change classes" and then she would slip back into school for her next class.[32]

While in high school, Pearl apparently had plans to attend Central State Teachers College at Edmond, Oklahoma, after graduation from high school. A newspaper article outlined her plans to commute via airplane from Marlow to Edmond and back each day. Her parents estimated that the trip would take fifty-five minutes one way, which was less time than they had spent walking to school when they were Pearl's age. But Pearl was not destined to commute to Central State or any other college at this time in her life. Indeed, her days as an aviator already were numbered. During a span of seven years, events on a global scale, such as the Great Depression of the 1930s, the deaths of key figures in Pearl's life, and her falling in love, combined to completely change the direction of Pearl's life.[33]

Chapter Five
▼▼▼

RICHES TO RAGS

A dramatic turn in Pearl's life came when she met a tall, lanky, handsome farmer named Lewis Scott, who was six years and six days older than Pearl. Scott was born in Nellie, a small community west of Marlow in Stephens County. His parents were William Lewis Scott and Sally Roxanna (Richardson) Scott. The elder Scotts were referred to by Pearl as Pa and Ma, and she affectionately called their son "Scottie." The Scott family was large, as Scottie had two sisters, five half sisters, and four half brothers. The Scott home and farm was near Marlow, "a half a mile west of Nabor Street," where they had a "big, two-story white house." It is not known how Pearl met Scottie.[1]

Once they became acquainted and began falling in love, Pearl used her flying skills to flirt with Scottie. Pearl managed to fly almost every day after school. She soon discovered that she often would see Scottie behind some mules plowing in one of the fields on his family's farm. She fashioned a small parachute that she used to drop notes to him from her Curtiss Robin. "I would buzz him and drop my note," Pearl recalled, and "he would sure have to hold his old plow mules."[2]

Scottie and Pearl did much of their "courting" at the Jones and Graves Drug Store. The store sold records and had a music room, where customers could listen to records before purchasing them. Pearl and Scottie en-

Pearl, left, and Arnetta were attractive young women when this photo was taken ca. 1940. Approximately twenty-five years old at this time, Pearl already had been married nine years and was the mother of three children. (Courtesy Joseph Carter Brooks)

joyed listening to music in the music room, and that is where Scottie asked Pearl to marry him. Pearl said yes. She must have believed that her parents, who had plans for her to go to college, would not approve, but they decided to "tie the knot" anyway.[3]

On Thursday, February 5, 1931, when her parents thought she was taking a music lesson, Pearl and Scottie "ran off" and got married at Lawton in the First Methodist Church. Lydia Mae Stallons and Marvin Racheal were witnesses. George and Lucy were stunned when they heard the news. As Pearl noted, "Momma and Daddy weren't very happy with me getting married." Pearl was a married woman not quite two months past her sixteenth birthday. Sixty-eight years later, Pearl comment-

Pearl's husband, Lewis Scott, as he appeared in his middle to late twenties. (Courtesy Pearl Scott Collection)

ed on her marriage; "I got married before I finished high school and I am ashamed for marrying so young! I was 16. That was not uncommon then. But to people now it would be."[4]

For a while after they were married, Pearl and Scottie lived with his family. Friends helped them begin their married life together by having a "shivaree" for them and three other couples—Guy and Ruth Taylor, Asa and Leatrice Taylor, and Albert and Theda Stone—who had gotten married at about the same time. The men had to push their wives down Main Street of Marlow in wheelbarrows. When they got to the jail, which was a small building behind the City Hall, the "friends" locked up the new husbands. Albert Stone thought he would play a joke on the shivaree crowd. He had some tear gas with him, and he "pitched it out into the crowd." He soon realized that he had made a mistake when "the wind blew it right back in the jail on the guys."[5]

George and Lucy could not stay mad at Pearl. Before too much time passed, they got over their disappointment with her early marriage, and soon Pearl and Scottie had a home of their own. In fact, George gave Pearl two farms, former Indian allotments, and built her a new house on the farm located at the west end of Main Street in Marlow. The other farm was located "about two miles west on Caddo Street." Pearl and Scottie were ready to begin married life as farmers and start a family in the depths of the Great Depression, which had begun when the stock market crashed in October of 1929. By the time of their marriage, unemployment was rising dramatically and farm prices were plummeting.[6]

Pearl and Scottie's first child, Georgia Louise, was born on January 13, 1932 in the home of Pearl's parents. Pearl was barely seventeen. A year and a half later, on July 5, 1933, Pearl and Scottie had a son, Billy Joe, who was born at the Kiowa Indian Hospital in Lawton. Five months before her nineteenth birthday, Pearl was the mother of a toddler and a baby. Carter Roy, Scottie and Pearl's third and last child, was born on March 11, 1936, in Lawton. Pearl and Scottie would also endure the heartbreak of two miscarriages, which resulted in the loss of two baby boys.[7]

As some point, Pearl's children began referring to George, Sr. and Lucy as "Big Daddy" and "Big Mama." In later years, Bill Scott could not remember calling them any other name. In fact, all of their grandchildren and great-grandchildren affectionately referred to them in this manner.[8]

Not long after her marriage, Pearl resumed her aviation activities. Various articles referring to Mrs. Lewis Scott flying her father's Curtiss Robin airplane appeared in the Marlow newspaper. Typical of such articles was one reporting that "Mr. and Mrs. Lewis Scott and Tony Bayliss made a trip via airplane to Wilson. . . Mrs. Scott piloting . . ." the plane. The return trip, the story noted, "was made in thirty minutes." Another article reported that George Carter, "Marlow land man," and "his daughter, Mrs. Lewis Scott, will fly to Dallas, Sunday, in Mr. Carter's Curtiss Robin monoplane."[9]

Pearl's days as an aviator came to an end, however, at age eighteen. By then Pearl had a husband, a baby, and another child on the way. Shortly before the birth of her second baby, Pearl realized that she loved stunt flying and just could not resist doing it when she was in the air. She was "just too much of a daredevil." So Pearl walked away from one of the great passions of her life—flying. At age eighteen, she recognized and accepted that she had a family that she loved and that needed her.[10]

The same year that Pearl and Scottie began their lives together as

Scottie's parents, W. L. and Sally Scott, were affectionately knows as "Pa" and "Ma" to to Pearl and other family members. They are shown here sitting on the front porch of their home west of Marlow. (Courtesy Pearl Scott Collection)

farmers a severe drought began that would plague the central and southern plains from 1931 until the fall of 1939. Although Marlow was not in the area most dramatically impacted by inadequate rainfall, the farmers of the region suffered tremendously from the parched conditions that prevailed. The difficult economy affected farmers and townspeople alike, and everybody was forced to endure the amazing dust storms that rolled over much of the nation, including southwestern Oklahoma.

Far northwestern Oklahoma, the western half of Kansas, a small area of southwestern Nebraska, much of eastern Colorado, and a relatively small area of northeastern New Mexico were the heart of the Dust Bowl. It was in this area that poor farming techniques combined with a severe and prolonged drought to cause the top soil to begin blowing away in the powerful winds that frequented the region. Vast clouds of dust often traveled hundreds of miles and made life miserable for those unfortunates in the pathways. The agricultural economy of the Great Plains region was devastated, and this situation helped deepen and prolong the Great Depression. The difficulties of production combined with low prices for agricultural products to make tenant farming virtually impossible to sustain, and many share croppers from Oklahoma, Arkansas, and other states in the region joined a great migration of destitute families on Route 66 to find work in California.[11]

Dust began to blow in 1931, and fourteen dust storms were reported in 1932. That number would increase to thirty-eight in 1933. Southwestern Oklahoma was severely impacted by the drought, making subsistence as a farmer difficult. Moreover, many dust storms found their way to the Marlow area, and they were "just awful," Pearl later recalled. Massive clouds of dust rolling along the ground, "sometimes red looking and sometimes kind of white," could be seen in the distance, moving majestically toward Marlow.[12]

Pearl and Lewis "would have to shut doors and windows" regardless of the heat, "but still it came in, would pile up like snow banks, even at the doors." Pearl often had to wash the sand off dinner plates and out of coffee cups and glasses to prepare them for use, and she frequently "had to shake out the bed clothes to even go to bed" because "they would be covered in dust. I'd sprinkle our beds with water so we could get a little sleep." There were days when Pearl and her family "could hardly get out" of their house.[13]

Lewis and Pearl's primary farm activity that produced income was raising cattle. That quickly became a most difficult venture. Like others in the cattle business, Pearl and Lewis soon ran out of cattle feed, and "there was none to buy, everyone ran out." Grass could not grow in sufficient quantity on the parched pastures of the plains. Pearl and Lewis devised a desperate plan in an attempt to cope with the situation. They rented some additional pasture land east of Marlow from her father and then began rotating their cattle between their pasture on the west side of Marlow and the rented pasture, thus allowing some grass to grow in the pastures while the cattle were absent.[14]

Pearl and Scottie had city water available on their farm, but when the grass there was depleted, they would move the cattle to the rented pasture "six or seven miles" east of town. Pearl would pack a lunch and water for herself, Scottie, and hired hand Hubert "Beans" Gibson, and they would mount their horses and drive the cattle to the alternate pasture. Pearl quickly learned how to be a "cowboy" as the trio moved "about one hundred head or more of cattle" during these "cattle drives." The youthful Pearl viewed her cattle driving experience as "fun."[15]

While the cattle were on the rented pasture, Scottie and Beans use the Scott's pickup truck to go there each day to dig in the bed of the creek on that property to uncover some water for the cattle to drink. For most of these daily excursions, Pearl would pack a lunch and, along with the children, would accompany Scottie. The cattle would remain on the rented pasture for about ten days "to let a little grass grow at home," and then the three "cowboys" would drive them back to the home pasture. This rotation continued "till there was no grass" in either pasture.[16]

Finally, the federal government began purchasing cattle to assist desperate farmers and ranchers. The price Scottie and Pearl received was $5.00 a head, Pearl later recalled. Their choice was either sell the cattle or watch them starve to death. Government officials herded the cattle into the Scott's corral "and shot them, all of them, then dragged them to the creek and buried them. It was an awful sight to see," for Pearl and her family.[17]

Pearl and Scottie later were able to rebuild their cattle herd and resumed the movement of cattle from one pasture to the other. This resulted in the last cattle drive to take place in Marlow in 1938 or 1939, Pearl later recalled. Approximately two hundred head of cattle were driven down Marlow's Main Street "around 1:00 or 2:00" in the morning by Scottie, Howard Hill, Charlie Hill, Ralph Stone, and Beans Gibson from the east pasture to the Scott's home at the west end of Main Street.[18]

From the perspective of the Scott children, the Great Depression did not affect them because they had plenty to eat while the families of their school friends all had to be careful with their expenditures. They lived just a few blocks from their school, so they usually walked home for lunch. Yet Louise enjoyed the days when Pearl was busy, and the children could eat at school. One of Louise's favorite meals at school featured "cooked raisins and little white beans" as well as an apple or an orange.[19]

Pearl and Scottie had an orchard and a large garden, so Pearl canned the fruit and vegetables that the family did not consume when they were fresh. Pearl used some of the fruit to make jelly. They also had a cow that produced fresh milk, and Pearl recalled, "Gee! that thick cream was

Pearl and Lewis posed with various members of the Scott family in this photo in front of a broomcorn crop. Pearl is on the far right in the front row while Lewis is standing fourth from the right in the second row. Lewis' older brother Roy, standing to the far left, was a favorite of Pearl and her family. (Courtesy Pearl Scott Collection)

good." Chickens provided fresh eggs and occasional fried chicken dinners. Scottie raised hogs and most years killed four hogs during the winter. Pearl would can sausage and "fresh side meat," and they also had sugar cured ham. Corn from the garden was a tasty addition to the family's diet, Bill Scott recalled, "it used to be a lot sweeter than it is now." Corn also was taken to a local mill where it was ground into cornmeal that, Pearl remembered, "would make the best cornbread!"[20]

Another farm delicacy enjoyed especially by Scottie and Bill was "mountain oysters" or "calf fries." The testicles of castrated cattle were sliced, breaded, and fried and "all the men ate them. People never raised on a farm don't realize that . . . you ate everything grown on a farm." As an adult, Bill would describe harvesting, cooking, and eating calf fries and in the process "made a lot of people turn pale." Bill also loved eating a variety of fruit called "Indian Peaches because they were red, and when you canned them the juice was real red." Moreover, "they were sweet as can be." 'While the Great Depression wrought havoc with the economy, the Scott family had plenty to eat due to the hard work of Scottie and Pearl.[21]

Although Pearl had quit flying, her recent flying career and her association with the internationally-famous Wiley Post continued to bring her some attention. On August 15, 1935, Pearl's father called to ask her to come to his office to meet with Burrell Tibbs and Keith Kahle. Pearl and George knew Tibbs, the renowned, barnstorming aviator and mentor of Wiley Post, who had helped deliver Pearl's Curtiss Robin. Kahle was a reporter for an aviation magazine called *Taxi Strip*. He later founded Central Airlines and would be inducted into the Oklahoma Aviation Hall of Fame. Kahle had traveled to Marlow with Tibbs to interview George about their experiences with Wiley.[22]

Some years later, Tibbs recalled that he and Kahle were late for their meeting and found George Carter "unsmiling and not talkative and thought that was about us being late." Tibbs began talking about Post and Will Rogers, mentioning that they had embarked on a trip around the world together and speculating on when they would return. It was then, Tibbs recalled, that "Carter told me . . . about hearing of the plane crash in Alaska on the radio." Wiley's new airplane (the *Winnie Mae* had been retired) had crashed on takeoff at Point Barrow, Alaska, and both Wiley and Will were dead. Interestingly, in recalling the incident, Tibbs referred to George as an Indian.[23]

Pearl's recollection differed from that of Tibbs in that she remembered that her father received a phone call after Tibbs and Kahle had arrived, informing him that Wiley and Will had been killed in a plane crash in Alaska. However the news was received, it had a devastating impact on the four friends of Wiley gathered in George's office. Pearl remembered, "You talk about tears!" As she cried, Pearl recalled Wiley telling her, "Now Shorty, you fly that plane and don't let that plane fly you." Pearl then thought, "Wiley, you let that plane fly you." In one tragic accident, Oklahoma had lost its two favorite sons.[24]

The deaths of Wiley Post and Will Rogers plunged the nation into mourning. Rogers was arguably the most popular figure in America at the time of his death, and Post was internationally renowned as an aviation pioneer. Indeed, many considered him to be the world's greatest

A Carter family portrait ca. 1935. From left to right: Opaletta Carter Williamson, Jewell Arnetta Carter Brooks, Lucy Gibson Carter, George Carter, Jr., George Carter, Sr., and Eula Pearl Carter Scott. By this time, Lucy was known to her grandchildren as "Big Mama" and George, Sr., was called "Big Daddy." The prosperity of the family was reflected in the quality of their clothes, but events soon would reduce the family's wealth significantly. (Courtesy Art Williamson)

aviator. When Post's body was returned to Oklahoma via a Pan American Airlines airplane, 8,000 people were at the airport to pay their respects. From there, the body was taken to Watts and McAtee Funeral Home in Oklahoma City, where the following morning thousands passed the aviator's casket. The casket was then transported to Maysville, some sixty miles from Oklahoma City. Residents of cities and communities as well as farm folk lined the highway to pay tribute. In Maysville, thousands filed by his casket.[25]

The body was returned to Oklahoma City to lie in state in the rotunda of the state Capitol. There in the August heat, an estimated twenty thousand gathered to file by the casket. After a ceremony presided over by Governor E. W. Marland, Wiley's body was transported to the First Baptist Church in downtown Oklahoma City for the funeral. Oilman Frank Phillips chaired the 150 honorary pall bearers that included Oklahoma's United States Senators Thomas P. Gore and Elmer Thomas, Harold Gatty, famed aircraft manufacturer Walter Beech, aviation pioneer Paul Braniff, and United States Secretary of State Cordell Hull. Prominent aviators Amelia Earhart, Bennett Griffin, Jimmy Mattern, and Art Goebel also were among the mourners in attendance. The church seated two thousand and was jammed, while a throng of almost twenty thousand massed outside the church and listened to the service over loudspeakers that had been set up for that purpose. Some estimated that forty thousand were gathered within a two-block radius of the church. The service was broadcast on radio stations KOMA and WKY, and it was the largest funeral in Oklahoma history. Another ten thousand people waited at the cemetery where Wiley was laid to rest.[26]

Few people grieved more over Wiley's death than Pearl. In her development as an aviator and as a person, Wiley's influence was second only to that of her father. From her father's example and Wiley's pronouncements and deeds, she had adopted her personal motto, "Never give up!" Wiley had taught her to fly, had bolstered her confidence, and had treated her like a daughter. The Carter family drove to Oklahoma City for the funeral, but Pearl did not attend. She knew she "couldn't get up close" because of the massive crowd. Pearl did not want to go because she believed that to the masses "it was a curiosity; they didn't know him. They just went because it was Wiley Post. I didn't want that." [27]

Pearl got to see the *Winnie Mae* again a few years after Wiley's death. In 1939 she was able to visit the Smithsonian Institution in Washington, D. C., and there she saw the famous airplane on exhibit. Many thoughts and memories went through her mind as she gazed at the flying machine that had carried her friend to aviation immortality. She had many happy memories of Wiley and the many things he had taught her. She thought also of her father's special friendship with Wiley and of how she had served as "a bond between them, for I was their creation and both were proud of me." Such thoughts must have been especially moving for Pearl, for by this time she had lost not only Wiley but also her father.[28]

In the summer and fall of 1935, at about the time of Wiley Post's death, George Carter, Sr., began having trouble with his kidneys. His physician advised him to drink a bottle of beer every evening after work to "flush them out." Lucy and her friend Mae O'Quinn decided to surprise their husbands and brew their own beer. They made it in the basement of the Carter home, but, being novice brewers, they bottled the beer while it was still "green." Hidden in the tunnel between the main basement room and the storm shelter rooms, the brew continued to ferment, releasing gases and building pressure in the bottles. After a few days, the bottles began to explode.[29]

Upstairs, the family would hear a loud noise and George would ask about it. Lucy concocted several explanations until the explosions came so frequently that she had to tell him the truth. Lucy and Mae had to start over and eventually learned when to bottle their brew.[30]

George's regimen of a beer a day did not solve his kidney problems. Early in the morning on Tuesday, September 8, 1936, George became seriously ill and was rushed to the Patterson Hospital in Duncan where he died at 6 a.m. the following day of uretic poisoning. The news of his death shocked the Marlow community, as only his family and a few close friends knew that he had been hospitalized. The news of his passing was printed in a number of newspapers and was announced on local radio stations as well. His body laid in state for three days, and many came to pay their respects. During his funeral, all the stores in Marlow closed as did many of the offices in the Stephens County Courthouse.[31]

George's funeral was held at the First Methodist Church of Marlow. The Reverend Simeon Charleston of Duncan, a close family friend, officiated and was assisted by Reverend Guy Ames of Marlow. Among those attending were former Oklahoma Governors Martin E. Trapp and J. C. Walton and United States Senator Thomas P. Gore.[32]

Coming only thirteen months following the death of Wiley, George's sudden illness and death dealt Pearl a devastating blow. When her father died, Pearl wrote years later, "a part of me died too, there is just a part of me gone." Noting that she was a "part of him and he was a part of me," Pearl believed that was why her sisters, brother, and mother had been so good to her. "They understand and try to fill in that gap in my life, for they know I have never gotten over his death," she wrote. Her father had said that he wanted his flowers in "deeds and words while he was living and could enjoy them. Not to wait . . . to bring flowers to his grave to wither and die . . ." Pearl once heard George tell a friend that Pearl gave him his flowers while he could enjoy them, "so I can't take flowers" to his grave. George gave flowers "to everyone who knew him," and he gave his "special one" to Pearl, who thanked "God for giving me such a wonderful daddy."[33]

Pearl and her family were hit hard economically as well as emotionally by George's death. Pearl believed that George had between 350 and 450 farms, rent houses, and business buildings at the time of his death. This was in addition to personal property such as two airplanes and investments such as stocks and bonds. This would seem to have been plenty to have left his wife and children each with a sizable inheritance. Years later, Pearl would write that when her father died, "of course I inherited

Lucy posed for this photograph in the late 1930s with a number of her grandchildren, including Pearl's daughter Louise, standing to the left of Lucy, and Pearl's sons Carter, second from the right in the front row, and Billy, on the far right of the front row. (Courtesy Art Williamson)

a lot and was quite wealthy for a little while, only I didn't get the benefit of it, and everything I had was soon lost."[34]

Problems began when Lucy could not find George's will. He supposedly had made a will a year or so before he died, but it was nowhere to be found. George thus was considered to have died "intestate," and his estate went into probate with Lucy as the executor of the estate. In addition to the will, there were some deeds to property also missing. Pearl came to believe that much of the estate was lost to the family in the probate process, as individuals may have taken advantage of her mother, who was not sophisticated in business matters.[35]

▼▼▼

The status of George's finances at the time of his death in 1936 is difficult to ascertain. The Great Depression had a devastating impact on agriculture in general and share cropping operations in particular. Virtually all of George's farms were operated by share croppers who received a portion of the value of the crops they grew as payment for their labor while the remainder went to George. Agriculture did not prosper in the late 1920s, and after 1929 prices for various crops plummeted. This must have had a severe impact on George's income. In addition, it is clear that many of the farms he operated were leased by him from the land owners, many of whom were Indians who did not want to farm their land or deal with tenants. These leased farms and the income they generated would not have been in the estate as they were not owned by George. He also oversaw tenant farm operations for other land owners. For example, he operated five farms for his friend M. E. Trapp, former governor of Oklahoma.[36]

Just before the onset of the Great Depression, George had spent significant money for a Durant sports car, two airplanes, the construction of an airport and hangar on his land, and a full-time pilot. He continued flying regularly during the early part of the 1930s, a costly activity. If George's finances suffered from 1929 to 1936, that would not have been unusual for someone whose income was based heavily on sharecropping operations. Moreover, he likely would not have shared these difficulties with his family. In addition, Pearl recalled that he helped a number of his tenants with cash gifts during the Depression. George never mentioned these gifts, but people who had benefited from his generosity told his family about it later. He also put a significant amount of money into local banks to help them remain solvent.[37]

According to a document issued by the Estate Tax Division of the Oklahoma Tax Commission, George's estate at the time of his death was valued at $15,475.83. Of this amount, the bulk ($11,103.83) was in personal property while $4,257.00 was in "real estate, oil and gas leases, etc." By the time the final decree of the probate court was issued on April 26, 1937, the total value of the estate was listed at $8,236.51, of which Pearl was to receive a one-sixth share, or $1,372.75. Expenses to the estate had included funeral expenses, various legal fees, a monthly stipend to relative O. L. Bayliss for help in administering the estate, cash distribution to the heirs, the purchase of a new car, and various other expenses. While Pearl's share of the estate was a nice sum of money in 1937, it did not represent a particularly sizable inheritance. However it happened, the large bequest that Pearl and her mother and siblings might have expected certainly did not materialize.[38]

Lucy was married for a short time to Roy Hodges, who helped dissipate the family fortune. This photo was taken on property near Phoenix, Arizona, which Hodges apparently acquired while married to Lucy. In the front row, left to right, are Junior Jones and George Carter, Jr. In the back row, left to right, are Roy Hodges, Lucy, Arthur T. Williamson, and Opaletta, holding an unidentified child. (Courtesy Art Williamson)

As a relatively young widow, who probably was believed by many to command more wealth than she actually had, Lucy was an obvious target for individuals interested in her money. Moreover, she had been married since she was fifteen years old, had little formal education, and had never had to manage money. George, Sr., always had plenty, it seemed, and Lucy had charge accounts at various stores and pretty much purchased whatever she wanted. She had always had George to handle the money, and just over six months after his death, on March 24, 1937, she had another husband to oversee her finances.[39]

Lucy married Roy Hodges, an oilfield worker who apparently was more interested in spending Lucy's money than in working. The marriage was doomed to fail but not before causing Lucy and, no doubt, her children considerable anxiety. Lucy apparently was smitten by Hodges, even though he was in considerable legal trouble at the time of their marriage. While drinking, Hodges had struck and inadvertently killed a sixty-year-old man. Witnesses indicated that Hodges did not know the man, who in no way provoked Hodges into striking him. Recoiling from the blow he received from Hodges, Jasper McAfee's head struck a post, and he fell to the ground with a broken neck and died. Hodges was arrested the next day while staying at a friend's house in Oklahoma City and was subsequently charged with murder, tried, and convicted of manslaughter in the first degree. Hodges was sentenced to seven years in the state prison at McAlester.[40]

With the help of Lucy's money, Roy appealed his conviction to the State Court of Criminal Appeals and was represented by attorney Bob Howe of Oklahoma City. His conviction and sentence, however, were upheld on December 16, 1938. Hodges, fortified with his new spouse's resources, hired prominent attorneys O. A. Cargill, Howard K. Berry, and Bob Howe, all of Oklahoma City, and the firm of Ogden and Thompson of Ardmore to pursue a second appeal. This time the lawyers were successful in getting Hodges' sentence reduced to four years in a ruling on July 7, 1939.[41]

Ironically, Hodges had received several "leaves of absences" from the prison during the appeals process. During one such ten-day sojourn to Marlow, he threatened to kill Lucy unless she signed over a parcel of land to him so he could use that asset to obtain funds to allow him to procure a parole. She conveyed the property to Hodges, which he used to secure a loan of $750 to hire a lawyer in McAlester to help him in the parole process. When Hodges returned to prison, however, she filed for divorce, alleging that he had made "numerous threats on her life" to force her to convey the property to him. Moreover, she contended that Hodges was a habitual drunkard and had been "in the habit of coming come home at all hours of the day and night in the state of intoxication." Lucy also stated that he had abused her and her relatives, and that he was a "spend thrift" who had insisted since their marriage that Lucy convey some of her property to him so he could have "money to have a good time on."[42]

Hodges was served in prison with Lucy's petition for divorce on October 25 and chose not to contest the divorce or deny any of the allegations she made against him. Moreover, he conveyed the parcel of land that he had extorted from Lucy back to her. Lucy's decree of divorce and judgment was granted on November 8, 1940, and she received everything she had asked for in her petition, including sole ownership of all property that she

brought into the marriage
and had not already been
sold. Hodges also was "en-
joined and restrained" per-
petually from approaching,
harming, or molesting Lucy
in any way. Hodges was or-
dered to pay Lucy's attorney
fees and "all cost of this action." The divorce became final six months later, in May
of 1941, thus ending four difficult years for Lucy and, no
doubt, her children.[43]

*The Carter family posed in front of their tour-
ing car, ca. 1940. From left to right: Opaletta,
Pearl, Arnetta, George, Jr., and Lucy. (Courtesy Joseph Carter Brooks)*

Two months shy of her
twenty-first birthday, Pearl
had given up flying and had
lost Wiley Post and George
W. Carter, two of the three
most influential people in
shaping her life. Moreover,
six months later her mother
married Roy Hodges, which
proved to be a costly mistake
that took a heavy emotional
and financial toll. Pearl's
attitude toward Hodges was

*By the time of this family photograph in 1941,
Lucy apparently was free of Roy Hodges.
Enjoying a family gathering was, left to right:
Bobby Williamson, Lucy, George, Jr., George's
wife Catherine Parker, Pearl, Opaletta, Ar-
netta, and her husband Joe Wilson Brooks.
(Courtesy Joseph Carter Brooks)*

reflected in the fact that she never mentioned him once in all her writings
or interviews. Yet, she endured the situation and on at least one occasion
drove Lucy to McAlester to visit Hodges in prison.[44]

Lucy and her children felt sufficiently prosperous in 1939, however,
to drive to New York to see the world's fair during a respite from Lucy's
troubles with Hodges. Given the state of roads across the nation at that
time, the trip was quite an adventure, but Pearl, her sisters, brother,
and mother thoroughly enjoyed this time together. Among the wonders

they experienced at the fair was television, the commercial development of which would be delayed by World War II. Pearl and her family also enjoyed other stops along the way, including the Smithsonian Institution to see the *Winnie Mae* and Monticello, the home of Thomas Jefferson.[45]

Pearl had received a small inheritance to add to the gifts her father had given her after she married Lewis Scott, but if she assumed that she and her siblings would inherit significant wealth, she was destined to be disappointed. During the 1940s and 1950s, she would experience difficult times financially. Scottie invariably would be compared to Wiley and George, Sr., by Pearl, if only subconsciously, and it would have been difficult for most men to measure up to an international aviation hero and her amazingly talented father. Trying to "make it" as a small farmer in the 1930s and 1940s was exceedingly difficult, and Scottie ultimately would turn to work in the oil fields, which frequently took him away from home. Financial difficulties and separation ultimately would strain their marriage to the breaking point.

Chapter Six
▼▼▼

LIFE ON THE FARM

B y the time the United States was thrust into World War II as a result of the Japanese attack on Pearl Harbor on December 7, 1941, Pearl had entered the job market in Marlow to help with the family's finances. During this time Scottie began working in the oil fields of the region as a roughneck, eventually developing his skills and becoming a pipe fitter. His work took him away from home days at a time, leaving Pearl to raise the children, manage the household, and work outside the home. It was a challenging situation, but she was determined to help financially and be a good mother.

Pearl's first job outside the home was in Marlow as a waitress at the City Café operated by J. W. Taylor. The cafe, the "Hub of Marlow," was a popular establishment that was open twenty-four hours a day and "was always full of coffee drinkers." Many business deals were consummated there, and every Friday night during football season, the Marlow team would come there after the game for a meal. Local fans would come to visit with the boys, "win or lose," drink coffee, and talk about the game. During World War II, while Pearl worked there, the café was a popular spot for oilfield workers as well as soldiers on their way to and from Fort Sill near Lawton.[1]

Pearl worked from 6 p.m. to 6 a.m., a demanding, twelve-hour shift. The waitresses had a problem on Saturday evenings that Pearl helped to

Pearl was proud of her young family. In this photo taken in late 1936 or early 1937 are, left to right: Carter, Louise, and Billy. (Courtesy Pearl Scott Collection)

solve. Men would come to the café from Watt's Pool Hall after that establishment closed. They tended to stay until daylight, laying their arms on their table and going to sleep. Pearl and her co-workers "couldn't clean tables, or do our work." They addressed the problem one Saturday evening. Pearl and her friends "got some red fingernail polish . . . and when the men went to sleep, we painted their nails. We didn't have them from then on."[2]

Pearl later worked on Saturdays at a grocery store in Marlow owned by Karo Taylor. Initially, she worked from 8 a.m. to 12 midnight, but eventually the store changed its hours and closed at 6 p.m. on Saturdays. The store needed extra help on Saturdays because that was the day area farmers came to town to shop and sell their eggs and butter. Pearl and the other employees had to "candle" the eggs to see if any of them were fertile, thereby containing a chicken embryo. They also had to assemble the egg boxes, which came flat, and box the eggs for sale. They used an adding machine to total customers' purchases, and then punched the appropriate keys on the cash register and "cranked" it to record the amount and open the cash drawer. Many of the customers had charge accounts, so each item purchased had to be itemized on the charge slips. Some of the farmers who brought eggs and butter to the store traded them for groceries, while others took cash for their produce.[3]

Among other jobs Pearl held was that of secretary for Oscar Sparks, who operated a real estate office in Marlow. She also worked in the fall for three years at Harry Hill's Co-Op #1 cotton gin, one of six cotton gins in operation in Marlow in the 1940s. Pearl enjoyed the grocery store job more than others that she held during this period of her life because she had more opportunities to interact with large numbers of people.[4]

Although she had to work outside her home, Pearl always believed that being a mother was her first and most important responsibility. In addition to Pearl's three children, Beverly Carter spent a great deal of time at the Scott farm. Beverly was the daughter of Pearl's brother George and his wife, who were divorced when Beverly was five-years-old. At this time, George moved to Oklahoma City and on to other places for a number of years. Beverly remained in Marlow with her mother and became "close" to her Aunt Pearl. Beverly recalled that Pearl was the

By the 1940s Lewis Scott began working in the oilfields of the region, finding that work more profitable that farming full time. He began working as a roughneck, eventually developing his skills to become a pipe fitter. In this photograph, Scottie is in the right foreground, working on an oil well, ca. 1949. (Courtesy Pearl Scott Collection)

"type to hug you. . . . She loved me and I loved her. . . . So when dad came to town, called my mom, I would be over at Aunt Pearl's."[5]

In addition to her work in town, Pearl was mom and dad to her children. "That little woman knew what work was," Beverly Carter recalled. She had to work and take care of her children when she got home, but "she was so strong. She just kept going." Remembering her father's admonition never to say, "I can't," Pearl would tell Beverly and her children that, "Can't never did do anything."[6]

Penn Rabb, a classmate of Bill Scott, was a frequent visitor to the Scott farm, and he was impressed with Pearl as a mother. The youngster observed Pearl's attentiveness and obvious love for her two sons and daughter. "One of the most vivid memories I have of Pearl" is the "love and caring . . . she gave their children as they were growing up. . . . It is obvious that they were a very close-knit family." Others in the Marlow community, such as Jack and Betty Graves, observed Pearl's love for her family and her determination to be the best mother she possibly could be.[7]

Pearl became a talented seamstress so she could save money and make clothes for Louise, Bill, and Carter, as well as for herself. She made shirts for Bill and Carter, and pretty dresses and blouses for Louise and herself. She also made rodeo outfits for Louise and Carter. It was a practical talent, and Pearl loved both the creative and practical aspects of her craft.[8]

Pearl's children were her pride and joy. Her only daughter, Louise, also was her first child. Louise was active in a variety of organizations, including the Order of the Rainbow for Girls, the Brownies, and the school pep squad. A self-described "tomboy,"

Bill Scott's childhood comrade Penn Rabb, shown here in his football uniform in 1947, became a lifelong friend of Bill's. (Courtesy Pearl Scott Collection)

Louise loved horses from early childhood and had her own Shetland pony, as did her brothers. As she grew older, Louise became active in the Marlow Rodeo Club and was rodeo queen for two years. With her younger brother, Carter, Louise would follow the local rodeo circuit, riding her beautiful black stallion Scotty in parades. She "tried barrel racing but couldn't do it." She later sold her horse to Freckles Brown, a "long, tall, gangling kid" who practiced roping at the Scott farm. He later became a world champion bull rider.[9]

Pearl and Scottie's first son, Bill, also had a Shetland pony named Blackie, who was quite cantankerous and perhaps was a factor in Bill's ultimate interest in sports such as football instead of rodeo. The mischievous horse loved to run close to fence posts with barbed wire to "scrape" Bill off. Almost sixty years later, Bill still had scars on his knees from the barbed wire. Blackie also enjoyed running fast and then planting his front hooves, thereby stopping abruptly and sending Bill flying. One Saturday, the entire family was planning on going to town. Bill got cleaned up then decided he would ride his pony. After riding the horse for awhile on the farm, he rode up to a pool of rainwater that had formed on one of the terraces to let the horse, who was "all lathered up," get a drink of water. Blackie waded into the pool and laid down in the water and mud. Wet and muddy, Bill returned to the house, and his parents "weren't too happy" with him.[10]

The farm was a wonderful place for boys like Bill and Carter to grow up during the late 1930s and 1940s. There were several creeks that traversed the farm, and the boys "lived on those creeks." Later in life, Bill would declare that, "We learned a lot about life on those creeks. To this day I firmly believe that all boys ought to grow up on a farm with a creek on it." Friends such as Penn Rabb joined Bill and Carter and "spent many an hour along the creek behind the Scott's house" making what would become "many pleasant memories. . . ."[11]

When Bill and Carter were growing up, the best place in town to swim was a pond on their farm. Known as Scottie's Tank, the pond was a popular spot in the summer for many youngsters. An annual ritual was to see "what was the earliest we could stand to go in swimming," Penn Rabb recalled. Most years the water was too cold until the end of March. For a number of years, most of the boys in Marlow learned to swim and fish in Scottie's Tank. In later years, the City of Marlow constructed a municipal swimming pool just to the west of Scottie's Tank, which still can been seen just south of the road leading to the city pool.[12]

Bill frequently found something of interest as he explored the farm. While playing in the barn where his father kept feed for horses and cattle, Bill saw a large bull snake. He killed the snake but to his dismay soon learned that he had "killed daddy's pet." Scottie had let the snake live in the barn to control the population of rodents that were drawn to the grain. "From that point on I started respecting snakes," Bill recalled, because "he dusted my pants off pretty good."[13]

Bill learned other lessons growing up on the farm. While playing on the creek, he saw some cactus plants in bloom. Attracted by the pretty flowers, he put some of the cactus leaves in his pockets so he could take them to the house and got a load of cactus spines in his thighs. On another occasion, a red ant apparently crawled into Bill's pajamas while they were drying on the clothes line. That evening, when he went to bed, he put on his clean pajamas. He woke the family with a scream in the middle of the night when the ant stung him "where I would be embarrassed to show. It was like someone put a branding iron on me," Bill recalled.[14]

With Scottie often away on a job, Pearl handled much of the necessary discipline, including corporal punishment. Bill remembered "the last time mom spanked me" with one of Scottie's belts for some violation of her rules. "She was vigorously flailing the dust from the seat" of Bill's pants when he looked around at her, "smiled real big," and asked if she was about finished or perhaps getting tired? Pearl realized then that Bill had outgrown that form of punishment and exclaimed, "That's it! No more! You're too big now."[15]

In addition to playing and, as he got a little older, working on the farm, Bill was involved in a number of organizations and activities. Pearl strongly encouraged him to participate in as many worthwhile programs as pos-

Lewis Scott, ca. 1942. (Courtesy Pearl Scott Collection)

sible. He was a Cub Scout, a Boy Scout, a member of Demolay, a participant in various Methodist Church youth groups, a member of the Marlow High School Marching Band, and both a representative in student government and an assistant with the publication of the school annual his senior year. Pearl also encouraged Bill and the other children to appreciate music, ranging in genre from country to classical, history and other non-fiction literature, and "to respect talent of all sorts."[16]

Carter was the baby of the family and, like Louise, loved horses. When he was little, he and Bill used to "ride" the arms of a "plush, stuffed

Left to right: Carter, Louise, and Billy at play at their home at the end of West Main Street in Marlow. (Courtesy Bill Scott)

rocking chair" pretending to chase outlaws and tame wild broncos. He had a Shetland pony named Maggie, who entertained the family by coming to the back door of the house begging for biscuits and gravy. Although no one caught him doing it, Pearl suspected that Carter had fed Maggie biscuits and gravy, and the horse dearly loved that treat. Carter began riding Maggie "about the time he learned to walk." He had learned to ride earlier by pulling himself onto his big dog and riding it. Little Carter would ride Maggie in the Scott's fenced-in yard "all morning and that horse would come like a dog, would stay on the front porch most of the time."[17]

Carter was small for his age, and he did not develop an interest in playing football or basketball. Instead, he was devoted to rodeo. An active member of Marlow's Future Farmers of America chapter and the Marlow Roundup Club, Carter shared Louise's love of riding in rodeo parades. He had a little Palomino horse that he rode bareback with a blanket in place of a saddle, and he dressed as a Plains Indian. Carter "wore a loin cloth and painted his face . . . and legs." Pearl painted "Indian designs all over his horse." The butcher in the grocery store where Pearl worked at the time enjoyed helping her decorate Carter's steed.[18]

Most of the towns in the area of Marlow had active roundup or rodeo clubs, and when a community had a rodeo, they had a parade. Roundup club members from many communities were invited to ride, and townspeople turned out in large numbers to watch. "We'd all go to the parades," Pearl recalled, and Carter and Louise would take their horses and ride in the parades with their friends. It was in connection with one of these parades that Pearl demonstrated her determination to ensure that her children were treated fairly.[19]

▼▼▼

Carter and his friend, Claudell Wallace, were preparing to ride in a rodeo parade, had bathed their horses, and "got them all spruced up." A woman who apparently was a volunteer with the Roundup Club "wasn't going to let them go." Claudell and Carter went to Pearl, who was working in the grocery store, and told their story through sobs and tears. Louise observed that the woman "was an old bossy! It was none of her business," and "It kind of hit mom wrong." Pearl told her boss, "Be back in a minute" and stormed out of the store without removing her apron. She went immediately to the woman's apartment on the second floor of a nearby building and began pounding on the door— "and I don't know what all I said." People began poking their heads out of doors up and down the hallway, but the woman refused to open her door. Claudell and Carter did ride their horses in the parade.[20]

Scottie's older brother Roy Scott, ca. 1965. Bill and Carter knew him affectionately as "Uncle Roy." Both boys worked for Roy and admired and respected him. Pearl also loved him, and when he died in 1967 she grieved as if she had lost an older brother. (Courtesy Pearl Scott Collection)

Pearl had a difficult time keeping up with Carter when he was little because his Uncle Roy, Scottie's "old bachelor" half-brother, loved to come by the house and take Carter with him. Charlie Roy Scott had been the last of nine children born to Scottie's father and his father's first wife, while Scottie had been the second of three children that resulted from his father's second marriage. Roy had attended the public schools in Marlow and was a veteran infantryman who saw extensive combat in Europe during World War I. He returned to Marlow after the war, never married, and became a farmer for the rest of his life.[21]

Bill remembered Roy as a man who played a significant role in the lives of both Carter and Bill. He was characterized by his honesty, generosity, integrity, and work ethic. Roy "would never think of going back on his word and he expected the same" from Bill and Carter. "If a job was to be done, you stayed on that job until it was finished," Bill remembered. One of Roy's favorite expressions was, "Get to workin', we're burning up daylight!" Both boys had a wonderful relationship with Roy.[22]

When Carter was about four or five, he and his Uncle Roy "thought the sun rose and set in each other." Roy and a friend would come by the house, find Carter playing in the yard, and take him with them without telling Pearl. "No matter how much I fussed," Pearl recalled, "anytime Roy got ready to pick him up and take him, he did." On other occasions, Carter would escape from the yard and walk to a pool hall downtown where he knew he would usually find his uncle. Carter's three dogs would follow him to the pool hall and wait patiently for him at the door. Carter was "all ears" at the pool hall, and the men there would "have him saying some things that he got a spanking for."[23]

Uncle Roy sometimes would get both Carter and Bill. and they would help him with some task, such as gathering corn. On one such occasion, Carter was riding with Roy on his Farmall Model B Tractor. When they came to a fence gate, Roy got out and told Carter to get ready to drive the tractor through the gate after Roy got it opened. Carter somehow got the tractor going prematurely, kept hitting the clutch instead of the brake, and, as a result, drove the tractor into the gate, demolishing it. Roy was "cussing and raising Cain. It was a long time before Roy let Carter drive that tractor." When they got home, the boys told Pearl what happened. She asked Carter what Uncle Roy said, and Carter replied, "Oh mother, he said a lot of nasty words!"[24]

Carter's friend Claudell Wallace had an Uncle Irving, who happened to be a close friend of Uncle Roy. Occasionally they would "get on a toot together . . . and one time they were drunk out at Irving's" place. Claudell and Carter were afraid that Irving and Roy were going to get into one of their cars and go driving while drunk, so the boys took both cars and hid them. When Roy and Irving discovered that their cars were missing, they called the police and reported them stolen. Finally, they found the boys who confessed to hiding the cars.[25]

Pearl "loved and respected Roy. . . ." He would "advise her, tease her in his sly wit," and be "her friend" when needed. When Roy died in 1967, Pearl said that she felt as if she had lost an older brother, and his nephews and nieces all felt as it they had lost their "other daddy."[26]

Carter had a wonderful sense of humor and when teased by his older siblings would respond in kind. Louise and Bill would call him Carter's Little Pills, after a product called Carter's Little Liver Pills, and Corduroy, a take off on his name, Carter Roy. Carter countered with names like William Josephine for his brother Billy Joe. Some sixty years later, Louise sometimes still lovingly referred to Bill as William Josephine when writing him. Bill gave Carter another nickname as a result of one of Carter's FFA projects. Carter raised a pig and named him Alabam. Bill soon began calling Carter by the nickname "Alabam," and "He would get so mad!"[27]

The children did their share of chores, including washing dishes. Pearl needed their help in order to work outside the home. When Bill and Carter washed dishes Bill usually would let Carter wash and he would dry. Periodically, Bill could not resist the temptation to "roll a towel up and pop" Carter "on the rear." As those who have been on the receiving end of such an action can attest, a damp towel artfully popped can elicit considerable pain. Carter would grab a knife or anything close by and chase Bill, who fortunately was able to outrun his younger brother.[28]

One incident that occurred when Carter was about eight years old had a searing impact on his memory and his body. The bathroom in the Scott home featured a gas heater mounted in the wall. It was an open-flame heater with a front-mounted grill for safety. Carter was in the bathroom and had taken a bath. In the process of drying himself, he bent over and "his little rear end hit that grid!" Carter screamed at the top of his lungs, and Pearl "went running there and boy it burned him! I think he always had the scars." Pearl comforted Carter, telling him that it wasn't bad, "you just barely did touch it." Carter replied, "Well, Mom it hurts!" Assuring him that it didn't look bad, Pearl applied some salve to the burns. Carter asked, "Did you get it on there?" Pearl said that she had and Carter said, "Okay." He did not cry, Pearl believed, because he believed her when she told him that it did not look bad. But, Pearl later remembered, "It hurt me!"[29]

Both Carter and Bill got to experience the broomcorn harvest. Bill remembered that Carter was too young and small to work as a field hand, so he worked as a water boy. The work was done on their Uncle Clyde and Aunt Florence "Hootie" Lowe's farm. Hootie was Scottie's younger sister.

Pearl and Lucy, ca. 1943. With Scottie working away from home, Pearl put in long hours working outside the home, taking care of her children, and managing the day-to-day tasks involved in keeping house. Yet, she found time to stay close to her mother. (Courtesy Pearl Scott Collection)

Clyde had an old horse named Queen that would be equipped with water bags. Carter would fill the water bags and ride the horse to the workers so they could have a drink. Working in the summer heat, the "broomcorn johnnies" needed to drink plenty of water to prevent dehydration or heat stroke. Throughout the day, Carter would lead the horse back and forth, refilling the water bags and making them available where needed. Bill recalled that, "Everybody started playing tricks on him but he took it all in stride. . . . He was a hard worker."[30]

Bill had started working as a water boy on the broomcorn harvest when he was younger. He later worked as a field hand for the harvests that would last two or three days. The workers would go into the field early in the morning, and at the end of the day, the cut broomcorn would be hauled by wagon to a storage shed. At night the broomcorn was thrashed to remove the seeds. This process would last until about midnight. The hulls and fuzz would get inside the workers' clothing and cause them to itch. "Everyone would just go to the horse tanks and dive in to try to get that fuzz off. . . . It didn't take long to go to sleep." When the crew got through with the Lowe's crop, they would move over to the next farm to help their neighbors.[31]

Bill also remembered that the children would help Clyde and Hootie plant watermelons in the spring, and then "Come late June, we'd start gathering watermelons. They would load them in a pickup truck and take them to Rush Springs, just north of Marlow, to sell them. Rush Springs was known as the Watermelon Capital of the World." The Lowe's grew "big old Black Diamonds. . . . And you hoist those big babies all day long, come night time you are ready to hit the sack."[32]

Saturdays were important to the businesses in Marlow as rural residents in the area came to town for "Egg and Butter Day." Farmers would bring their eggs and butter to sell to the grocery stores, to shop, and to visit with town friends and others from around the county. Drawings for cash or merchandise frequently were held on Saturdays, adding to the excitement. In this photo taken during the early 1930s, the Harlow Dry Goods Company is advertising a $10,000 sale and a drawing for a $75.00 bedroom suite. This photo likely was taken the day of the drawing. (Courtesy Marlow Chamber of Commerce)

Pearl followed her mother's example of taking her children to the First Methodist Church of Marlow every Sunday. Pearl was a lifelong member of the church, and the religious teachings and values of the church would remain with her children throughout their lives. Pearl had each of her children baptized when they were two months old. If anything were to happen to them, she wanted to have had them already baptized.[33]

Growing up in Marlow was a joy for the children. The children in Marlow of the Great Depression and World War II era were "all loyal, highly loyal to each other," Bill remembered. For this particular generation of kids in Marlow, "everybody was the same. We didn't know we had it so bad until someone told us."[34]

The children especially looked forward to "egg and butter day" (Saturday) when "everyone took their eggs and butter to the grocery store to trade for groceries." People strolled the streets to shop and visit, and children played with their friends from town and from the surrounding countryside. In addition, at about 6 p.m., the Chamber of Commerce sponsored a drawing for cash, usually about $50.00 provided by the merchants. Tickets for the drawing were obtained by making purchases from participating businesses. When someone "who didn't need it" would win the cash, some of the disappointed would mutter, "Them that has gets." But they would return with renewed hope the following Saturday. Most people would remain in town Saturday night and Pearl noted that, "Sometimes you could hardly walk down the street it was so crowded."[35]

Halloween was especially fun, as the youngsters would go "trick or treating" with children and many adults going downtown in costumes. One Halloween, Marlow resident Ralph Stone dressed as a woman so effectively that no one recognized him. He went into the City Café, Pearl recalled, hugged and kissed the men "and embarrassed them so much. He had on a wig, high heels and all."[36]

Pearl thought Stone's antics were hilarious. She always loved a good joke or story. Indeed, members of the Scott family frequently played "practical" jokes on one another. One evening, Pearl and Scottie went to a football game while the children went to a see a movie. The children arrived home first after having seen a "scary" movie and decided to have some fun with their parents. They rigged up "a dummy thing" and propped it up in Bill's bed with "blood" all over it. When Pearl and Scottie arrived home, they entered through the back door, which opened into a bedroom. There was just sufficient light from a heater for them to see "Bill" with "blood" all over him. Pearl and Scottie were horrified; the sight almost "scared us to death!" Pearl remembered. After recovering from the shock, Pearl and Scottie made it clear that this particular joke was not very funny, and, according to Louise, "That was the last time we ever pulled anything like that!"[37]

Chapter Seven
▼▼▼

THE HORRORS
OF WAR

W orld War II suddenly intruded upon American families on December 7, 1941, when the Empire of Japan attacked United
States Naval and Army Air Corps installations in Hawaii. The war soon
brought rationing of gasoline, tires, shoes, sugar, and other items in order to maximize supplies available for the war effort. Growing rapidly,
Pearl's children would need shoes about every six months. To conserve
shoe leather, the boys happily went barefoot from the time school was
dismissed in the spring until it started again in the fall. To ease the
shortage of sugar, Scottie planted sugar cane.[1]

Maximum petroleum production was encouraged to support the war
effort, and Scottie found it more profitable to work in the oil fields full
time than farming. And Pearl's brother George was being trained for
combat in Europe. Pearl had lost her father and Wiley Post within the
last six years, and, though she maintained a brave front, she was terrified
that George, Jr., would be killed. Yet, she was proud of him for serving
his country.

George had joined the 45th Infantry Division of the Oklahoma National Guard at the age of seventeen in 1938, and his unit was mobilized
and sent to train at Fort Sill near Lawton, Oklahoma, before the attack

Just under three months prior to his twenty-third birthday, George Carter, Jr.
posed for this photo in England only a few days prior to participating in the D-
Day invasion of France on June 6, 1944. On that day, he would witness unspeak-
able horrors and become a war hero. (Courtesy Marlow Chamber of Commerce)

▼▼▼

on Pearl Harbor. When his unit was sent overseas, however, George was hospitalized with a bone infection and was not allowed go with his comrades, despite his protests. After his recovery, he was assigned to the 5th Combat Engineers Combat Special Brigade, attached to the 16th Infantry Regiment of the United States Army's First Infantry Division, known as "The Big Red One." As fate would have it, when the allies invaded Europe on June 6, 1944, George's brigade was among those assigned to clearing a portion of Omaha Beach of obstacles placed there by entrenched German forces. George would be a part of the largest amphibious assault in world history.[2]

After a few days of training in England, George and thousands of other troops began moving to the coast where they boarded ships to be transported to a spot a few hundred yards off the French coast. At that point they climbed down rope ladders into the landing crafts that would carry them to the beaches of Normandy. The sea was choppy, and the men were loaded with field packs, rifles, ammunition, gas masks, and other items that made the descent into the landing craft difficult. George's unit was in one of the first boats loaded, so they had to circle for some time until all the craft were loaded. During this time, the choppy sea caused the landing craft to bob up and down, and almost all the men "got seasick and nauseated . . . and pretty soon that stuff was inches deep in the bottom of the boat and slopping over everything." The vomit combined with seawater that slopped over the sides of the boat to make the bottom of the craft so slick that it was difficult for the men to stand. George was so seasick that he "didn't care if he ever got to the beach or not."[3]

Finally all the landing craft were loaded and began heading toward their destinations. The target of George's unit was the Easy Red portion of Omaha Beach. As they moved toward shore, the allied ships opened fire on German positions and allied aircraft roared overhead to strafe and bomb the entrenched enemy. "It seemed like the whole navy opened up over our heads," George remembered, and "the Germans opened up as we got closer. They had concrete bunkers, big gun emplacements, trenches connecting them all, barbed wire on the beach and anti-personnel mines. . . ." Some of the landing craft were struck by artillery, rifle or machine gun fire before reaching the beach. In many instances, as soon as the landing ramps were dropped, exposing the men inside the boats, the Germans began pouring machine gun and rifle fire into them.[4]

George's landing craft struck a sand bar some forty yards from the beach. The "sailor that was driving the landing barge lowered the ramp and shouted 'get gone boys'!" The men charged out of the craft and into the chaos of combat. Almost immediately, the sand bar gave way to deep water and the men, as heavily loaded as they were, found themselves in serious trouble. A number of soldiers drowned that day, but George kept his head, got rid of virtually everything that was weighing him down, and began swimming for shore.[5]

However, he soon heard a cry for help from his "best buddy" who "couldn't swim too good and he still had most of his equipment on." George swam to him, helped him shuck his gear, and with eventual assistance from another soldier, got the half-drowned man to shore. As the three men struggled out of the water, a photographer assigned to document the invasion snapped a photograph of them. The photo was published in the army's magazine *Yank* and sixty years later would be prominently displayed at the D-Day Museum in New Orleans, Louisiana. Amid the ongoing carnage on the beach, George worked to revive his friend, who spit out a great deal of sea water and recovered. George also would be photographed later that day, pulling to shore a life raft filled with wounded men. He also helped resuscitate several other men who had nearly drowned. In all, he was credited with saving the lives of at least seven of his comrades while men continued to fall all around him.[6]

After helping others, George and his friend equipped themselves by taking helmets, rifles, ammunition, and other gear from fallen comrades. "There were guns and equipment lying all over the beach because there were so many casualties," George later recalled. The horrors of the combat at Omaha Beach during the D-Day invasion are well documented, and George was in the middle of the heavy action among the desperate, the daring, the dead, and the dying. "We couldn't get off the beach for most of the day," George recalled. "The Germans had what they called pill boxes, and boy they had firepower to beat the band." George was particularly impressed by the deadly accuracy of the German 88-millimeter artillery field piece. German anti-personnel mines, especially the variety

UNITED STATES OF AMERICA
OFFICE OF PRICE ADMINISTRATION

24407 DW

WAR RATION BOOK No. 3 *Void if altered*

OFFICE
OF
PRICE ADM.
R-123

Identification of person to whom issued: PRINT IN FULL

Lillie *Scott*
(First name)   (Middle name)   (Last name)

Street number or rural route 505 h 5th

City or post office Marlow State Okla.

R. R.

AGE	SEX	WEIGHT Lbs.	HEIGHT Ft. In.	OCCUPATION

SIGNATURE
(Person to whom book is issued. If such person is unable to sign because of age or incapacity, another may sign in his behalf.)

WARNING
This book is the property of the United States Government. It is unlawful to sell it to any other person, or to use it or permit anyone else to use it, except to obtain rationed goods in accordance with regulations of the Office of Price Administration. Any person who finds a lost War Ration Book must return it to the War Price and Rationing Board which issued it. Persons who violate rationing regulations are subject to $10,000 fine or imprisonment, or both.

OPA Form No. R-130

LOCAL BOARD ACTION

Issued by _____ 1—10—45
(Local board number)   (Date)
STEPHENS COUNTY

Street address WAR PRICE & RATIONING BOARD No. 5528

City DUNCAN, OKLAHOMA State

Beulah Lantz
(Signature of issuing officer)

While Pearl, Scottie, and the rest of the family worried about George, Jr., who was serving on the front lines in Europe during World War II, they also had to deal with rationing of a wide range of products at home in order to make more goods available for the war effort. Gasoline, tires, shoes, various types of food, and many other items were rationed. This is one of the ration books the Scott's had during the War. (Courtesy Pearl Scott Collection)

called "Bouncing Betty" by the Americans, also impressed George. When stepped on by a soldier, this variety of mine would do nothing until the unfortunate victim took his foot off the mine. Then it would bounce about waist high and explode.[7]

Pearl and other residents of Marlow were alerted to the news of the invasion of Europe by the town's tornado siren, which emitted a prolonged wail to herald the arrival of D-Day. Pearl knew that George was among the Americans landing on the beaches and that there was a good chance of him being seriously wounded or killed. All she and millions of other anxious Americans could do was stay close to their radios and wait, worry, and pray that their friends or loved ones would survive.[8]

George saw continued combat through France as a member of a twelve-man squad on a .50 caliber machine gun. Among his duties was

▼▼▼

setting up and emplacing the gun "for greatest firepower against enemy attack." He also "loaded, aimed and fired" the weapon, and during a lull in the fighting, he "stripped down, cleaned and oiled" the weapon to ensure its proper operation. George ended the war in a small French village on the border with Germany before returning to Marlow as a decorated war hero. Yet, for George, none of the combat he experienced after D-Day approached the intensity and horror of what he endured on Omaha Beach. Among the well-deserved medals and citations he received by the war's end was the Bronze Star with a "V" for valor.[9]

Pearl, ca. 1945.
(Courtesy Bill Scott)

After World War II ended, Louise, Bill, and Carter continued to enjoy their friends and life on the farm. Louise was a member of the B. W. Club in high school. This was an invitation-only organization for girls. Penn Rabb remembered that, although it was supposed to be a secret, everyone knew that B.W. stood for "Brainless Wonders." New members of the club had to be voted in by the existing members, and there was an initiation period for one week each year. Initiates had to wear tow sacks, could not wash or comb their hair for the week, and had to wear eggs in their bras. Of course, the boys "couldn't wait to smash the eggs." The club met once a week and sponsored an annual dance to which the girls invited boys. The school did not have a senior prom while Louise was in high school because the local Baptist and Church of Christ congregations frowned upon dancing, so the B. W. Club dance was the social event of the year.[10]

Louise and her friends did not limit their dancing to the annual B. W. dance, however. Almost every Friday night, they would go to one of the girl's homes, such as Shirley Taylor's house, and "roll the carpet back and have a big dance, there in that one house, with the parents there." Louise and her friends "made their own entertainment."[11]

During the summer broomcorn harvest, Louise helped cook for the broomcorn hands on Uncle Clyde and Aunt Hootie's farm. Broomcorn harvesters would bring blankets and sleep on the ground, so as to be in place to eat breakfast and start to work early. Work would continue all day until late in the evening. The workers had to be fed, and Louise and the other women would rise at 3:30 in the morning to start preparing breakfast for up to fifty people. The workers would rise at daylight, eat breakfast, and work until lunch break. Louise helped prepare the noon meal, which included tomatoes, vegetables, and plenty of iced tea and often featured fried

Pearl's children, ca. 1948. Left to right: Carter, Bill, and Louise. Years later, a friend of Bill's would recall that in high school Louise was a "very pretty girl" who attracted a great deal of interest from the boys. (Courtesy Bill Scott)

chicken or beef—"stuff that stuck to your ribs"—cooked on wood stoves. "It did get hot!" Louise recalled in later years.[12]

Described as a "very pretty girl" with a "lovely complexion," Louise was a popular girl who "always had the boys interested in her." After graduation from high school, Louise married Billy Guy Thompson of Bray, Oklahoma, a World War II veteran who had served in the United States Army Air Corps. Eventually residing in Alabama, Billy Guy and Louise became the parents of three boys and one girl. Inspired by their Grandmother Pearl and their helicopter-pilot father, all three boys became aviators.[13]

Scottie had been a football player, and his love for the sport influenced Bill to play. Marlow did not have football as an organized sport for students below the ninth grade, but Bill and his buddies got together almost every Saturday morning at the football field to play. "We might have 20 guys on each side," Bill remembered, "but that's where we learned to tackle, no pads, no nothing, but we got pretty rough. There were a lot of broken noses and busted up ribs." He began playing as a freshman, and by his junior year he was starting at the right halfback position. Later, in track he was a hurdler, a quarter miler, and a member of the mile relay team. He also played basketball and during his junior year participated on Marlow's first baseball team. However, he was first and foremost a

Louise used the occasion of this photograph in 1951 to "show off" her wedding ring. (Courtesy Pearl Scott Collection)

football player. But his athletic and academic career would be interrupted when he was called to serve his country in Korea.[14]

Bill had joined the National Guard during his junior year in high school. Jobs for young men were not plentiful, and service in the Guard would bring in some extra cash. Moreover, some of his buddies were seventeen and had joined, while other friends had falsified their age on the application form and joined early. Bill also joined early at the age of sixteen in the spring of 1950. In June of that year, the Korean War broke out and Bill's unit was federalized for service as infantrymen in a land "we'd never heard of. . . ." They were to begin their service on September 1 of that year. [15]

Many of Bill's classmates also were in the National Guard and thus would miss their senior years of high school. Because local officials knew which of the young men were underage, each of them was given the opportunity to correct their records and consequently not go to war. A number of them took the opportunity to do just that, but eight opted to serve. Pearl and Scottie were required to sign papers to allow Bill to serve, and Pearl agonized over the decision. She was terrified that if she signed he might get killed. But she also realized that he could get drafted and perhaps get killed anyway. Finally, she determined that "if that's what he wants he is old enough to realize what he is doing."[16]

On the night Marlow's Company G, 179th Infantry Regiment, 45th Infantry Division departed Marlow for active service, "the boys marched from the National Guard Armory to the train depot. . . . Main Street was lined on both sides" with people "to see them off," Pearl remembered. The mood of the crowd was somber as most of those present remembered the horrors of World War II. The only sound to be heard was the rhythmic footfalls of the marching men. Louise remembered that "you could have heard a pin drop. All you could hear is their feet hitting, marching. I never want to see that again."[17]

It must have been especially difficult for Pearl to watch her son departing for combat, when her brother George was already in Korea. Following World War II, George had worked as a painter and as a roughneck for Johnson and Gay, drilling contractors headquartered in Duncan. He reenlisted in the army on March 29, 1949, as a paratrooper, observing that you were paid more money if you made jumps. Noting his extensive combat experience, the army quickly offered George an advance in rank to train troops. He accepted this opportunity and thus never trained as a paratrooper. Over the coming months he served at bases in Virginia, Texas, New York, and Massachusetts as a drill sergeant.[18]

When the Korean War broke out, the army needed officers with combat experience, so George was sent to Japan as a platoon sergeant in B Company, Fifth Cavalry Regiment, First Cavalry Division. By the time Bill was departing Marlow for Camp Polk, George found himself facing the infamous Hill 303 near the Naktong River, the village of Waegwan, and the strategic Waegwan Bridge. At the moment, he was the ranking member of his platoon. The location had been the site of a brutal massacre of American POWs by North Korean forces on August 17, 1950. Adjacent to the Waegwan Bridge over the Naktong River, Hill 303 was strategically important and was fought over with control shifting between the Americans and their South Korean allies and the Chinese and their North Korean allies. George and his platoon were part of a force that was in place on September 4 with the mission of regaining control of the hill.[19]

Waiting to attack the enemy, George was in radio contact with his company commander, who assured him that before advancing on the enemy, "we'll give you an artillery barrage, an air strike, and another artillery barrage. All you will have to do is wade in." The artillery barrages and air strike, however, never came. Then the order came via radio to, "Take 'em on in, Sarge." George knew that the well-entrenched enemy held the high ground and that he and his men would be attacking uphill over ground offering little cover. He replied, "What do you mean? We can't hit that without any backup." The officer responded, "That is a direct order. Go on in." George believed in military discipline and knew that violation of a direct order likely would lead to court marshal proceedings against him. Thus, he passed along the order to attack.[20]

George and his command had just started advancing up Hill 303 when the enemy opened fire with deadly results. "Boy they were really mowing us down, killing my boys and all," George recalled. At one point, George turned to one side to motion his men forward, and he was hit by enemy rifle fire. The bullet entered his left shoulder and exited through his back. His left lung was punctured and three ribs were fractured. George was bleeding profusely, was in pain, but remained conscious.[21]

Recalling what he had heard about enemy treatment of prisoners, George determined that he would not be taken alive. He pulled the pins from two hand grenades and held down the levers, knowing that once he let go of the levers, the grenades would explode in about five seconds. He waited, thinking that if the enemy closed on him, he would allow the grenades to detonate, killing some of them as well as himself. After some time, it appeared that he would not be captured, and he decided to get rid of the grenades by tossing them over a cliff. He threw them one at a time, and in each case the grenades "just barely went over the cliff before exploding."[22]

At great risk, two of George's men crawled up to him and found blood running out of his mouth and a large exit wound in his back. One of the men said, "Hold on, Sarge, we're going to get you back." The men were able to drag George to safety where he was loaded on a stretcher in a jeep. By this time he had stopped coughing blood, and he was surprised to be greeted by another soldier on a stretcher who earlier had been trained by George. George was taken to an old church that had become a field hospital. It was so crowded that he had to wait in a nearby apple orchard for awhile. He finally got into the hospital where medics "patched" him up so he could be taken to a hospital in Japan. He was there about thirty days and then was flown back to the United States.[23]

The army hospital at Fort Sam Houston, Texas, was full, so he was sent to a naval hospital at Corpus Christi, Texas, where he was to remain for five months. While there he was visited by Pearl and other members of the family, including his daughter Beverly. George eventually recovered from his wounds, although he was considered to be 50 percent disabled. While in the hospital, George received notification from the adjutant general of the United States Army on November 17, 1950, that he would receive the Purple Heart. He also received a medical discharge and a military pension. He received his Purple Heart during a formal ceremony at Fort Sill, Oklahoma, just before he was honorably discharged from the service.[24]

Although George recovered reasonably well physically, the experience of leading young men in his platoon on a virtual suicide mission took a heavy psychological toll on him. For a number of years he drank heavily. His daughter years later recalled how her father would come home intoxicated late at night and lay down and cry, sobbing "My boys! My boys!" George's heroic service on behalf of his country was not forgotten by his family. In 2002 his nephew Bill wrote a tribute on behalf of the entire family to let him know "how much we love you, respect you and thank you . . . for all you have done to preserve our country and its freedoms, as well as helping to free Europe and keep South Korea from tyranny." George always found it ironic that the military action in Korea has been officially referred to as a United Nations-sponsored "police action" or as the "Korean Conflict." To George and the other men and women who served there, "It was a war alright!"[25]

The sobering news that his Uncle George had been severely wounded came to Bill not long after he arrived with Company G at Camp Polk, Louisiana, for six months of intensive training before being sent to Japan for advanced training. Bill and his friend Penn Rabb lived in the same barracks at Camp Polk and "became extremely close" during this time. While they were there, Thanksgiving was celebrated, and Penn's parents were unable to travel to Camp Polk for the occasion. But he was included in the group with Bill, who was joined by Pearl, Scottie, Louise, Carter, and one of Bill's classmates and close friends Joe "Joe Boy" Hogan. The Company G cooks prepared a Thanksgiving dinner for the troops and their guests, and the holiday visit was a special treat for Bill and Penn. Penn's parents would be able to visit him the next weekend.[26]

On the Saturday following Thanksgiving, the Scott family, Penn, and

Mack Corcoran (another soldier from Marlow in Company G) went to Lake Charles, Louisiana. There they "enjoyed a delicious lunch of . . . Louisiana shrimp." Unfortunately, Carter became ill and, as Bill put it, "gave" the shrimp "back to the Cajuns with gusto (partially digested!). . . . I don't ever remember him" ever "eating any more shrimp. . . ." Seeing his family certainly raised Bill's spirits.[27]

George Carter, Jr., left, and Bill Scott were able to visit while George was recovering in Japan from serious battlefield wounds he suffered in combat during the Korean War. Bill was in training in Japan, awaiting deployment to the combat zone. (Courtesy Pearl Scott Collection)

Several weddings were held in the chapel at the camp, including one that involved Corporal Harold Staats of Company G. Bill and Penn both were good friends of Staats, so the two solders served as witnesses while Staats and Wilma Fine of Bray, Oklahoma, "tied the knot." Later, Bill and Penn debated who had served as best man and as "maid of honor."[28]

The troops learned that at the end of March they would leave Camp Polk for Japan and some additional training before going on to Korea to fight. A special ceremony was held on March 26 when the entire 45th Infantry Division passed in review before Oklahoma Governor Johnston Murray and other dignitaries. Not long after the troops returned to their barracks, rain began falling and, Penn Rabb recalled, "The gloomy weather matched the mood of the soldiers and their families." Bill's spirits were brightened by the fact that Pearl, Scottie, Louise, and Carter had driven to Camp Polk to witness the review and visit.[29]

Pearl and Scottie took a number of photographs while visiting Bill and two days later departed for Marlow. Bill was confined to base because three days later he and his buddies found themselves on a train headed to New Orleans, where they would board a navy ship *Marine Lynx* for the long trip to Japan. Pearl later told Bill that the day she and her family left Camp Polk was "one of the saddest days of her life, seeing me for the last time before shipping out. It was a long way home to Marlow

The Marine Lynx *was the troop ship used by the United States Navy to transport Bill Scott and his comrades from Louisiana to Japan, on their way to fighting in the Korean War. (Courtesy navsource.org/archives)*

for her." Pearl undoubtedly feared that she may have seen Bill alive for the last time.[30]

As the troops boarded the ship on the afternoon of March 30, they received a musical salute, which included the playing of "Boomer Sooner," from the 45th Infantry Division Band. The *Marine Lynx* then eased away from the dock and proceeded down the Mississippi River to the Gulf of Mexico on its way to the Panama Canal. Ocean travel was a new experience for Bill, and he kept a diary of the trip. In the Gulf the following day, he got his "first glimpse of the ocean," and he also saw flying fish for the first time. Finally, he observed two matters that were important to all the troops, "The chow is pretty good. The weather is hot." After a brief stop at the Balboa Naval Base at the west end of the Panama Canal, the voyage continued, and on April 4 Bill saw the Pacific Ocean for the first time. The next stop was San Diego, California, where the ship was rerouted to get a man who had contracted meningitis off the ship.[31]

While crossing the Pacific Ocean, a regimen of classes and physical training was established. Weapons were cleaned daily to protect them from the corrosive effects of the salt air. The ship was able to travel at a speed of about 12 knots. About half way to Japan, a fire in one of the galleys destroyed approximately half of the food supply, so the men's rations were somewhat reduced. Moreover, the ship was so crowded that long lines were a feature at every meal, and some of the men thought the food was so bad that they preferred eating the emergency rations stored in the ship's lifeboats. Sleeping quarters also were crowded and the sea often was rough. Finally, the ship arrived at Muroran on the Japanese island of Hokkaido on April 28 The following day, the men boarded trains for a four-hour ride to Camp Chitose.[32]

On Christmas Day, 1951, Louise Scott tried on the present, a Japanese kimono, that her brother Bill had sent her from Japan. Scottie is in the background. On the back of the photo is the note, "She's trying to grin but was kinda cold." Although the family did not know it, by Christmas Bill had departed Japan earlier in the month and was already in Korea. (Courtesy Pearl Scott Collection)

Company G trained intensively at a variety of camps for the remainder of the spring, through the summer, and into the winter. They had just finished winter training and were about to be issued snow shoes and skis when they received the orders that would send them into combat. The 45th Infantry Division departed for Korea in early December, landing at Inchon, South Korea on December 11.[33]

Over the coming months Bill and the men of Company G were involved in heavy fighting for control of hills such as Old Baldy, Pork Chop, T-Bone, Hassakol, Hill 200, and Outpost Erie. The combat was intense, and Bill recalled, "We lost a lot of men. Fortunately only one man from Marlow was killed. Could have been a lot worse considering the situations we were involved in. . . ." In combat, Bill lost sight of "the big picture;" instead "you see only the war around you. . . when you are cold and fighting the Chinese for survival." Your family "was the men on your right and your left. . . and your main concern was that you don't want to let your buddies down." At times, while standing watch, it was so cold that Bill and his comrades wore their sleeping bags while standing in the trenches.[34]

Bill fortunately made it through his tour without getting wounded. He even had one experience, though not funny at the time, that he could laugh about later. He volunteered to go out on a night ambush patrol near an ir-

Bill Scott at age eighteen was on the front lines in Korea overlooking Pork Chop and T-Bone Hills. (Courtesy Pearl Scott Collection)

rigation ditch, even though he was the leader of a 60-milimeter mortar squad and as such was not usually expected to participate in such patrols. A signal was agreed upon which was to be used by the first man to spot enemy soldiers. Stationed at the left flank of the ambush detail for about an hour, Bill, now a sergeant, heard water splashing closer and closer in the irrigation ditch. He took his M-1 rifle off "safety" and tapped the signal to the others. With tension running high, he watched intently to spot the approaching enemy. Bill thought he was a dead man when something suddenly raced up his leg and into his face. He soon realized that he had not been attacked by an enemy soldier; instead, he speculated that his assailant had been a rat, perhaps being chased by an owl.[35]

Bill received orders to "rotate home" in May of 1952. At the replacement depot, he received clean clothes and was thrilled to find clean showers with "soap and hot water, yet!" Here the troops lived in a tent city surrounded by barbed wire. The food was "barely tolerable," and the soldiers' stomachs had shrunk during their time in action. Consequently, the soldiers dumped much of what was served to them into garbage cans.

While waiting in the inevitable line to dump his uneaten food, Bill noticed a large group of old people and children just outside the fence. Because of the war, food was scarce and these people appeared to be starving. As Bill waited in line, he saw a youngster go under the fence and race to one of the garbage cans with a pail. He quickly scooped as much food from the garbage as he could and ran for the fence. A South Korean guard intercepted the child and began beating him with a club. Bill lost his temper, proceeded to run the guard down, and started to "beat the hell out of him." Others joined him, and they gave the Korean guards a good thrashing. Afterward, they moved the garbage cans next to the fence, where they still remained when Bill and his comrades departed this facility. Soon Bill and others going home sailed to Sasebo, Japan, to await the ship that would take them home.[36]

Like his father, Scottie, Bill loved football. He is shown here in his uniform on the old practice field located at the rear of Marlow's grade school building. He did not become a star player, however, until his senior year, after he returned from serving his country in Korea. (Courtesy Pearl Scott Collection)

Upon arrival at Sasebo, Bill had his "first hot, GREAT meal since we set foot on Korean soil." The mess sergeant gave special attention to Bill and others who were wearing their Combat Infantryman's Badges. They were placed at the head of the line and told to get what they wanted and to come back for more. Selections included "steak cooked to order, chicken, seafood, chef salads," and much more. That meal, Bill recalled more than fifty years later, "was the most memorable meal I ever had, bar none."[37]

For several days, the men enjoyed the food and bunks that featured sheets and pillows, and then the men were loaded on the ship *General Weigel* for transport to San Francisco, California. When he arrived there,

Bill Scott's telegram to his mother, letting her know when he would be arriving by train at Lawton, a message that Pearl and her family received with jubilation. *(Courtesy Pearl Scott Collection)*

Bill telephoned home to inform Pearl and the family that he was back in the United States and was on his way home. His date of departure had not been known to the family; consequently, Pearl was so relieved and emotional that she could barely talk to Bill on the phone. After several days at Camp Stoneman, California, Bill and his cohorts boarded a troop train bound for Fort Sill. Bill was assigned to the only yellow car in the train, and somewhere in Arizona or New Mexico, when the train was stopped to take on water for the steam engine, he managed to send a telegram to let Pearl and Scottie know when he was to arrive in Lawton. He was met at the depot station there by Pearl, Scottie, Louise, Carter, "Joe Boy" Hogan, and Penn Rabb. Excited, Bill was standing on the step of the coach while the train was still moving slowly. Forgetting that his duffel bag weighed at least sixty pounds, he shouted for Joe Boy to catch it and then tossed it to him. When the bag hit Joe Boy, "all that weight knocked him sprawling," but luckily he was not injured.[38]

▼▼▼

In June of 2000, George, Jr., traveled with three nephews to the opening of the D-Day Museum in New Orleans, Louisiana. Shown here waiting in an airport are, left to right: Dan Williamson, George Carter, Jr., Bob Williamson, and Art Williamson. At the museum, they saw a movie about the D-Day experience. In a letter to Bill Scott, George noted that the film showed "men getting wounded, bodies floating in the water and bodies on the beach." Everyone cried, and Bob put his arm around George and patted his arm. After the movie, Art introduced George, and he received a standing ovation. Also, George and his nephews found a large photograph of George helping another soldier pull a wounded comrade on to the beach. (Courtesy Pearl Scott Collection)

After an emotional reunion, it was time to go home to Marlow. Scottie recently had purchased a new Chevrolet automobile, and he was "so proud of it." Scottie insisted Bill, who had not driven a vehicle in two years, drive the Chevy. As they got underway, Scottie kept encouraging Bill to drive faster. Bill thought that they were traveling "plenty fast" until he looked at the speedometer and realized they were "only going twenty-five or thirty miles per hour." Bill would increase his speed but soon would get caught up in the conversation and slow down again, only to be reminded to speed up. After what seemed like an especially long trip, with their speed cycling between slow and slower, the Scotts finally arrived home. Soon thereafter, Pearl presented Bill with three scrapbooks containing photographs and news clippings focusing respectively on his time at Camp Polk, the training period in Japan, and his combat in Korea. Pearl was relieved that George and Bill had survived their service in Korea and that Bill was ready to complete high school.[39]

▼▼▼

Chapter Eight

EMPTY NEST AND DIVORCE

Bill had earned his GED (Graduate Equivalence Diploma) while in Japan. Nonetheless, he wanted to return to Marlow High School and receive his high school diploma. Pearl was pleased with the idea of having Bill at home another year, since she had always encouraged her children to obtain as much education as possible. Moreover, Bill wanted to play football, and he would help establish Marlow's tradition as a football powerhouse.[1]

Not long after returning to Marlow, Bill and Jim Newman, a friend and fellow veteran, were working out at the high school, trying to get into shape for football. There they met Marlow's newly hired football coach, Sevil Pickett, a descendant of Confederate General George Pickett, who led "Pickett's Charge" during the Civil War Battle of Gettysburg. Pickett quickly identified the two former soldiers and informed them they were going to be leaders on his team. Bill, who weighed about 150 pounds, was tabbed to play right guard and pulling guard in Pickett's single wing offense.[2]

Bill and his friends soon learned that Pickett had planned a special, preseason, one-week football camp that would test the physical resources and resolve of even combat-tested veterans like himself, Glen Robertson, and Newman. The camp was held near Cache, Oklahoma, in the Wich-

Pearl dressed for Easter services at the First Methodist Church in Marlow in 1953. (Courtesy Pearl Scott Collection)

▼▼▼

ita Mountains. "The camp was down in a valley, Bill recalled, "You can imagine how hot it was . . . ." The team departed Marlow on a Sunday in August and spent Sunday evening at the camp, settling in and reviewing

As a Korean War veteran, Bill Scott returned to Marlow and became a star football player, earning All-State honors and a scholarship to Eastern New Mexico State University. This is his official All-State photograph. (Courtesy Pearl Scott Collection)

plays. The following morning, they were awakened early and were practicing in full pads at 6 a.m. after breakfast. They practiced until 10 a.m., took a four-hour break for lunch and rest, and resumed practicing at 2 p.m. in the heat. The second practice ended at 6 p.m. This schedule was maintained every day though the following Saturday. There were many who lost their lunches during the afternoon practices, but in the end Bill remembered that they all loved Coach Pickett. "No one ever said anything about quitting," Bill recalled. "Even if they had, where were they going to go over there in Cache all by themselves?"[3]

Marlow's football team compiled a record of eight wins, three losses, and two ties that year, winning two games in the state playoffs. Bill was described as being "one of those raw-boned types of guys who were tough as nails after having been in the army." His outstanding play was recognized by his being honored as an All-State player at his position. Pearl and Scotty attended every home and away game during this special year and were proud of Bill's determination to excel.[4]

Bill's excellence on the gridiron was recognized by coaches at Eastern New Mexico University at Portales, New Mexico, who offered him a scholarship. He weighed 170 pounds when he arrived there. He "looked at those great big old guys playing guard and decided to become an end." He played four years in college, graduating in 1957 with a degree in journalism, and later played three years of semi-professional football in Alabama. Pearl and Scottie managed to travel to Portales for two homecoming games during Bill's time there.[5]

Money was tight for Bill during his college years. He was on a football scholarship and was receiving support though the G. I. Bill of Rights pro-

Bill Scott and his wife, Linda, posed for this photograph in 1967. They were married in 1965. (Courtesy Pearl Scott Collection)

gram. But finances were a problem, especially after he got married before graduation and started a family. He never complained, "a trait taught by mom," and got a job in the off-season, writing sports for a local newspaper. Money also was tight for Pearl and her family, so Pearl worked in a store in Marlow to earn extra money. Still, Bill recalled decades later, that "Mom . . . would send me, unannounced, her entire paycheck about every three weeks."[6]

After Bill's first marriage ended in divorce several years before he moved to Alabama, he met his second wife Linda. He held a number of interesting jobs over the years before accepting employment with the Reynolds Metal Company. His company moved him to Virginia where he eventually retired.[7]

While his Uncle George and his brother Bill were away because of their involvement in the Korean War, Carter pursued his high school career. He was not interested in playing football, but he loved rodeo. The Future Farmers of America (FFA) had a rodeo circuit, and as a member of the Marlow Chapter of FFA, Carter eagerly participated in the sport as a bull rider. Pearl did not enjoy watching Carter try to stay on the powerful beasts for eight seconds, which was considered a complete ride. She went with him to a rodeo at Cyril, Oklahoma, and was understandably frightened when she saw him perform. Small, short, and tough, Carter was a good bull rider, and he continued to ride as often as he could after he graduated from high school.[8]

During his sophomore year in high school, Carter and his friend Claudell Wallace began learning how to drive trucks. They were taught by Claudell's uncles, whose business was hauling cattle to the stockyards in Oklahoma City for local farmers and ranchers. Carter enjoyed driving trucks, and he enjoyed traveling. By his senior year, he was earning extra money driving trucks, and he ultimately would settle into truck driving as a career.[9]

Carter Scott ca. 1954. A recent high school graduate, Carter quickly found work installing dial telephone systems. However, he especially enjoyed the freedom of the open road as a truck driver and made that his lifelong career. (Courtesy Pearl Scott Collection)

In May of 1954, near the end of Carter's senior year in high school, tragedy struck the Scott household. Their house burned, and they lost almost everything. The loss of irreplaceable family items and other valued possessions hit Pearl hard, although she was grateful that no one was injured. She later told Louise that "you don't know what it is like, watching your home burn up and there are things in there that you can never get back." Pearl had some items in a cedar chest that were saved from the flames. Years later Pearl "cried about that fire a couple of times" while telling granddaughter Beverly Louise Scott about the fire. The cause of the blaze was never determined officially, but Pearl and Scottie suspected the fire might have been caused by a malfunctioning bathroom heater. After the fire Pearl, Scottie, and Carter moved in with Scottie's parents until they could find a rent house in town in which to live.[10]

In addition to coping with the aftermath of the fire, Pearl soon had another concern involving Carter with which she had to deal. Pearl "caught him crying and he told me he wasn't going to get to graduate. Carter's grades were good . . . but he had been absent two days more than he should have." Pearl went into action, showing up at the high school every morning to argue with the administrators about Carter's situation. The FFA teacher pointed out that for one of the two days in question, Carter had been on an FFA trip. Pearl persistently pummeled the principal with protests, went to the school board, and threatened to discuss the matter with appropriate officials in Oklahoma City. Finally, "to get rid of me," Pearl believed, Carter was allowed to graduate.[11]

Pearl knew that Carter probably would not return to school the next fall under any circumstances, so she was thrilled by the decision to let

After Carter had graduated from high school and their house had burned, Pearl found there was nothing to keep her in Marlow while Scottie was on the road, so she and Scottie purchased a small house trailer and moved from one construction job to the next. By this time, Scottie's work took him to all parts of the nation. He is shown here with friend Noble Crownover in the state of Washington in 1955. Both men are sporting injuries that resulted from an accident on the job. (Pearl Scott Collection)

Carter graduate with his class. She was determined that each of her children receive at least a high school diploma perhaps because she had not graduated from high school herself. The night Carter "graduated and they handed him his diploma, he looked around at" Pearl "and just grinned!"[12]

Given the necessity of working outside the home and playing a larger role in raising her three children with Scottie being away at work much of the time, Pearl still managed to remain relatively active in the Marlow community. In addition to her faithful attendance at the First Methodist Church, she was particularly active in the Veterans of Foreign Wars Auxiliary and the American Legion Auxiliary. The local American Legion Post constructed a new building and began raising money to pay for it. Among their fundraising activities were dances. Pearl and other members of the auxiliary "sold tickets, checked hats and coats, and served ice and cokes to help." Dancers enjoyed some outstanding music, including one dance played by Les Brown and His Band of Renown and several appearances by Bob Wills and His Texas Playboys. Pearl and her family also enjoyed other musicians who played in Marlow or at the Sky View in Duncan, including saxophonist Ernie Fields and his band and the Glenn Miller Band, led by Tex Beneke.[13]

Community involvement became virtually impossible, however, in the summer of 1954. With all three children out of high school and their house destroyed, Pearl and Scottie acquired a small house trailer. This would allow Pearl and Carter to travel with Scottie to jobs all across the nation. By this time, Scottie was a skilled pipefitter, whose work had expanded far beyond the oil fields. The United States was locked in a "Cold War" with the Soviet Union and was expanding its military capabilities and installations. Included in this effort was the construction of special "silos" to house intercontinental ballistic missiles that were equipped with nuclear warheads. Scottie obtained work on these and other defense installations in the states of Washington, Georgia, South Carolina, and other locations.

This photo of the famed Louis Armstrong was autographed to Pearl in 1957 at Colorado Springs, Colorado. She must have had the good fortune to attend a performance by Armstrong while she and Scottie were in Colorado on a job. (Courtesy Marlow Chamber of Commerce)

They also lived for a time at Colorado Springs, Colorado, while the United States Air Force Academy was being constructed. The couple moved from job to job, sometimes returning to Marlow if there was sufficient time between jobs.[14]

▼▼▼

After graduating from high school, Carter worked as a truck driver for several months and then in 1955 accompanied Pearl and Scottie to Longview, Washington. While there he became friends with a young man from Portland, Oregon, who had obtained a job installing a new type of telephone system for the Stromberg-Carlson Corporation. The new system supported the new dial telephone technology, so with the probability that telephone systems throughout the nation would be converting to dial phones, the future looked bright for this company. Carter successfully applied for a job as a telephone equipment installer and moved to Portland. When Scottie's job in Washington ended, Carter was "climbing up the ladder" with his employer and decided to remain in Portland. Scottie and Pearl returned to Marlow alone.[15]

Although Pearl and Scottie followed his work, they returned to Marlow when they had a sufficient break between jobs. Here they are enjoying a meal in the home of Scottie's parents in December 1957. (Courtesy Pearl Scott Collection)

In 1957, Carter was transferred to Elko, Nevada, and there he married Anita June Heath of Rush Springs, Oklahoma. Carter was transferred to Oklahoma by Stromberg-Carlson in 1958, and he was drafted into the army late in that year. By this time, Pearl probably thought she would never have to worry about having anyone in her family involved with the situation in Korea. Nonetheless, after taking basic training at Camp Chaffee, Arkansas, Carter found himself on duty on the southern boundary of the Demilitarized Zone, a dangerous place during the uneasy truce between North and South Korea. He served as a truck driver hauling road repair equipment and supplies. He received his discharge in 1960 and entered the inactive reserve. During the Cuban missile crisis, he was called back into active service for six months, after which he was able to resume his employment with Stomberg-Carlson. By then he and Nita had one child, Carl Lewis.[16]

As a truck driver, Carter became highly proficient. Here he is standing in front of his truck with a special load that he was to deliver to a location on the West Coast. This load required a unique, customized trailer, special permits, and a highly skilled driver. Carter was one of a limited number of drivers permitted to handle such loads. (Courtesy Pearl Scott Collection)

Carter and Nita acquired a mobile home to ease the process of moving frequently. In late 1963, however, the nomadic lifestyle became burdensome for the family, which now included a daughter, Teresa Ann. Bill encouraged Carter to move to Florence, Alabama, to work for the Reynolds Aluminum Corporation, where Bill was employed. Carter and his family did move to Alabama, but he did not enjoy working inside on a fixed schedule with a supervisor looking over his shoulder. When a "wildcat" strike against the company took place, he siezed the opportunity to leave and began working as a truck driver again, an occupation that he particularly enjoyed. He continued in that line of work until he retired at the age of sixty-two, still living in Alabama.[17]

Carter maintained his sense of humor throughout his working years and into retirement. While family friend Penn Rabb was recovering from a hip replacement procedure, he received a phone call from Carter, who also had recently undergone hip replacement surgery. He had called to challenge his friend to a race. This was typical of Carter, "who was always a bit mischievous. You could always tell when Carter had something on his mind because his eyes would flash and he would grin," Rabb recalled.[18]

With Carter no longer living with Pearl and Scottie, the couple continued their itinerant pattern of following Scottie's work and living in their little house trailer. By this time, however, their marriage was in serious trouble. The years of financial difficulties, combined with years of being separated because of Scottie's being on the road, had taken a large toll on their relationship. In 1960 Pearl decided to move back to Marlow by herself, rent a house, and get a job to support herself. She would travel no more with Scottie. One day in 1961, while Scottie was working in Colorado, she filed for divorce. When Scottie was served with the divorce papers, he drove to Marlow to talk to Pearl. He did not want their marriage of thirty years to end and said to Pearl, "Don't do this." Pearl replied, "I have to." She later confided to a niece that telling Scottie their marriage was over "hurt her" but "she had made up her mind."[19]

Pearl and Scottie posed for this portrait during happier times, ca. 1957. Telling Scottie in 1961 that she was divorcing him was difficult for Pearl, but she believed that they no longer could live together. (Courtesy Pearl Scott Collection)

Pearl was only forty-six years old when her marriage with Scottie ended. She had gone from riches as a teen aviator to rags as a divorced woman with few assets. She was somewhat bitter about her financial status, noting that she had lost "my farms, my home, my everything. Even the pick-up was wrecked on a drunken spree." She blamed Scottie for these circumstances. Although she played a role in the loss of her real estate by signing mortgage papers with Scottie, she indicated that she had felt forced to do it. Scottie was not the businessman that her father had been, and he suffered in comparison. But few individuals were as astute in financial matters as her father, and Scottie had to cope with making ends meet as a farmer in the Great Depression and later as a pipefitter, following the work wherever it led him. In later years, Pearl would indicate that they married too young. As the years passed, Pearl realized that she missed Scottie, that he had loved her and their children, and that she still loved him.[20]

After her divorce, Pearl noted that she had gone from "riches to rags" but indicated that she was still the same person as before. She knew that she had been and still was capable of doing significant things and that, as taught by her father, she would never say, "I can't." She would "go on helping people" to the best of her abilities and was grateful for the many friends she had made over the years. She had retained her sense of humor and her ability "to laugh and be myself." She enjoyed good health. She felt young enough to "go out dancing and have fun in anything I do." She enjoyed fishing like her mother, and she could "cook a good meal." She could sew anything she wanted and was pleased that she still had "a nice figure" and could "dress modern." And she could "talk to anyone about almost any thing." She also had three children whom she treasured and who loved her and Scottie.[21]

At this point in her life, Pearl believed that "Except for a few years I've had a good life and still have. So money doesn't buy the most important things in life after all. . . . A Person is what they are in their heart, and I am just me and I . . . hope I never change." Although her life had taken a major turn in direction, Pearl was determined to face the future with optimism.[22]

Nonetheless, the next six years of Pearl's life were somewhat unsettled. Not long after her divorce, Pearl moved to Paramount, California, to be near her mother and her sister Arnetta. Her brother George also was living in California at that time. She then moved to Alabama and lived with Louise and her family for awhile. Bill had gotten divorced from his first wife and was also living in Alabama and having a rough period of adjustment. She wanted to help Bill and see her grandchildren. Carter and his wife also had moved to Alabama. After several years in Alabama, Pearl missed Marlow and decided to move back "home."[23]

"Home" temporarily would be an "Indian house" in Duncan, Pearl informed her son Bill in a letter. She indicated that she would be getting a job, but she did not know what it would be. Moreover, she noted that she wished she could just stay home for awhile and rest: "I am so tired, tired of going to work and back every day." Another reason she was returning was that her mother, who now was living in Duncan, was ill and needed Pearl. It appeared her mother's cancer had reappeared, and a biopsy would be taken to be certain. Her mother had said that she would wait for Pearl to tell her what to do. Pearl wished that her mother had not said that, "for I don't know what is best. . . . I do know I am going home to her as soon as I can. . . . That's my mama, and I am going back to her." Fortunately, her mother's condition was not as dire as Pearl had thought because she lived until November of 1980, when she died in a nursing home at Marlow.[24]

Pearl also noted that she had finally gotten over having shingles, a painful, blistering rash caused by the same virus that produced chicken-pox. Although the rash covered only a limited area, it could make individuals feel tired and even depressed. The disease had run its course, but Pearl noted that she still had "scars from under my right breast to the middle of my back." Given her recent divorce, her mother's condition, and her battle with shingles, it is not surprising that Pearl would wish she could just stay home and rest instead of trudging off to work every day.[25]

While in Alabama, Pearl attempted to conquer a lifelong phobia. Although she had no fear of cavorting through the air while stunt flying in her Curtiss Robin, she was "terrified" of water and had never learned to swim. On one occasion, a family outing to a lake, Carter and Louise talk-ed Pearl into trying to water ski. They fitted her with flotation devices so she could not sink, and Pearl decided to give it a try. After receiving some coaching, Pearl got into position and latched onto the tow rope. When the boat began pulling her, Pearl failed to pull herself up and as a result began plowing the water with her head. In a panic, she maintained a death grip on the tow rope and continued to part the water with her head until the boat was stopped. When asked why she had not released the tow rope, she replied, "You never told me to release it!" At this point, she no longer had any interest in learning to water ski.[26]

By January of 1967, Pearl had been divorced for almost six years and was fifty-two years old. After moving back home from Alabama, she had met A. J. Kizarr, who was five years younger than Pearl, and the couple found that they had some common interests, such as fishing. They mar-ried and A. J. agreed to move to Alabama so Pearl could be close to her children and grandchildren. Although they may have loved each other or at least were comfortable together at first, the relationship was not des-tined to last. Pearl's description of her experience when astronaut Neil

Armstrong stepped on the moon seems to indicate that her relationship with A. J. fell somewhat short of love.[27]

As American astronauts prepared to land on the moon on July 20, 1969, Pearl remembered Wiley Post's pressure suit that he described while visiting with Pearl and her father and the wonderful times they had shared. She also remembered vividly how her father had predicted

While living in Alabama, Pearl worked in a Gibson's Discount Center in 1966. (Courtesy Pearl Scott Collection)

that radio someday would have pictures, "and now we have television." He also envisioned that man would eventually walk on the moon. Just over forty years later, Pearl watched in amazement as the lunar landing was televised live. Before Neil Armstrong actually descended the ladder of the lunar module, Pearl stepped outside so she could see her television and look at the same time directly at the moon. Pearl then had the "strangest, funniest feeling" and was convinced that her father was standing there with her and telling her, "See honey, I told you it would happen some day."[28]

The hair on Pearl's arms "just stood up," and "for just a little while" Pearl had "the safe, secure and being loved feeling" she "hadn't had since" her daddy died. For the first time in years, Pearl cried for her father. She later recalled that "I know he was there with me for a few minutes, and we were seeing it together, just like we used to do." Although Pearl had remarried, she apparently had not regained the "being loved feeling" that she missed so dearly.[29]

While in Alabama with A. J., Pearl worked in a Gibson's Discount Center. And she enjoyed being with her family. One unexpected bonus of living in Alabama came in 1970 when her grandsons—Craig, Billy Roy, and Scott Thompson—arranged to take her up in a private airplane. Once they were in the air, Craig told her she was going to fly the plane, but she thought he was "kidding." However, he soon turned the controls over to her, saying, "Grandma, its all yours." After thirty-seven years, Pearl was thrilled to be flying once again. For Pearl, "It took just a little while before

it all came back. After that it felt as though I had never quit." She later was able to fly the plane at night, a new experience for her. Because she did not have a pilot's license, she was not allowed to take off or land the plane, but she had great fun flying it.[30]

Pearl was proud of the fact that Louise's sons—Craig, Billy Roy, and Scott—all were aviation enthusiasts and pilots. One day in 1970 her grandsons and Louise arranged for her to fly once again. Pearl went up in a private airplane piloted by Craig with Pearl in the co-pilot's seat and Louise in a passenger's seat. Once in the air, Craig turned the controls over to Pearl, and she was thrilled to be flying again after having been grounded for thirty-seven years. Craig and Pearl are shown here just after landing. (Courtesy Pearl Scott Papers)

Pearl later acknowledged that although she had not flown in decades, the "flying fever" had never left her. Flying again was "the best gift" that Craig could ever give Pearl: "For my grandson to fly and let me, with him beside me and my daughter in the plane." Pearl had never understood people who were afraid of flying because "The thrill I get from flight far outweighs any fear."[31]

While reconnecting with her aviation past was deeply satisfying for Pearl, her second stay in Alabama was relatively short. Pearl and A. J. returned to Oklahoma in 1972 to reside in Marlow, most likely to be near her mother again. The move soon would prove to be instrumental in Pearl's reaching another major turning point in her life.

Chapter Nine
▼▼▼

FOR THE PEOPLE

N ot long after returning to Oklahoma, Pearl was revisited by another lifelong phobia. Pearl had been afraid of storms since she
had witnessed the destruction of her childhood home by a tornado. The
two-story structure, then under construction, had been flattened by the
ferocious funnel. One day in the spring of 1972, there was a significant
tornado outbreak, with numerous funnels spotted in various parts of
the state. Pearl's granddaughter Beverly Scott recalled spending most
of the day either in or standing beside a storm shelter. At one point
Pearl and Beverly saw several tornados at the same time, and Pearl "was
so terrified." On this day, Pearl may have wondered if she should have
remained in Alabama. However, developments within the government
of the Chickasaw Nation during the time she had been in Alabama set
the stage for Pearl to reconnect with her Native American heritage and
launch a new career.[1]

Before her new career could get underway, Pearl's marriage to A. J.
Kizarr reached a crisis. In August she filed for divorce on grounds of in-
compatibility and asked for the furniture and the 1964 Chevrolet that she
brought into the marriage. She also sought and received a restraining order against A. J., barring him from "interfering with or molesting" Pearl
"in any manner." That same order required A. J. to remove his clothes
and personal effects from their home, and the sheriff was directed to see

*As a Community Health Representative for the Chickasaw Nation, Pearl worked
long hours and spent some of her own money for gasoline and food in order to
help as many Indian people as possible. (Courtesy Pearl Scott Papers)*

that A. J. moved out of the home. Although their marriage was effectively over, the divorce would not be finalized until 1980.[2]

Pearl's new career that would begin in October had its origins in efforts of Overton James, governor of the Chickasaw Nation. In the late 1960s, the Chickasaws had a small government consisting of a governor, James, and a small number of employees. Federal policy for American Indians had begun to turn toward encouraging them to manage their own affairs, and tribal governments were on the verge of a new era of vigor and growth. In 1968, James had been successful in working with the Indian Health Service (IHS) to establish Indian clinics at Tishomingo and Coalgate. Another new program launched in 1968 by IHS was the Community Health Representative Program, commonly referred to as the CHR program. And the individuals hired to work in this program often were called CHRs.[3]

CHRs officially were to visit with Indian people within their assigned geographical areas, provide health-care related information, and determine if the people needed to see a physician for any sort of treatment. However, Governor James made it clear that the job would involve much more than that. He informed potential CHRs that the job would be challenging but potentially rewarding because they would be assisting Indian people in need. For remuneration of $700 a month plus 10 cents a mile, these individuals would be the foot soldiers of the Chickasaw Nation, making direct contact with the people. Although their responsibilities would primarily involve health-related matters, they would be expected to answer questions or be able to refer people to the appropriate person. "If you are visiting a family who is living in a shack, tell them about our housing authority, see if they qualify and help them fill out an application for housing," James told them. "If you are really helping people," James said, "word will spread; you will be on call 24 hours a day." James's words would prove to be prophetic.[4]

By 1972, the Chickasaw Nation's CHR program had grown to seven CHRs and two family planning representatives. Among these early employees was Pat Woods of Sulphur, who had responsibility for Grady and Stephens counties. Starting work in January of 1972, she traveled from her home each day to meet with Indian people of all tribes living in the

Overton James, Governor of the Chickasaw Nation, visiting with his friend Carl Albert of McAlester, Oklahoma, Speaker of the United States House of Representatives. James in the 1960s and 1970s played a prominent role in the revival of the Chickasaw Nation, leading to the participation of the Chickasaws in a national program to hire and train Native American Community Health Representatives to work with needy Indian individuals and families. This new program would provide Pearl an opportunity to do demanding but rewarding work on behalf of Indian people throughout a three-county area. (Courtesy Chickasaw Nation Archives)

area to build a rapport with them, to assess their needs, and to help them access resources within and outside their own communities that could help them. She found people living in extreme poverty with a wide range of needs. The work was rewarding for her, but after working there for "about seven or eight months," it was determined that the area should be worked by someone who lived there. This became especially apparent as the anticipated 24-hour nature of the job became a reality. Mrs. Woods began looking for her replacement, who would free her to take an administrative position in the Nation's health department.[5]

The chairman of the Chickasaw-Choctaw Alliance at this time happened to be Marlow Police Chief Harvey York. Mrs. Woods asked York who he thought would be a good candidate for the CHR position, and he recommended Pearl. He noted that she knew the Indian people in the area and that she enjoyed helping people. Pearl was "thrilled to death" and quickly accepted the offer because she "always wanted to help people, because we grew up helping people." She officially became a CHR in October of 1972. With her acceptance of the CHR position, Pearl began an association with the Chickasaw Nation that would endure the remainder of her life.[6]

Before Pearl could begin working in the field, she was required to undergo an intensive training program at the Desert Willow Training Center, located near Tucson, Arizona. Operated by the Indian Health

Service, the Desert Willow facility essentially was "a big dude ranch. It had . . . little houses where people would stay and had a large kitchen and a big auditorium." All new community health representatives from various tribes throughout the United States were trained at Desert Willow, and Pearl and her forty-seven classmates spent one month there going to "school day and night." At age fifty-seven, Pearl was the oldest of the trainees.[7]

Pearl and her fellow students were trained in health education and communication skills, concepts of health and diseases, environmental health, mental health, community development, CHR

Pearl posed for this photograph as she entered the Desert Willow Training Center near Tucson, Arizona, in 1972 to begin training to become a community health representative, or CHR, for the Chickasaw Nation in 1972. There she would interact with Indians representing tribes from throughout the United States. Always eager to learn, Pearl enjoyed both the formal training she received and the informal gatherings during which she learned about the cultures of the other tribes represented among the students. (Courtesy Pearl Scott Collection)

program issues and problems, home nursing, and first aid. Just as she had been as a child, Pearl was eager to learn and thoroughly enjoyed the experience. A typical day began with rising early, eating breakfast, and beginning classes. After a lunch break, classes would resume for the afternoon. The trainees next would have their evening meal, get a break for "two or three hours," and receive additional instruction in the evening.[8]

After classes ended in the evening, Pearl and her new friends would go to a large building called "The Roost." There they would socialize and "Indian dance." Pearl especially enjoyed these gatherings, because it afforded her the opportunity to visit with other students about the history and culture of the various tribes that they represented. The Navajos had

Pearl, on the far right, enjoyed learning how to "Indian dance" during her time at the Desert Willow Training Center. Her social time with fellow students such as these enhanced her pride in her Chickasaw heritage in particular and in American Indian heritage in general. (Courtesy Pearl Scott Collection)

"brought their drums and they would sing and dance and have a big time. . . ." Pearl learned how to dance during these sessions, and her pride in her American Indian heritage was greatly enhanced. When she returned to Marlow, she became more active in Indian events, and when her younger sister Arnetta returned to Marlow to live in 1980, the sisters "got shawls and moccasins and we'd go to Walters and all different places that had powwows" and danced and socialized.[9]

Pearl chaired the committee that planned the graduation ceremony for her class of forty-eight individuals from many more tribes than the seventeen states from which they came. The ceremony was a joyous occasion for Pearl, as she was ready to go home and get to work. The class motto, which was printed in the graduation program, seemed to indicate that Pearl and her fellow trainees had some understanding of the challenges that awaited them:

> With the Patience of Job,
>> With the Wisdom of Solomon,
>>> With the Strength of Sampson,
>>>> I will strive to help My People

Pearl returned to Oklahoma ready to serve her people, but her training did not end with her graduation from the CHR training program at Desert Willow.[10]

During the following year, she attended nineteen different workshops or seminars on subjects, including home safety and sanitation, rabies and spraying, drug abuse, audiology, mental health, and venereal diseases. By the end of 1978, she had participated in 106 such training sessions, many of which were multi-day programs over an amazing range of topics. A number of seminars were held on college and university campuses throughout Oklahoma, and Pearl reveled in the environment and in learning new information that she could use to help people. A typical example was a five-day seminar on cooperative management of health problems, held at Eastern Oklahoma State College at Wilburton. Participants took courses sponsored by the Indian Health Service on prenatal and neonatal care, child care, cardio vascular assessment, diabetes and immobilization, family planning, venereal diseases and counseling, revised standard first aid and safety, and the use and care of equipment in the home. For Pearl, renewing her education in this manner was exciting.[11]

Pearl's job was to see that the Indian people in her area, whether they were Chickasaw or any other tribe, knew about the health services that were available to them. Living in Pearl's service area were members of eighteen different tribes. She and her fellow CHRs became the "liaison between the health services and the individual." She was trained to spot health problems and help her clients understand how to get the help they needed. In addition, Pearl often was the only person an elder might see in a day's time, so her visits became important to those individuals socially and medically. Some of the elderly people Pearl visited could not clean their houses or yards, so Pearl did it for them. Often she would help them wash clothes.[12]

When asked some years later what her CHR job had entailed, Pearl exclaimed, "Name it! We vaccinated dogs. We vaccinated cats. We gave people shots. We'd take their temperatures. Well, we'd go with them and help them get anything they needed. We were even taught how to deliver babies." Pearl was never called upon to deliver a baby, but she was prepared to do so if needed.[13]

Pearl's granddaughter Beverly lived with Pearl for a year during the time Pearl was a CHR and, when she was not in school, usually rode with Pearl while she was making her rounds. Beverly was amazed by the miles Pearl put on her vehicle. She drove to meetings in Sulphur and other locations throughout the Chickasaw Nation. She crisscrossed

Stephens County, Grady County, and part of Jefferson County, calling on Indian families and individuals. She transported people to the IHS hospital in Lawton or to the clinic in Tishomingo when there was no other alternative. Frequently, she "drove up and down dirt tracks" to get to the homes of her clients. Pearl often exceeded the mileage limits that were placed on the CHRs, but she continued to drive, paying for the extra gasoline and maintenance of her car out of her own pocket "because people needed help."[14]

Pearl often found families living in grinding poverty at the end of those dirt trails. Many times they had little or no food, and Pearl could not ignore the hunger she found, especially among the children. Paying for the food out of her own funds, she would often buy groceries to deliver to the desperate families. "When you see kids hungry," Pearl said, "you're going to feed them." Often the children's fathers would "put their arms around" Pearl's neck "and just cry because I got their kids some groceries to eat. It was pitiful." Pearl's finances often were strained; "I had to do without a car payment sometimes, put it off until the next month, but I just could not see those kids go hungry."[15]

Pearl encountered many problems. Many of the people she encountered not only were impoverished but also were depressed, "lost, fallen through the cracks." Pearl worked hard to find them, give them hope, and help those who would accept it. Alcoholism was a significant problem, and there were those who were difficult, if not impossible, to help. Pearl would "never stop offering" to help, "but if they said 'Get out of here' then off we went, but she would always be sure she left some sort of food or something."[16]

It was typical for CHRs to work long, irregular hours. An 8-hour day was an exception rather than the norm. Often Pearl would be up early in the morning to take a client to the clinic in Tishomingo or, after it was built, to the Carl Albert Indian Health Facility in Ada. She might be out late that evening, finishing her rounds for the day, or even venturing out in the middle of the night, responding to a telephone call for help. Beverly recalled that the phone would ring at 2 or 3 a.m., and "it would be somebody needing help. She'd jump up, get dressed, get in the car and go break up a family fight" or respond to some other crisis—"someone is drunk or in jail. She just worked all the time." Pearl and her fellow CHRs quickly became involved in much more than health matters because they were the Chickasaw Nation's "front-line troops. . . . They were the contact with the people." "That phone never stopped ringing" when Beverly lived with Pearl.[17]

Pearl was impacted emotionally when her first husband, Lewis Scott, died on November 7, 1975, in Duncan. On the day he was buried in the Marlow Cemetery, Marlowites experienced one of the biggest snow storms the community had seen in years. That evening, Pearl "sat there . . . thinking I had to get out there and shovel that snow off of him." Pearl "cried and cried" that evening for Scottie and felt that he was "cold" and needed her. After fourteen years of separation, Pearl still loved Scottie. Perhaps their difficulties had faded with time, but she "still had that deep passion" for him that had stirred her soul as a young bride and mother. Many years later as Pearl began to contemplate her own death, she mentioned the idea to her daughter Louise of having Scottie's body moved so it could be buried next to her. Scottie was the father of her children and he remained the love of her life.[18]

Pearl responded to emotional trauma such as her troubled marriage and the death of Scottie by working ever harder on behalf of her clients. Among the various services Pearl provided was conducting rabies clinics on a regular basis. Pearl would spread the word orally and through local newspapers, and people would bring their dogs to be vaccinated against the dreaded disease. Sometimes she administered the shots herself, and other times she would have help from the IHS clinic at Tishomingo. On other occasions, Pearl would vaccinate the animals while visiting the homes of clients.[19]

Pearl also inspected children to see if they had lice in their hair. When she found lice, she would wash their hair and scrub their scalps with a special shampoo to kill the lice. "And then we had to spray their houses for bugs," Pearl recalled. "You do that for two or three houses, why you just almost feel them crawling on you."[20]

Pearl and her fellow workers were supposed to have Saturdays and Sundays off. However, Pearl and the other CHRs frequently organized dinners in one community or another throughout the Chickasaw Nation on Saturday evenings to attract clients to socialize and to hear a speaker with knowledge that could benefit them. At their personal expense, the CHRs would purchase the food, cook the dinner, wash the dishes, and organize the program. "We'd cook a big meal, have a big meeting, and everybody would come. And we'd have some kind of person that could help them . . . that would teach them something." Indian churches, a housing authority community building, a school cafeteria, or some other facility would be secured. The dinner would be publicized in local newspapers and by "word of mouth," and the events were highly successful.[21]

After the idea was proved to be workable and the Chickasaw Nation became more successful financially, such dinners were catered, but Pearl and her co-workers had donated their time and money to get the program started. "Oh we worked like everything," Pearl recalled, "but you could go to bed at night and think you helped so and so." Because the dinners were held in communities throughout the thirteen-county area that comprises the Chickasaw Nation, Pearl often would arrive home late at night after helping with these events. "We did it for the people, to get the Chickasaw Nation on its feet," Pearl recalled, "not just for the check, we were dedicated."[22]

Pearl also organized special events for specific constituent groups. One example of such an event was a Stephens County Elderly Indian Conference Dinner for Indian individuals fifty-five and older. Anyone needing transportation to the event was instructed to telephone Pearl. Information that would benefit older Indians was disseminated. Speakers included Cy Harris, director of Chickasaw Nation Health Services; and representatives from the Social Security Administration, Oklahoma Welfare Department, and the local Community Action program: an otitis media technician, and Pearl as a community health representative.[23]

Pearl also established a special clothing room in the Chickasaw Community Center in Marlow. Here clothing obtained from various sources was made available to Indian people who needed it. Again, Pearl placed stories in local newspapers to remind her clients of the availability of this resource and when it would be open. In addition to having clothing and shoes available free of charge, Pearl noted in one story that "there also will be some bedsprings and mattresses, baby clothes, underwear, curtain, drapes, and miscellaneous items available. . . ."[24]

Pearl developed a strong relationship with the *Marlow Review*. As a result, she was able to publicize her efforts in the paper through press releases and through open letters. One such letter was printed with the headline "Letter to the People!" She used the letter to publicize the clothing room, tell when she would be there to operate it, and outline how to make appointments for transportation to the hospital in Lawton. Pearl also used the newspaper to solicit clothes for the clothing room. In one such item in the paper's "Here N' There" column, she specifically asked for shoes and clothes for school age children. The clothing items were delivered to her house or to the Chickasaw Community Building in Marlow. Of course, she included her phone number for those who needed "pick-up service."[25]

Pearl always enjoyed getting together with her sisters whenever possible. Here she is enjoying a visit with them. From left to right: Opaletta, a Louisiana friend of Arnetta's son Joe Carter Brooks, Arnetta, and Pearl posed for the photographer, presumably Joe Carter Brooks, in front of Pearl's home in 1977. (Courtesy Joseph Carter Brooks)

By 1977 Pearl was providing transportation to the IHS hospital in Lawton on Tuesdays and Thursdays, provided that the clients scheduled their appointments more than one week in advance. This allowed Pearl to establish her itinerary for the week by the preceding Wednesday so that her schedule could be sent to the Chickasaw Nation Health Department headquarters in Ada. She still occasionally transported clients to the clinic at Tishomingo as well.[26]

Pearl also worked to benefit the entire Marlow community whenever possible. On one occasion, the local Home Demonstration Club asked Pearl if she could secure the use of a room in the Chickasaw Community Building for the Stephens County Health Department to use as a clinic one day a week. Pearl went to the head of the Chickasaw Nation Housing Authority and the governor of the Chickasaw Nation and obtained use of the room at no cost.[27]

Pearl's work occasionally afforded her opportunity to meet outstanding people. One such instance occurred in 1976 when she attended a retirement dinner for Carl Albert, the former congressman and speaker of the United States House of Representatives. Albert had been a great friend of the Chickasaw Nation. Pearl was impressed by the fact that the "Little Giant from Bugtussle" was not much taller than herself and that "He was such a polite person." Albert was "down-to-earth," and Pearl took the opportunity to get him to autograph several of the dinner programs. Pearl encountered Albert again in 1980 during the celebration of the opening of the Carl Albert Indian Health Facility in Ada. She was appointed by Chickasaw Governor James to serve as a guide for Albert and several other dignitaries in attendance. [28]

Another pleasant diversion from Pearl's heavy work schedule came in June of 1978, when she was invited to be a part of a Chickasaw delegation headed by Governor James to retrace the route of the original Chickasaw Trail of Tears. Murray State College (MSC), located at Tishomingo, provided the bus and gasoline for the trip. MSC President Clyde Kindel accompanied the group that also included other Chickasaw Nation employees, tribal leaders, and representatives from East Central State College at Ada.[29]

The tour officially began at Jackson, Mississippi, where Governor James was made honorary mayor and given a key to the city. From there the group journeyed to the Natchez Trace, where they were honored by a reception and historical presentations by park rangers, one of whom joined them on their bus as they traveled the historic trade route. When they reached the point where they were to leave the Natchez Trace to travel on to Pontotoc, the heart of their ancestral homelands in Mississippi, they were met and accompanied by three highway patrol cars and about twenty cars decorated with banners and loaded with citizens of Pontotoc. The tour members found Pontotoc festooned with decorations, including a large welcoming banner spanning Main Street and people lining the streets carrying signs welcoming the visitors. Two days of programs ensued, during which the visiting delegation was honored in various ways and given gifts including historical artifacts and items for placement in a special Chickasaw Nation Memorial Garden and Museum being planned for the Murray College campus.[30]

One program was held in the school auditorium, and it attracted a "standing room only" audience. The mayor of the community and Governor James exchanged gifts and speeches. Chickasaw "Princess" Barbara Boster gave the Lord's Prayer in sign language while it was being recited by Geraldine Greenwood. John Jack then led eight members of the delegation who sang in Chickasaw. The program was closed with all present singing "This Land is Your Land" and "The Star Spangled Banner." A reception followed, during which a local author gave Pearl an autographed copy of his book on Chickasaw Chief Tishomingo. During another program the following day, an elderly man gave her a red rock that was said to have been used by Chickasaws to make war paint.[31]

From Pontotoc, the group traveled to Memphis, Tennessee, where again they participated in festivities in their honor, and then moved on to Little Rock, Arkansas, following the route many of their ancestors had used when they were forced to leave Mississippi for Indian Territory so many years in the past. Historic sites were toured along the way. The following day the group continued along the historic Trail of Tears route, eventually returning to Ada. Pearl enjoyed every minute of the trip, "It was a thrill, and I wished my great grandparents might have known what a better world it is today than when they had to leave there 151 years ago."[32]

In December of 1978, Pearl was honored to be included in the publication *Personalities of the South*. Considerable space in her biographical entry was devoted to her unique, early aviation career. Her work on behalf of the Chickasaw Nation also was highlighted, including the extensive training she had undergone in order to serve her people more effectively.[33]

Pearl's workload had increased by this time because in October Pearl and Lillian Fowler, another CHR whom Pearl admired as a wonderful cook and dedicated worker, were appointed as "full-time" nutrition specialists for the Chickasaw Nation. Both women were to continue working as CHRs. Pearl and Lillian's focus was on reducing the startlingly high incidence of diabetes among Indians through proper diet. Pearl had received a food and nutrition certificate from Oklahoma State University and had attended several workshops on nutrition and diabetes. She also had already helped conduct special "nutrition and diabetic dinners" sponsored by the Chickasaw Nation Health Department. In her new responsibility, Pearl would conduct dinners and in-home demonstrations on "how to prepare well balanced and nutritious dinners without having to purchase a lot of special food items." Pearl also noted that she would be "available to help any diabetic with their diet, Indian or non-Indian."[34]

The same newspaper article that announced Pearl's new expertise also noted that she would be in Ada on Wednesdays and Thursdays for the next eight weeks, attending a course on physical therapy. Clients who needed to contact her on those days were encouraged to call her either before 8 a.m. or after 6 p.m. Pearl's popularity among her clients was such that she surely must have received a significant number of phone calls early in the morning or at night on those particular days. [35]

In 1979 a writer for *Memphis Magazine* spent a day with Pearl as part of his research for an article on the Chickasaws. Quoting Pearl as saying, "I don't think I have ever met a stranger," Kenneth Neill observed that Pearl was "one of those special people whose enthusiasm for life is infectious, the perfect antidote for a bout of melancholia." After reviewing her aviation history, he noted that Pearl had "the energy (and appearance) of a woman half her age."[36]

During their day together, Pearl and Neill visited a "young Comanche woman who was wearing a 'Custer had it coming' t-shirt" and a Choctaw elder who "spoke fondly of his childhood days in 'I. T—Indian Territory.'" They also called on an elderly Choctaw woman who had lost both legs due to complications from diabetes and a "sad-eyed Chickasaw woman whose husband had just deserted her, leaving her with four children at the age of twenty." The duo finally visited a Choctaw household where Pearl tried to explain to a mother whose son wanted to be an upholsterer how to obtain a loan through a special Indian Small Business Loan program. "Both of us sensed that nothing will come of the conversation," Neill wrote. Pearl concluded that, "It's all up to the individual. All we can do is try to get them to help themselves."[37]

Pearl's kindnesses extended beyond her clients. When needed, she consistently helped neighbors, friends in the community, and members of her family. She also could not turn away stray cats or dogs, and many of them were fed at her home. Her granddaugh-

ter Beverly watched her "spread many small kind-nesses . . . and words of encouragement."[38]

Pearl's hectic schedule and long hours caused problems in her already strained marriage to A. J. Kizarr, who resented Pearl's long hours at work and her late night and weekend excursions on be-half of her clients. He wanted a companion, and Pearl often was not there. He began drinking, at times heavily, of which Pearl disapproved. On one such occasion, A. J. and Pearl's brother George had gotten drunk together and called Pearl to come get them. Pearl brought them home, and when A. J. said "something smart" to Pearl when he was getting out of the car, she slapped him as hard as she could. George immediately curled up in a ball and said "Oh sister, don't hit me!" While George thought this was funny, Pearl failed to see the humor in the situation.[39]

Pearl's retirement as a community health representative did not end her service to the Chickasaw Nation. With the continued evolution of the Chickasaw Nation's government, new opportunities for service soon would arise, and Pearl again would serve her people. (Courtesy Marlow Chamber of Commerce)

By December of 1979, Pearl was ready to end her marriage to A. J. In her divorce petition, signed by Pearl on December 18 and filed with the Stephens County Court on December 26, she stated that "a state of complete and irreconcilable in-compatibility" had arisen between the two parties, "and [that] by reason of the acts of the Defendant and the resulting irremediable breakdown of the marital relationship," she no longer could continue to live with A. J. She also petitioned to be allowed to return to her prior name of Eula Pearl Scott. In addition, she was to retain her personal possessions, house-hold goods, appliances, furniture, fishing and camping equipment, and 1976 Chevrolet Malibu. A. J. was to keep his personal possessions. A. J. waived "all lawful time requirements for a divorce and pleading rights," and the final divorce decree was issued on January 7, 1980. All the terms outlined in Pearl's petition were granted by the court. Her difficult marriage finally was ended. [40]

By 1980 Pearl was tired. The long hours and miles on the road had taken a toll as had her martial problems. Just a few months after her divorce was granted, she decided to retire at age sixty-five from her positions as a CHR and nutrition specialist. By all accounts, Pearl had done an outstanding job. Upon her retirement, Chickasaw Governor James expressed his "sincere appreciation" for her "eight years of devoted services." Moreover, he told Pearl that her "untiring efforts and dedication to assisting Indian people has been an inspiration to us all." Lieutenant Governor Bill Anoatubby, who had served as health department director, accounting director, controller, and special assistant to the governor, remembered Pearl as being a "diligent, hard working community health representative" who "went above and beyond the call of duty when it came to doing her job."[41]

Pearl's efforts on behalf of the Chickasaw people were also observed and appreciated by individuals outside the Indian community. For example, Marlow banker, D. B. Green, recalled that as a youth he had been impressed with Pearl. To him, she was a "larger than life" figure who usually wore clothing reflecting her Chickasaw heritage and was "very charismatic." Green recalled how, "Pearl could walk into a room or a restaurant and everybody knew her. . . She had a great confidence and a great gift of gab. . . . She could just work every table in a restaurant." For Green, Pearl was his introduction into Indian culture. As an adult, Green observed Pearl's work as a community health representative and her subsequent activities on behalf of her people and came to develop a "real appreciation for her and for her protecting her heritage and being very proud of her culture and never abandoning that."[42]

An article on Pearl's retirement in *The Chickasaw Times* reviewed her life and service to the nation. In the caption under her picture, after noting that "she will be missed," the anonymous writer observed, "We know Pearl though—she will never really retire." That statement would prove to be prophetic.[43]

Chapter Ten
▼▼▼

CONTINUED SERVICE

The completion of a Chickasaw Nation housing project in Duncan played a major role in the timing of Pearl's retirement as a CHR. She successfully applied for the secretarial position at the housing project, which enabled her at age sixty-five to work more normal hours and not drive an average of two thousand miles per month, as she had done over the previous eight years. The job required Pearl to perform a variety of tasks, including collecting rent payments, making bank deposits, communicating with residents on behalf of the administrators of the project, and all the usual duties of an executive secretary. The job provided Pearl with an opportunity to continue working on behalf of the Chickasaw Nation while maintaining a more normal work schedule, leaving her time for community activities and her sisters and brother. In 1983, political developments in the Chickasaw Nation, however, presented a new opportunity for Pearl to serve her people.[1]

For much of the period from 1905 to 1979, the Chickasaw government had consisted primarily of a governor, whose principal function by federal mandate was to close out the tribe's business. Policy toward the Indian nations fluctuated from one presidential administration to the next, but President Richard Nixon set federal policy in the direction of

Pearl enjoyed her service in the tribal legislature, despite the fusses that inevitably take place in political bodies such as councils and legislatures. She enjoyed meeting as many of her constituents as possible and looking for ways to enhance health care and educational opportunities for the Chickasaw people. (Courtesy Chickasaw Nation Archives)

▼▼▼

recognition of tribal sovereignty. Consequently, Overton James, who had been appointed governor of the Chickasaw Nation in 1963 by President John F. Kennedy, found increasing opportunities to expand the role of the Chickasaw Nation in service to its citizens. The establishment of the Chickasaw Nation Housing Authority and the community health representatives programs in the early 1970s significantly elevated the importance of the Chickasaw government, and a new constitution for the nation was established in 1979. The governor remained the dominant force, as he had knowledge, experience, and contacts, while members of the new tribal council had little of those commodities of power. The office of Lieutenant Governor also was established at this time, and James selected Bill J. Anoatubby to become the first to fill this office.[2]

In 1983, a new constitution, intended to establish a more balanced government with executive, legislative, and judicial branches, was approved by a vote of the Chickasaw electorate. The Chickasaw Nation was divided into four legislative districts along historical lines—Panola, Pickens, Pontotoc, and Tishomingo—and the number of legislative seats for each district was apportioned based on population. The legislature would consist of one house with thirteen representatives. The executive department would be headed by a governor and lieutenant governor, who would stand for election as a team. The judiciary would feature three judges, who would rule as needed on the constitutionality of resolutions and laws passed by the legislature and signed by the governor. The governor could veto laws or resolutions passed by the legislature, which, in turn, could override a veto with a minimum of nine votes. In short, the Chickasaw constitution was intended to establish a system of checks and balances along the lines of the United States government and the fifty state governments. Of course, the relative power of the three branches would evolve over time and would be a matter of contention, as it has been in the federal and state governments.[3]

The Pickens District was large in geographical area, ranging from the southern half of Grady County to the eastern boundary of Marshall County and including all or parts of Garvin, Murray, Carter, Love, Jefferson, and Stephens counties. Far western portions of Grady, Stephens, and Jefferson counties were not included in the Chickasaw Nation. Con-

With the establishment of the Chickasaw Constitution of 1983, the election of a Chickasaw tribal legislature was mandated. Governor Overton James, seated, and Bill Anoatubby, to the immediate left of James, who was running for election as lieutenant governor, determined that Pearl's experience as a CHR and the respect she commanded among the Chickasaw people in her area made her an ideal candidate for the legislature. They asked Pearl to consider running for one of the Pickens District seats. She agreed to do so and was successful. (Courtesy Chickasaw Nation Archives)

sequently, Pearl's home town of Marlow was situated near the western boundary of the Nation and Pickens District. Although Pickens was the largest legislative district in land area, it received only three seats of the total of thirteen based on its population relative to the other districts.[4]

Governor James selected Bill Anoatubby as his running mate for the elections of 1983, which would determine who would serve in the elective offices in all three branches of government. Both James and Anoatubby were familiar with Pearl's dedicated work as a community health representative and her enthusiasm for continued growth of the tribal government's ability to help the Chickasaw people. Consequently, James telephoned Pearl and asked her to run for Seat #2 in the Pickens District. Anoatubby later recalled that Pearl was "the perfect candidate" because of her experience and status as a leader. People had continued to come to her for help and advice after her retirement from the CHR program.

She was "in touch with the community," and it was an "easy transition for her to move into the legislature. . . ." Pearl saw the idea of serving in the legislature as yet another interesting opportunity to help her people, so she agreed to enter the race.[5]

Pearl announced her candidacy for the Chickasaw Tribal Legislature in *The Chickasaw Times* and in other publications. In the tribal newspaper, she emphasized that her mother was an enrolled Chickasaw and that she had lived in Marlow most of her life. She also discussed her three children and mentioned that she had ten grandchildren and four great grandchildren. After devoting a paragraph to her aviation career and connection to Wiley Post, she described her work experience on behalf of the Chickasaw Nation, her education, her community activities, and her honors and recognition. Finally, she emphasized her dedication "to my people" and noted that she would work hard to see that the needs of the people were met. She planned to travel and meet with people from communities throughout the Pickens District.[6]

In a published letter to the voters, Pearl observed that she knew "first-hand the problems faced by our people. . . ." She pledged that as a legislator she would "work for better living conditions, more jobs, increased health services, and . . . a per capita payment from the Arkansas Riverbed settlement" if and when such funds were to become available. The Cherokee, Choctaw, and Chickasaw tribes each had claimed ownership of a portion of the Arkansas Riverbed and hoped to receive a significant sum of money to settle those claims.[7]

Pearl's opponents in this election were Turquoise S. "Coy" Colbert, Stanford Wade, and Emil J. Farve. When the vote was counted, Colbert had received 124 votes, Pearl had garnered 114 votes, Wade had received 56 votes, and Farve had tallied 36 votes. Although Colbert, who was perhaps aided somewhat by having a last name that was prominent in Chickasaw history, had the most votes, he did not receive a majority of the votes cast and thus faced a runoff election against Pearl, who finished a close second.[8]

A lifelong resident of the Mannsville, Oklahoma, area, Colbert's father was an enrolled Chickasaw. Colbert noted that he was retired and would work full time for his constituents. He highlighted his work experience in construction over a period of forty-two years, stressed the importance of tribal businesses, and pledged to foster unity among Chickasaws. He also observed that he lived by the Ten Commandments and the Golden Rule and that he would run a clean campaign.[9]

Pearl placed an ad in the *Marlow Review* to thank voters who had supported her and urged them to vote for her again in the runoff election scheduled for November 5. In an open letter to Pickens District voters, Pearl asked for support, indicating that she wanted to be their "voice" in the Chickasaw government and to work with them to "make the future a secure one for our children." She also pledged to work with Governor James and Lt. Governor Anoatubby to devise a system of per capita payments when the Arkansas Riverbed issue was resolved. Other major points were that she would work to see that Chickasaw housing programs were continued, that "we take every opportunity to provide employment and training for our people, and that we continue to provide good, decent health care to those who need and deserve help."[10]

Prior to the runoff election, Pickens District voters received a letter signed by Governor James and Lt. Governor Anoatubby urging support for Pearl. Running as a team in the general election, they had received 1,502 of the 2,500 votes cast. Of the three other candidate tickets in the race, their closest competitors had received 639 votes. Consequently, such an endorsement from James and Anoatubby undoubtedly carried a great deal of weight with voters. In their letter, they praised Pearl as "The finest example of dedication to our future. . . ." Pearl, they observed, had "shared in many of our tribal developments in the past. . . and is will known and liked by many." Moreover, "Her appeal is directly related to her sincere interest in our people, by her dedication and resolve to DO something." James and Anoatubby strongly emphasized that "Pearl is not controlled by any special interest group" and concluded, "We need Pearl."[11]

In an article in the *Marlow Review* just three days prior to the election, Pearl indicated that she intended to continue serving her people "in any manner possible." During her time when she would not be meeting in legislative sessions or committees, she "would be doing whatever is necessary to help her fellow Chickasaws." And this might even include doing some of the same type work she had done as a CHR, including "vaccinating dogs, spraying houses, etc." Pearl also noted that the other two Pickens District legislators elected in the general election were from the eastern end of the district. If Pearl were not elected, the western region of the district would not be represented in the legislature. Consequently, she hoped the voters "will try to provide some balance . . . by voting for a western Chickasaw." Noting Pearl's eleven years of service to the Chickasaw Nation to date, the author of the article observed that, "During that span, her name has become a household item throughout the three western counties, something which will have to aid her in her candidacy."[12]

With the valuable endorsement of James and Anoatubby and the steadfast loyalty of those who knew her, Pearl defeated Colbert in the runoff election by a count of 189 to 165. In the days following the election, Pearl received congratulatory communications from many, including a letter from Overton M. "Buck" Cheadle, a former Marlow resident who had been elected to the legislature in October, representing the Pontotoc District. Cheadle would prove to be a good friend and ally of Pearl's in the legislature. He told Pearl that he was "so happy for both you and the Tribal Legislature. I know you will be a good contributing member." Because of being involved in a runoff election, Pearl had missed the first meeting of the legislature in October, but she was on hand for the November 18 meeting. At the beginning of the meeting, Pearl and several other runoff contest winners were sworn in and began their service to the Chickasaw Nation.[13]

Pearl and most of the other legislators had little experience to guide them in their conduct of legislative business. "None of us had ever done anything like that," Pearl observed. Consequently, Gary Childers of the executive department staff conducted sessions with legislators one night per week over several weeks to teach them about Robert's Rules of Order, long established guidelines for conducting meetings. Pearl was impressed with Childers, and a strong friendship between the two began that would endure the remainder of Pearl's life. Years later, Pearl would remark, "That Gary, you just can't beat him." Childers had known Pearl when she was a CHR, but they had not worked together previously. The sessions with the legislators on parliamentary procedure were the first time "Pearl and I got hooked up really well, "Childers remembered. Pearl took to that stuff like a duck takes to water. . . . So she and I got to working together on a lot of things." The new legislators learned quickly and soon were ready to tackle their responsibilities.[14]

Although Pearl was sixty-eight when she began her legislative service, she was excited and energized by her new responsibility. Except for an occasional special session, the legislature would meet only once a month, with a few committee meetings during the intervening period. Pearl, nonetheless, viewed legislative service as a full-time job. She was determined to participate in as many community meetings as possible in her district, and some outside her district, in order to interact with the people she was representing. Moreover, her phone, which had never stopped ringing after she retired as a CHR, continued to ring as her constituents kept seeking her help on all manner of problems. Pearl worked hard to help callers resolve their problems, either by referring them to their current CHR or by directing them to an appropriate local or tribal official. Often, she would make the contact herself to ensure that her constituent received proper attention. Regarding Pearl's enthusiasm and energy level as a legislator, Childers recalled, "She was great. I don't know any other way to put it."[15]

In November of 1983, during Pearl's first meeting with the legislature, she voted for Robert Stephens to be chairperson of the tribal legislature and Harold Hensley to be secretary of that body. Jess Green, the other candidate for chairperson, was a newcomer to Chickasaw government, while Stephens was a veteran of the previous tribal council and was considered to be an ally of Governor James. It was logical that Pearl would support Stephens, given that she had been recruited by James and was supported by him in the campaign.[16]

In time, she was destined to clash with Hensley over the issue of travel policy, but during their first two years, the legislators were largely consumed with getting organized and defining the role of the legislature in tribal government. The legislators did not have their own staff to draft resolutions or laws, so they relied on the executive department, specifically Gary Childers, for that service. In addition, they heard reports from the governor and lieutenant governor, who often presented specific resolutions for approval. Committee chairmen also presented reports each session and frequently introduced issues for the legislature to consider.[17]

The Chickasaw Constitution mandated that legislators were to serve three-year terms. Moreover, the terms of approximately a third of them would expire each year. To establish this rotation, it was necessary for the original thirteen legislators to have a drawing to assign initial one-year, two-year, or three-year terms. The Pickens District had three legislators, and after the drawing only one of them would have an initial three-year term. One of them would have a two-year term and the other would have a one-year term. Pearl drew the one-year term and would have to stand for election in October of 1984 if she wished to continue her service in the legislature.[18]

Harold Hensley of Ardmore and Pearl clashed over several matters during her first four years in the Chickasaw tribal legislature, including the travel reimbursement policy established by the law makers. (Courtesy Chickasaw Nation Archives)

Pearl was appointed to the finance and personnel committee chaired by Hensley. This committee's responsibilities involved reviewing and establishing salary scales for all employees of the Chickasaw Nation and to examining and critiquing the annual budget prepared by the governor. In addition to the regular monthly sessions, Stephens instituted a system by which all the legislators met at Sulphur once a month and split into their various committees to conduct committee business. Sometimes these meetings "degenerated into gripe sessions featuring Chickasaw citizens often cussing out the members," Stephens later recalled. The Finance and Personnel Committee sometimes met more frequently, and some of their meetings were attended by Governor James and Lt. Governor Anoatubby.[19]

In addition, Pearl began a pattern of meeting frequently with various civic and church groups to inform their members about tribal activities and to learn about concerns and views of her constituents. An example of such a meeting was that of the Southwest Choctaws in Marlow on December 6, 1983. This organization had members representing a number of tribes, including Chickasaws. Pearl was on the agenda to report on

Chickasaw tribal activities while her friend Harvey York would discuss matters of interest to the Choctaws. Pearl also traveled to numerous out-of-town community meetings, such as one at Lebanon in Marshall County, some 114 miles from Marlow, in March of 1984.[20]

Pearl enjoyed her work as a legislator and quickly determined that she would stand for election for a full three-year term in 1984. When the filing period for candidates ended, Pearl had not drawn an opponent. Consequently, she could pursue her work without worrying about another election until 1987. Throughout this period, Pearl enthusiastically supported many tribal efforts initiated by the executive department to obtain funds from various federal funding agencies to support programs to enhance the quality of life of the Chickasaw people. Because of her personal experience, she was a strong advocate for the CHR program. Often she would call Gary Childers to get a detailed explanation of the purpose of a particular grant proposal, and then she would be its "champion" in the legislature in support of the effort. "In the beginning that was her main thing," Childers recalled, "to get as many services for the Chickasaw people as she could get. She worked very closely with Governor James on a lot of those issues. . . and she had some really good friends in the legislature too." From Childers's perspective, "Pearl knew everything that was going on."[21]

Just as Pearl was getting her second legislative term in high gear, she received a welcome reminder of her personal aviation heritage. In early March of 1984, she received a letter from George E. Haddaway, founder of the History of Aviation Collection of the University of Texas at Dallas. Haddaway indicated that Mrs. Linda Harwill of Marlow had informed him about Pearl's "very exciting aviation background." He then extended an invitation to her to visit the History of Aviation Collection and asked her to provide a "complete file on your aviation experiences. . . . We have an excellent collection on Women in Aviation and certainly would appreciate having a complete file on . . . Eula Pearl Carter Scott." Pearl did provide information for the archival collection and was both pleased and honored that her aviation exploits had been remembered.[22]

Pearl took her legislative responsibilities seriously. From November 1983 to August 1985, she did not miss a meeting of the legislature until an illness forced her to be absent. By that time the legislature, or at least a growing faction of it, was becoming increasingly confrontational with the executive department. This, in large part, was a natural response of legislators wanting to test and expand the power of the legislature in relation to that of the executive branch. Such power struggles have ebbed and flowed throughout the history of the United States at the federal and state levels of government. As in most "balanced" governments, competition for power between the branches, especially the executive and legislative, was inevitable. As early as May 1984, there was growing conflict over who should control the content of the tribal newspaper, *The Chickasaw Times*.[23]

Governor James had controlled the paper since its inception in 1963. He had used the publication to promote the development of the Chickasaw Nation. Legislators began to believe that the legislative branch should have more input into the content of the newspaper. They recognized that it was an increasingly important means of communicating with their constituents and that the governor could have a significant impact on how they were perceived individually and collectively by his traditional dominance of the newspaper's content. Other potential political rivals undoubtedly believed that James could use the newspaper to boost his image and political stature within the tribe.[24]

Governor James responded to such concerns in his monthly column in the paper, in which he emphasized that "The stories in this newspaper do not dwell on bad news." In fact, it "has long been the policy of the paper to provide good news coverage; to show the rest of the world the good things being accomplished by a group of people dedicated to serving others." Other media were forced to sell their services, James observed, and thus had to compete for business in their quest for growth. He suggested that bad news sold and thus the other media tended to dwell on that. *The Chickasaw Times*, however, was provided free of charge to the Chickasaw people, he argued, and thus *"The Chickasaw Times* will continue in its efforts to bring you the finest in good news coverage."[25]

Continued concern on the part of legislators was reflected in the report of Pearl's friend Overton Cheadle, chairman of the legislature's Rules & Ethics Committee, during the July 19, 1984, meeting of the legislature. Cheadle indicated that he had been campaigning and visiting with Chickasaw people and that many of them had indicated that they did not understand "everything the legislature is doing." Some of them, Cheadle asserted, had asked that more information on legislative activities be put into *The Chickasaw Times*. Cheadle noted that he thought Gary Childers or someone in public affairs would be willing to attend legislative sessions, take notes, and provide stories on the legislature's work to the tribal newspaper. Governor James, who was in attendance, suggested that *The Chickasaw Times* could assign a reporter to cover the meetings. Legislator Jess Green noted that all resolutions acted upon by the legislature should be listed in the newspaper. Legislative Chairperson Robert Stephens ended the discussion by appointing Cheadle to visit with Childers to work out the details. Nevertheless, conflict between the governor and the legislature over content of *The Chickasaw Times* would continue to simmer and would finally reach a boil in 1986.[26]

. During the same July meeting, a controversy arose concerning whether or not Childers, who had been designated to serve as secretary of the election committee, should have the power to rule on the eligibility of candidates to run for a particular office. Some legislators argued that the tribal court should rule on issues of candidate eligibility rather than allowing an employee of the executive branch to have such authority. After considerable discussion, the legislators voted seven to six in favor of Childers for election committee secretary with the responsibility of making decisions regarding candidate eligibility. Pearl voted with the majority in support of Childers and, implicitly, the executive branch.[27]

During the year, Pearl and the other legislators reviewed, discussed, and voted on a wide range of issues including the establishment of written personnel policies, regulations dealing with bingo operations, the operations of the Chickasaw Motor Inn at Sulphur, the possible establishment of tribal smoke shop operations, and numerous other tribal affairs. Governor James and Lieutenant Governor Anoatubby continued to appear at the monthly legislative sessions to deliver their reports and answer questions. Pearl did not speak a great deal in debates, but she continued her quiet efforts to help the Chickasaw people in general and her end of the Pickens District in particular. For example, during the November

16, 1984, meeting, she complained to Governor James that on November 12, the scheduled truck from the tribe's food distribution program never arrived. Consequently, people waited and were never notified that the truck would not run that day. James noted that the twelfth was a holiday and that the truck should have been rescheduled to another date.[28]

Although Pearl did not draw an opponent in 1984 and thus appeared automatically elected to a new three-year term, for a period of time it appeared that she might not be allowed to begin serving in November of 1984 as scheduled. The area director of the Bureau of Indian Affairs (BIA) decided that his agency would not recognize as valid the election of Pearl and other legislators whose names were not printed on the election ballot, even though they would have been the only choice shown on the ballot for their particular office. Of course, this was yet another reminder of the power that the BIA exercised over tribal governments despite the progress that had been made over the past two decades. The Chickasaw Nation appealed this decision, and with the support of local BIA official Zane Browning, the decision was reversed.[29]

As it had previously, the tribal legislature in 1985 continued to function primarily in response to executive department initiatives, although later in that year the first significant clashes over legislative and executive powers would occur. Support for Governor James already had begun to erode as the legislature sought to establish its role in tribal decision making. That erosion was accelerated in February of 1985 when James was served with a federal indictment containing ten charges of mail fraud and one count of extortion. James proclaimed his innocence, assured the Chickasaw people that no tribal funds were involved in any way, and expressed regret for the embarrassment the circumstance had caused. Those who already tended to oppose James assumed he was guilty and hardened their opposition. His supporters were shocked by the allegations and some of them, including Pearl, began moving to a more neutral position in their view of him.[30]

James's trial did not begin until August, so he had to endure six months of speculation and rumor. When the trial finally began on August 13 in the court of United States District Judge Ralph Thompson in Oklahoma City, James, through his attorney, argued that the funds he had received were campaign contributions and were used as such. The government did not allege that any tribal funds were involved, and they did not show that any private citizen or business received any benefits as a result of the contributions. James readily admitted that he made a mistake in the way the funds were handled but forcefully maintained that he was innocent of all the charges. Character witnesses who testified for James included former Speaker of the United States House of Representatives Carl B. Albert and Chickasaw Nation Judge Haskell Paul.[31]

After approximately twenty-seven hours of deliberation, the jury reported to Judge Thompson that they were hopelessly deadlocked and Thompson declared a mistrial. Federal prosecutors announced that the case would be retried. James indicated that he would continue the fight because he was guilty of poor judgment, not a crime. Tribal legislator Jess Green, himself a state judge, later pointed out that James had never taken money from the tribe but had taken campaign contributions just like state and federal politicians, including his friend and model Carl Albert. New federal charges were filed against James less than a month later, but as a result of various legal circumstances, James's case would not be resolved until November 1988. This situation caused him considerable political difficulty.[32]

Tensions between James and the tribal legislature were heightened when Pearl's friend "Buck" Cheadle was elected to the chairmanship of the legislature in October of 1985. Although Cheadle had been brought into the Chickasaw government by James and had served on the previous tribal council, he had become a political rival of James. The selection of Cheadle, who was known among the legislators as being less friendly toward James than Stephens had been, was a setback for James. At the annual meeting of the Chickasaw Nation held at Byng on October 5, James forcefully proclaimed his innocence and indicated that he would stand for reelection upon the expiration of his present term in 1987. Special awards from tribal employees were presented to James, Lieutenant Governor Anoatubby, and Pat Woods "for their dedication and hard work."[33]

Pearl attended the annual meeting along with a "crowd of thousands" and enjoyed the festivities. She also attended the Inter-Tribal Council of the Five Civilized Tribes meeting held at Sulphur on October 10 and 11.

This was an "invitation only" meeting that featured a special presentation honoring Carl Albert for all he had done on behalf of the Indian people of Oklahoma and other special presentations by representatives of various

governmental agencies and by the council's executive committee, of which James was a member.[34]

In early December, James announced that he would not stand for reelection in 1987. Included in the same newspaper story was the announcement that Lt. Governor Anoatubby would be a candidate for the office of governor. James was not present at the December meeting of the tribal legislature, but Anoatubby was present and found himself in a hostile environment, especially during the "Citizen Comments" portion of the meeting. Anoatubby was assailed verbally by several individuals whose presence perhaps had been orchestrated by certain members of the legislature. He withstood these assaults without losing his composure, but he must have wondered if he should reconsider his plans for the future. From that point until James was out of office, both he and Anoatubby submitted reports to the legislature in writing and did not appear personally.[35]

Overton M. "Buck" Cheadle, a former resident of Marlow and friend of Pearl's, would prove to be a strong ally in the tribal legislature. (Courtesy Chickasaw Nation Archives)

There was some resentment against Cheadle on the part of particular supporters of the administration for his allowing the attacks on Anoatubby at the November meeting to get out of hand. This culminated in a motion by Harold Hensley to censure Cheadle. Hensley argued that one of the individuals who had attacked Anoatubby had also verbally attacked a legislator during a committee meeting. Hensley alleged that Cheadle had known in advance about the earlier attack yet indicated that he had been shocked into inaction when that person assailed Anoatubby. Only two legislators voted in support of Hensley's motion, Hensley and Robert Stephens. Pearl voted "no" on the motion, supporting Cheadle, along with the other eight legislators present.[36]

A major point of contention between the legislature and the governor that developed early in 1986 was Enactment 13, popularly called "The

▼▼▼

Right to Know Act." Late in 1985, Legislator Barney Abbott had asked for a list of all employees of the tribe, detailing their salary, tribal affiliation, and blood quantum. Instead, he received a list of salary ranges. In response, he introduced Enactment 13. Harold Hensley moved to table the motion to approve the legislation until Abbott explained satisfactorily why he wanted this information. Abbott indicated that there were inequities in salary among people doing the same jobs. He believed that friends and supporters of the governor were being unfairly favored. James believed that Abbott and others wanted to elevate salaries of their friends. Moreover, he asserted that the function of the legislature was to approve salary ranges, while is was the responsibility of the executive department to hire employees and set specific salaries. Enactment 13 passed by a ten to three majority, with Pearl voting "no."[37]

Later that same month, James vetoed Enactment 13, and the following month the legislature overrode the veto. This time, Pearl voted to override the veto. In fact, the only legislator to vote against the override was Hensley. James petitioned the Chickasaw tribal court to rule on the constitutionality of Enactment 13. On July 29, the court held a special hearing with about fifty citizens in attendance, and the court found "The Right to Know Act" to be "improper, null and void" on the grounds that the Chickasaw Constitution empowers the executive branch with devising the annual budget while the legislature could approve, alter, or reject it. Enactment 13 represented, in the opinion of the court, a usurpation of the powers of the executive branch. James had won this battle, but another confrontation already was underway.[38]

The power struggle between the legislature and the executive department reached a head with a controversy over the editorial content and policies of *The Chickasaw Times*, the official newspaper of the tribe that was published monthly and distributed to all Chickasaw citizens. Legislators wanted significantly more control over the content of the publication and correctly viewed it as the most effective means of communicating with citizens of the Chickasaw Nation. James and the legislators could not reach agreement on any changes in editorial policy or content of the newspaper, so during the August 15 session of the legislature, the newspaper issue arose again during consideration of the tribal budget for

Fiscal Year 1987. Federal funding that previously paid a portion of the newspaper's cost had been lost for 1987, so the budget request included $6,000 for the newspaper. Several legislators observed that they needed time to talk to their constituents about whether the newspaper should be continued under the present circumstances. Consequently, the budget resolution was tabled, apparently by common consent since no roll call vote was recorded. The Chickasaw Times had become the focal point of the conflict between the legislative and executive branches.[39]

A special session of the legislature convened to deal with the budget. The governor had modified the budget, leaving out the newspaper appropriation because he and the lawmakers could not reach agreement on editorial policies. The budget without the funding for the newspapers was voted on and passed by a ten-to- two vote, with Pearl voting with the majority. Hensley and Stephens remained loyal to the governor and voted against the budget because the newspaper had been excluded.[40]

Pearl and the other legislators were shocked when they saw the next issue of The Chickasaw Times. The first page consisted of two large headlines, "Legislature Votes to 'Kill' The Chickasaw Times," and "This is the Last Issue You Will Receive!!!" An editorial on page two blasted the legislature's "degrading and despicable action" and observed that the legislators have exhibited a "lack of knowledge, a general 'don't care' attitude and disinterest in the good of the Chickasaw people." The editorial concluded by urging "readers to write the legislators and tell them how you are receiving this latest action of theirs. . . . If this paper should ever be started again, if will be your letters, phone calls and comments which will do it." Another headline, "The Following Members of the Chickasaw Tribal Legislature Voted to Kill The Chickasaw Times," was followed by a list of the names, addresses, and phone numbers of the offending legislators, including Pearl. A separate "letter" in the newspaper praised the gallantry of legislators Hensley and Stephens who "stood their ground" on behalf of the publication.[41]

The legislators soon prepared a report that was mailed to tribal members to tell their side of the newspaper controversy. Ten of them, including Pearl, affixed their signatures to the report that pointed out that the legislators "for months" had attempted to "persuade the Executive Department to be a little more open about the editorial content" of the paper. Quoted in a newspaper story, Cheadle offered some hope for compromise, "We can always revise our budget. . . . We want it and they want it and I think the people want it. We just want about 50 percent of it."[42]

Perhaps realizing that he would be unable to effect a compromise with James to revive *The Chickasaw Times*, Cheadle declined to seek reelection as chairperson of the tribal legislature in October. The new chairperson, Wilson Seawright, appointed a committee to meet with the governor on the newspaper issue. A compromise was reached and embodied in Enactment 18, which was passed by the legislature and signed by the governor. The "General Philosophy" of the paper called for it to be "fair, impartial," and informative, and "No person or collection of persons shall be allowed to dominate the *Times* in any form or fashion." The enactment also provided that each branch of the Chickasaw government would have a minimum of two pages of commentary and information per issue; political or campaign statements would be limited to the special election issue; and the editor would work cooperatively, but independently, with all entities of the Chickasaw Nation.[43]

In his written report to the legislature in January 1987, James reported that a new editor, Emil Farve, had been hired and that the first issue of the revived newspaper would be distributed later that month. Lieutenant Governor Anoatubby in his written report that same month noted that he was pleased that *The Chickasaw Times* had been resurrected. Sounding a spirit of compromise and cooperation that foreshadowed his political approach in the future, Anoatubby observed that this progress had been achieved "through the cooperative efforts of both the executive and legislative departments." He believed that "with cooperation, we can work out most any of our differences. Rest assured that I stand ready to work with you." Anoatubby also noted that the newspaper had "new features designed to inform the Chickasaw people on all aspects of our tribal government," and pledged his continued full support to the publication of the newspaper.[44]

In the January 1987 issue of *The Chickasaw Times*, and in ensuing issues, a column by chairperson of the legislature Wilson Seawright was a regular feature, as were reports on the activities and deliberations of the legislature. In the March 20, 1987, session of the legislature, Pearl seconded the motion to extend funding of the newspaper. The controversy over the tribal newsletter had been resolved, and Pearl was delighted that the people were receiving a "reformed" publication. But the conflict between the executive and legislative branches over several issues would continue in 1987, and Pearl would be caught up in an internal fuss among legislative factions during the course of that year.[45]

Evidence of the ongoing tensions abounds in the minutes of the tribal legislature in 1987. During the "citizens' comments" portion of the May 15 meeting, Pearl's sister Jewell Arnetta Brooks, who often traveled with Pearl to various Chickasaw meetings and functions, observed that she had attended almost all of the legislative sessions over the past three years and, referring to earlier discussions about travel policies and expenses, observed that "Legislators who go on business trips for the tribe helped the people" and that she supported them "100 percent." Earlier in that meeting, Hensley had suggested that the travel expenses of three legislators who had attended a conference in Sparks, Nevada, amounted to wasting the tribe's money.[46]

Arnetta also noted that some of the legislators had left early and wondered if their pay would be "docked" for leaving early. The legislators who had departed before the end of the meeting were Tim Colbert, Robert Stephens, and Harold Hensley. Seawright indicated that there was no rule covering this situation and that the legislators in question would not have their pay docked. He went on to indicate the reasons for their leaving early, including the fact that Hensley "had to attend a golf game."[47]

Arnetta did not have a combative personality, and it was, therefore, quite remarkable for her to have spoken in this manner in a public forum. Perhaps Pearl and Arnetta already knew in May that Hensley was reviewing Pearl's travel expenses, or Arnetta's comments simply may have reflected the ongoing tension between the legislative factions. At any rate, Hensley responded during the June 19 session of the legislature with an attack on Pearl and her travel expenses. Although Pearl was listed as present for the meeting, she was not present for Hensley's report and the subsequent action. Hensley pointed out that Pearl recently had been reimbursed in the amount of $173.02 for travel expenses to the following meeting and events: "an elder's day at Ada, a ground breaking at Carter Seminary in Ardmore, a committee meeting in Sulphur, a railroad hearing at Ardmore, a Carter Seminary awards banquet at Sulphur, and a legislative meeting at Ada." Hensley questioned whether expenses for those activities that were not legislative meetings should be paid. He believed that $115.62 had been overpaid.[48]

Chairperson Seawright observed that the travel policy of the legislature was that "we can pay if it is a legitimate tribal legislative business. From the sound of those, it was legitimate business." Hensley argued that it was not legitimate to file claims for travel to events that were not called meetings of the legislature. Pearl, of course, believed that legislators should participate in as many events involving Chickasaw citizens as possible in order to maintain lines of communication with the people they represented. Moreover, she could not afford to absorb such travel expenses personally.[49]

Pearl was more than ready to respond at the July meeting. She told the legislators that her trips to various tribal events were justified and that she would continue attending them. Her travel costs merely proved that she was interested in tribal affairs and was doing a good job. She noted that Hensley had asserted that he never had charged anything for travel, but the records showed that he requested a reimbursement for travel in the amount of $23.65 for his travel expenses in June. Moreover, she observed that her total expenses for the year, including salary, travel, and communications, amounted to only $68.74 more than Hensley's total expenses. Her travel expenses were higher, she said, because Marlow was farther from the tribal headquarters in Ada than was Hensley's home in Ardmore. Traveling to committee meetings in Sulphur also entailed more distance from Marlow than from Ardmore. Of course, Hensley would not claim any travel expenses to Sulphur, she said, because "he never attends any of the committee meetings." Also, she observed that Hensley's telephone expenses were higher than hers.[50]

After considerable discussion, Stephens stated that the travel policy needed clarification and that the rules committee should review it and make any recommendations to the legislature at a subsequent meeting. Chairperson Seawright accepted Stephens's suggestion and assigned the task of reviewing the rules governing travel to the rules and ethics committee, chaired by Overton Cheadle. During the August 21 meeting, Cheadle reported that his committee had reviewed the travel policy and, after much discussion, had decided that the present policy was a good one and had no revisions to suggest. The travel policy controversy thus ended with Pearl feeling vindicated.[51]

Despite the wrangling between the governor and the legislature, a significant accomplishment was achieved in early 1987 when it was announced that the Chickasaw Nation would receive a little more than $2,000,000 as its share of a settlement on claims for compensation relating to abandoned railroad station grounds. Prior to the turn of the century, the federal government had required the Chickasaws and other Indian nations to surrender lands for railroad tracks and depots. The land was supposed to be returned to the various Indian nations if and when the railroads ceased to use the land, or, in lieu of returning the land, compensation was to be paid. However, by the 1980s many depots no longer were being used, and the railroads had either sold the properties or had retained the land themselves. Thus, the Chickasaws and Choctaws had undertaken surveys to determine how much land was involved and its value. The two Indian nations had pursued legal action to obtain compensation for the "abandoned" parcels of land.[52]

In the months following the settlement announcement, hearings were held in various parts of the Chickasaw Nation to receive input from the citizens of the tribe. As a result, the legislature devised four options to be voted on by the people in August of that year. The most popular option proved to be the one that provided for tax-free payments of $1,000 each to the estimated 325 surviving original enrollees of the tribe. The remainder of the settlement fund, approximately $1,700,000, was to be divided equally to establish endowments for educational programs and for tribal programs and operations. Some eighteen years later, Pearl would take particular pride in this accomplishment of the Chickasaw tribal government.[53]

Pearl had enjoyed her service in the legislature, and when the time came for filing for re-election, she knew she wanted to continue serving the people in this manner. Although she now was seventy-two-years old, she knew she had plenty of energy and experience to be effective for at least another three years. This time, however, she drew a formidable opponent, and she would not have the endorsement of James or Anoatubby. Pearl had supported the efforts of James and Anoatubby on many projects and programs, but she had opposed the administration in the controversy over *The Chickasaw Times* and other matters involving the relative power of the legislature versus the executive department. And she assumed that Lt. Governor Bill Anoatubby, now running for the governorship, would be "just like James," perhaps even controlled to a large extent by the former governor if he were to be elected.[54]

Pearl's opponent was David Stout of Madill. A seven-eights Chickasaw, Stout was a graduate of Southeastern Oklahoma State University at Durant and he had a distinguished military record. He also had experience in the U. S. Civil Service and argued that this background would enable him to be effective in helping the tribe work closely with state and federal officials and agencies. In the introductory information that he wrote for the Special Election Edition of the tribal newspaper, he noted that he was retired and thus would have time to travel the district and meet the voters. He indicated that "Too many people I have visited with tell me that they have never even met their legislator. . . . You need a legislator interested enough in your needs to make every effort to get to know you."[55]

Pearl must have found it ironic that her opponent was criticizing her for not making an effort to meet the voters when she had been criticized for her extensive travels only a few months earlier. Indeed, Pearl loved to meet people and had traveled extensively and spent a great deal of time doing that during her four years as a legislator. Nonetheless, she knew her opponent would be formidable and she would have a difficult fight on her hands.

In her campaign introduction in the same Special Election Edition of *The Chickasaw Times*, Pearl again discussed her family background, her status as a widow, and the fact that she had three children, ten grandchildren, and eight great grandchildren. She also listed her many community activities and her aviation heritage before discussing her fifteen years of service to the tribe. She pointed out that she had been the only legislator from the western part of the nation and that she understood the needs of the people in that area. She noted that her experience in the legislature would benefit her constituents in the future and that she hoped she could continue her service to the people. Finally, she concluded by noting that she was running "on my past record and merits, and I intend to run a clean campaign and do no mud slinging. . . . To do

Having both of her sisters residing in Marlow was a great joy to Pearl. Here they are enjoying visiting with each other in front of Pearl's home in 1985. From left to right: Opaletta, Arnetta, and Pearl.

that means a person doesn't believe in themselves or their abilities to do the job. . . . It shows the character of the person."[56]

Pearl also prepared a brochure, which she could distribute when making personal campaign appearances or mail to voters. The first panel of the flyer featured a photograph of Pearl, a drawing of a door key, and the text, "Pearl Scott: the KEY to Superb Representation in the Chickasaw Tribal Legislature." On another panel in the brochure, it was proclaimed that Pearl "Brings These Qualities To Her Work for US: Dedication, Devotion, Experience, Hard Work, Commitment to Tribal Goals and Ideals, Training, and Knowledge and Skills." Text in the brochure also detailed her experience, her dedication to and concern for the Chickasaw people, and her vision for the future. In the latter category, she stressed the importance of education and health care. The flyer concluded with a letter from Pearl to "My Dear Chickasaw Friends."[57]

Pearl received the enthusiastic support of her home-town newspaper, the *Marlow Review*. In an article announcing her reelection bid, Pearl stated that "During my years of working for the tribe and for our people, I'm proud to have had a part in helping to get us where we are today." Moreover, she said, "My ambition is to continue to serve all our people in the future, as I have in the past." She also produced an advertisement for the newspapers in her part of the Pickens District to remind voters that if reelected she would be the only legislator representing the western part of the Chickasaw Nation. In the second paragraph of the ad, she endorsed legislative colleagues Wilson Seawright and Overton Cheadle for governor and lieutenant governor, respectively.[58]

Seawright and Cheadle had stood by Pearl during the travel claims controversy, and Cheadle had been a friend of long standing. Pearl knew both of these candidates better than she knew Bill Anoatubby and his running mate Kennedy Brown. Cheadle had written a Legislator Profile column on Pearl for the April issue of *The Chickasaw Times* in an attempt to help her get some additional publicity the month before candidates began announcing their intentions for the August election. Her loyalty to Seawright and Cheadle did not help her campaign, however, as the Anoatubby-Brown ticket won handily, receiving 55 percent of the votes cast as opposed to 32 percent for Seawright and Cheadle. A third candidate ticket in the race, consisting of Kenneth Keel and L. M. Cass, received 13 percent of the vote.[59]

Nevertheless, with no help from the most powerful candidates at the head of the ballot, Pearl received 49 percent of the vote to her opponent's 51 percent. Pearl's backing of the "wrong" ticket for the executive department likely cost her sufficient votes to swing the election. At any rate, Pearl attended the final meeting of her second legislative term on October 1. It was a special occasion because it was the first meeting of the legislature in the new legislative building which had been constructed on the campus of the tribal headquarters in Ada. Pearl took the occasion to speak briefly about the progress that been made from when she started as a community health representative in 1972. At that time, she and her colleagues did not have a building in which to meet, so now it was particularly meaningful to her to be a part of the first legislature to meet in the new legislative building. After this meeting, Pearl became a private citizen once again, but she remained interested and active in tribal affairs. She also began observing the new governor.[60]

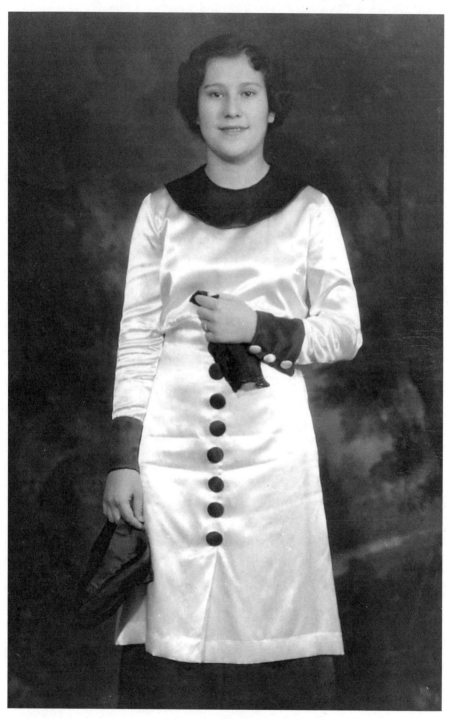

Chapter Eleven
▼▼▼

TEMPORARY RETIREMENT

W hile recovering from the disappointment of losing her re-election bid by such a close margin, Pearl received some news that put her electoral loss into perspective. In late November of 1987, Pearl's younger sister Arnetta was diagnosed with colon cancer at the Indian Health Service hospital at Lawton. Arnetta's son Joe Carter Brooks came from New York to be with his mother as did friends and relatives from many states, including her granddaughter Arne from California. Pearl and Arnetta's son Ronald Trent Brooks drove from Marlow to visit Arnetta as often as they could.[1]

On the evening of February 3, 1988, Pearl and Trent had to leave early because of a heavy snow. Arnetta had lost consciousness. Joe Carter had a bed in his mother's room so he could be with her continuously. That evening in her darkened room, Arnetta began reciting the names of loved ones as if she saw them in front of her, and then she stopped breathing with Joe Carter holding her hand. She was sixty-nine at the time of her death in the early hours of February 4. Joe Carter called George, Jr.'s home in Marlow where George, Jr., Pearl, and Trent were sitting vigil, and the news, while not unexpected, nonetheless was devastating to Pearl and the rest of the family. Pearl confided to Joe Carter that she had lost not only a sister but also her best friend.[2]

Arnetta Carter as she appeared ca. 1935. A note with the original photo indicated that she was the "Football Queen" her senior year in high school. (Courtesy Art Williamson)

▼▼▼
169

Arnetta was three and a half years younger than Pearl. She had begun her college education at Central State Normal College (now University of Central Oklahoma) at Edmond, Oklahoma, where, through their
mutual major in education, she met Joe Wilson Brooks. They married
on October 6, 1937, and, after Joe graduated, lived in various locations
in Oklahoma and in California, where Joe taught math and coached basketball. They had two children, Joseph Carter (born in 1942) and Ronald
Trent (born in 1946).[3]

Arnetta picked up additional college credits where she could and received her bachelor's degree from Central State in 1952 and her teaching
certificate the following year. At her graduation, she made the dean's list
and had forty-two hours toward a master's degree. Joe was diagnosed
with schizophrenia in the 1950s and became progressively more emotionally abusive. The family had moved frequently because Joe's condition
made it impossible for him to hold a job for long, and Arnetta's mother,
Lucy, lived with them periodically to help care for the children. Arnetta
and Joe divorced in 1960, ironically only a short time before Pearl divorced Scottie. Joe was killed in a mugging incident in Long Beach, California, in 1970.[4]

Arnetta taught kindergarten in Bellflower, California, from 1953 to
her retirement in 1980 at the age of sixty-two. She then moved to Marlow to be close to Lucy, who was seriously ill. Lucy died in November of
that same year. Arnetta lived across the street from Pearl. The two sisters, along with Opaletta and George, Jr., now also lived in Marlow, and
they enjoyed each other's company. Unlike Pearl, Arnetta had traveled
widely. She had visited every state except Alaska as well as cities such
as London, Paris, and Madrid. She went to Madrid when her son Joseph
Carter Brooks had earned a Fulbright Scholarship to study in Spain. She
also loved traveling to New York to visit Joe Carter. On her wall in Marlow, Arnetta hung a hefty necklace consisting of charms in the shape of
each state she had visited. She also had a rock and flower garden, and
she liked to collect a rock for her garden from each of the interesting
places she visited in her travels.[5]

In Marlow, Arnetta became interested in her Chickasaw heritage
and frequently traveled with Pearl to her legislative sessions, commit-

tee meetings, powwows, and numerous other events and functions. She was a lovely woman with a friendly disposition who, like Pearl, enjoyed learning. The two sisters enjoyed each other's company. Arnetta's granddaughter observed that when Arnetta and Pearl were together "they were like two school girls laughing and giggling. . . you couldn't help but be happy when they were around." In addition to participating in Chickasaw activities, they enjoyed doing genealogical research together.[6]

Arnetta Carter Brooks and Lucy Carter posed for the camera in 1965 at Paramount, California, were Arnetta was an accomplished educator. Lucy lived with Arnetta in California periodically to help Arnetta care for her children. (Courtesy Joseph Carter Brooks)

Arnetta was delighted with the birth in 1972 of her granddaughter, Elizabeth Arne Brooks, Ronald Trent's daughter. Ronald, however, like his father, was diagnosed with schizophrenia, and his condition worsened in the 1980s, requiring Arnetta to care for him and grandaughter Arne. On one occasion, he unsuccessfully attempted to commit suicide. He ultimately did kill himself by hanging in 1992. Arnetta never complained about her ongoing responsibilities in caring for her son or granddaughter. She had to deal with the heartbreak of mental illness, but she found joy in her love of children, the accomplishments of Joe Carter, being with her granddaughter Arne, her travels, and her activities with Pearl in her later years. The personal rewards she reaped in being with and teaching youngsters was reflected in the epitaph on her tombstone: "She Loved the Little Children."[7]

About the time of Arnetta's death, Pearl began worrying about her older sister Opaletta. By early 1988, Opaletta began having some difficulties, such as getting lost while driving her car to places that had

Despite the stress caused by her husband's and son's schizophrenia, Arnetta, right, shown here with Pearl, always maintained a positive outlook on life. Throughout her life, her brothers, sisters, and their families preferred using her middle name, Arnetta, but her husband and children preferred using her first name, Jewell. In this photo, she displayed her usual smile and friendly demeanor. (Courtesy Art Williamson)

been familiar in the past. Her son Art soon thereafter had the difficult but necessary task of taking her car keys from her. At seventy-six, she began a decline that would end with her death of a respiratory ailment in February 1992.[8]

Opaletta, like Pearl, had married when she was sixteen. Her husband was Arthur T. Williamson of Rush Springs, whose father, Dan Williamson, was city marshal of that nearby community. Opal met her future husband when he accompanied Findley Walden, who was dating Pearl at the time, on a trip to Marlow. Pearl and Findley's relationship did not blossom into marriage, but Opal and Arthur fell in love, married, and eventually had seven children—Bobby Lynn, Wanda Lee, Lucy Larue, Danny Wayne, Artaletta, Jackie, and Arthur Lewis.[9]

Like Pearl and Arnetta, Opaletta received farms when she married in 1928. The couple lived in Marlow for a short time after they were married while Arthur was getting his farming operation established. They soon moved to the farm, and the young couple settled down to life as farmers, although Arthur also took flying lessons, learning to fly George Carter's Eaglerock biplane. Farming during the Great Depression proved challenging for the couple as they raised broomcorn and cotton. They also raised some cattle and even tried sheep for a while without much profit. In fact, a number of sheep froze to death one winter when an unusually strong, late freeze occurred after the sheep had been sheared.[10]

By 1941 Opal and Arthur's marriage was strained and the couple separated. Farming operations were not successful because prices for their crops and livestock plummeted. Both farms eventually were lost. Financial strains certainly played a significant role in their difficulties. Soon thereafter, the Japanese bombed Pearl Harbor, plunging the United States into World War II. Arthur volunteered for service early in 1942, motivated by patriotism and, perhaps in part, by his marital troubles at home.[11]

After basic training Arthur was shipped to Australia and then found himself on a three-man machine gun crew fighting the Japanese on the island of New Guinea. Fighting jungle heat, deep mud, and the Japanese, Arthur and the other men were injured when a mortar shell landed near

Pearl's older sister, Opaletta Carter Williamson, and her husband, Arthur T. Williamson, posed for this photograph ca. 1951. Arthur fought in the Pacific Theater during World War II, suffered significant battlefield injuries, and contracted meningitis, while Opaletta worked at the Douglas Aircraft Plant in Oklahoma City. (Courtesy Bob Williamson)

them, buried itself in the mud, and then exploded. Only one of the men was actually wounded by shrapnel, but Arthur and a second soldier were blasted by a wall of heavy mud that bruised them severely and put them into a military field hospital. Arthur later explained that the impact of the thick mud felt as if someone had struck him in the head with a two-by-four piece of lumber. While in the hospital, Arthur contracted meningitis. For him, the war was over.[12]

The disease left Arthur completely deaf in one ear and with only 20 percent of normal hearing in the other. Moreover, his sense of balance was disrupted. After six months of rehabilitation, he regained his equi-

▼▼▼

librium but his hearing was permanently impaired. During his rehabilitation he was taught how to read lips. Arthur returned home, but Opaletta no longer resided in Marlow. She had obtained a job at the Douglas Aircraft plant in Oklahoma City and was earning good wages. Because she could not take care of the children and work full-time, she put the children in an orphanage in Oklahoma City, with the idea of reuniting the family as soon as possible.[13]

Arthur moved to Oklahoma City, got a job at the Douglas Plant, and the family was reunited. The couple's youngest child, Art, was three years old when Arthur returned to the family, and he has vivid memories of his father walking into the room, of having a daddy at home for the first time that he could remember, and of sitting in his father's lap and being curious about the battery kit that powered his dad's hearing aid.[14]

At the end of the war, their jobs at the Douglas Plant ended, but Arthur, receiving preference as a disabled veteran, obtained work at Tinker Air Force Base while Opaletta began working for the A. F. Williams Furniture store as an upholsterer, using skills she had learned at the Douglas plant. Later, she quit working at the store and did contract upholstery work at home for Williams Furniture and others. In 1954, Opaletta and Arthur decided to become entrepreneurs and purchased a "mom and pop" café on N. E. 23rd Street in Oklahoma City. They soon discovered that the café required a tremendous amount of work and time for a relatively small return. The operated it for just under a year and then sold it.[15]

Soon after selling the café, Arthur secured a job at Shepherd Air Force Base at Wichita Fall, Texas. He moved there while Opaletta remained in Oklahoma City for another year to let Art graduate from high school. She moved to Wichita Falls in 1956, where she worked doing upholstery work at home for the local Sears store and another furniture store. The coupled lived in Wichita Falls until 1964, when they retired and moved to Marlow. During this time in Wichita Falls, their daughter Jackie Lightener died at age 27, and Arthur and Opaletta adopted her two children, Michael and Donna, ages nine and seven respectively. The death of Jackie was a major blow to her parents, and it seemed that Arthur's health deteriorated significantly after that. A victim of what likely was Alzheimer's disease, he had to be institutionalized in 1967, when

This Williamson family photograph was taken in 1955. Left to right: Bob, Arthur T., Opaletta, and Arthur L. Opaletta and Arthur T. moved to Wichita Falls, Texas, in the mid-1950s and lived there until retiring and moving to Marlow in 1964. Unfortunately, Arthur apparently was a victim of Alzheimer's disease, and it was necessary for Opaletta to institutionalize him in 1967. (Courtesy Art Williamson)

Opaletta no longer could physically care for him. He died in the Veterans' Home at Sulphur in 1974.[16]

Michael was a senior in high school at the time of Arthur's death and Donna was a sophomore. After Donna's graduation in 1976, Opaletta at age sixty-four lived by herself, but she had her two sisters and her brother George, Jr., nearby. The sisters kept in touch with each other daily and when possible traveled, went to dinner, shopped, and visited with each other. Opaletta began declining in 1988, a situation that perhaps was accelerated somewhat by Arnetta's death. Pearl loved her sisters and enjoyed their company. It was exceedingly painful for her to lose Arnetta in 1988 and Opaletta in 1992. At the time of her death, Opaletta had twenty-one grandchildren, forty-four great grandchildren, and one great-great-grandchild.[17]

While grieving over the death of Arnetta and worrying about the health of Opaletta, Pearl retained her interest in the ongoing development of the Chickasaw Nation. As Governor Anoatubby took office, she had real concerns because he had been lieutenant gover- nor under Governor James, and she feared "he'd be just like James." Like some oth- ers who had opposed James during the later years of his service as governor, Pearl believed that he would still be running the nation's af- fairs through Anoatubby. So Pearl "sat back and watched" Governor Anoatubby "and he made a good one. So when he

Opaletta taking it easy ca. 1986. She enjoyed being near her sisters and brother after return- ing to Marlow, and many of her children lived nearby. (Courtesy Bob Williamson)

ran the next time I voted for him and have ever since." Pearl determined that "Bill is a good man; he really is a good man, a good leader."[18]

Anoatubby quickly demonstrated his willingness to mend fences with those who had opposed him. Shortly after his election as governor, he attended a legislative meeting and made a short presentation, stressing his desire to work cooperatively with the legislature for the good of the Chickasaw people. Pointing out that it was imperative for the governor and legislators to "trust one another and cooperate," Anoatubby pledged that he was "willing to go half way, in fact, more than half way. You will see." He also made an effort to reach out to Pearl. He remembered that she wanted the nation to continue to progress, and he soon discov- ered that they "were on the same page as far as dealing with the issues of tribal government and the needs of our community." As time went on, Anoatubby became "Governor Bill" to her, and they became personal friends and political allies.[19]

Pearl's historical and spiritual bond with Wiley Post remained strong throughout her life. In 1988 while visiting her son Bill in Virginia, she had the opportunity to visit the Smithsonian Institution once again. Ac- companied by Bill and members of the family, Pearl and the others began touring Smithsonian Air and Space Museum. Bill knew that when the group turned a certain corner, they would see the *Winnie Mae* and Wiley's

While on a trip to visit her family in Alabama and Virginia, Pearl particularly enjoyed visiting Washington, D. C. in 1988. While there, she toured the Smithsonian Institution and had an emotional reunion with her past while viewing an exhibit honoring Wiley Post, the Winnie Mae, and his development of the pressure suit. Here she posed for a photograph with Nita Scott, Carter's wife, in front of the legendary aircraft that she had flown more than fifty years earlier. (Courtesy Pearl Scott Collection)

original pressure suit directly in front of them. He managed to maneuver Pearl to the front of the group. When they turned the corner, he heard Pearl gasp, and he could see tears in her eyes. Knowing that Pearl would want to linger, he told her that he and the others would move on and come back for her in a few minutes. When they returned, Bill quickly realized that Pearl, for the moment, was not with them. She had a distant look in her eyes, for she had mentally traveled back in time to be with Wiley. Bill and the others departed again, leaving Pearl in her reverie. When they returned the second time, Bill saw that she had returned to the present, and the group continued their tour.[20]

Pearl was honored for her historical connection to Wiley Post in 1989, when she was one of one hundred Americans invited by the National Aeronautical and Space Administration to visit its headquarters in Florida to celebrate the life of Wiley Post. For Pearl, visiting NASA was a thrill, and to be included among a relatively small group to honor

Pearl's brother, George, also was hit hard by the deaths of his sisters Arnetta and Opaletta. George and Pearl supported each other through these difficult circumstances. This portrait of George was taken in 1986 when George was sixty-five. He wrote on the back of the photo, "To my sister Pearl, I love you." (Courtesy Pearl Scott Papers)

Wiley's memory was especially meaningful to her. She also was invited to attend as a special guest a ceremony in Oklahoma City on July 1, 1991, honoring the sixtieth anniversary of Post's and Gatty's flight around the world. The ceremony was held at the Oklahoma Historical Society, housed in the Wiley Post Building. These events set the stage for even more meaningful honors that she would receive in the future in recognition of her aviation exploits.[21]

While she was "retired" from public service, Pearl found more time to be active in the Marlow community. She received an opportunity to hone her writing skills when she was asked by the publisher of the *Marlow Review* to write a series of columns for the paper titled "Memories of Marlow. . . From then to now." The first of these columns appeared in the May 17, 1990, edition of the paper. The columns were written as a part of the community's "Homecoming '90" celebration. In four different columns, Pearl wrote about her family's history, events she had witnessed, community institutions, personalities, and customs through the years. Her final column appeared in the June 21, 1990, edition of the paper. She concluded it by expressing her pride in Marlow, "It's such a pretty, clean, community-minded and friendly town. Be proud to call it your 'home town.' It has the best schools, churches and good people to run the town."[22]

Pearl was thrilled with the response to her columns. At the outset, she had "no idea" that she would receive "so many calls from people about them . . . even long distance calls and letters." After her first two columns, many people urged her to write more, telling her that they were waiting for more. Pearl was "overwhelmed. Every time I go to the gro-

While in Washington, D. C., in 1988, Pearl also visited the White House. Here she is taking a break with her daughters-in-law Nita Scott (Carter's wife) and Linda Scott (Bill's spouse). (Courtesy Pearl Scott Collection)

cery store or anywhere people stop me and compliment me . . . it brings back memories to them." She also noted that the columns have let "'new comers' (20 or 30 years in Marlow) know more about Marlow." Pearl was indeed proud of her writings and was pleased that so many enjoyed her work.[23]

While she was writing her columns for the local newspaper, Pearl also was expressing privately her hope to be selected to receive a special honor: "I would give anything to be Homecoming '90 Queen, it would be the icing on the cake for me." She had been nominated, but she noted that an individual was supposed to be a graduate of Marlow High School to receive that honor, "so that lets me out, I guess. I'm hoping the committee will make an exception."[24]

As it happened, the committee did make an exception for Pearl. She was selected as Homecoming '90 Queen, and Dr. C. N. Talley, a 1917 graduate of Marlow High School, was named Homecoming '90 King. The celebration featured a variety of events, including a "sock hop in the grade school cafeteria," during which bobby sox, poodle skirts, and pony tails were back in fashion. A flag football game was held, featuring a team of men who had graduated from Marlow High School in even numbered years, playing a team consisting of those who had graduated in odd numbered years. At half-time of this Homecoming '90 Bowl, Pearl and Dr. Talley were crowned queen and king, with Pearl's crown being a Marlow Outlaw football helmet that she wore canted back on her head so that the face mask of the helmet circled the top of her forehead. After she was "crowned," Pearl planted a kiss on Dr. Tally's cheek.[25]

Pearl and Dr. Talley served as grand marshals of the Fourth of July parade, which was part of the Homecoming '90 celebration. They rode in the back seat of an antique convertible with the top down so they could be seen and wave to the crowd. The parade was described as the biggest in Marlow's history, "with more beauty queens and political candidates than you can shake a stick at." The parade highlighted a variety of groups, including the Duncan Antique Car Club, The Okie Trail Riders of Lawton, the Lawton Shriners Tin Lizzie Patrol, and the Duncan Shriners Clowns. The surprise of the parade, however, came when D. B. Green, president of the State National Bank of Marlow, presented his "Lawn Chair Brigade." The "normally sedate" bank employees "unfolded lawn chairs, planted themselves down for a brisk round of sedentary aerobics and then picked up their furniture to resume the procession.[26]

The celebration ended that evening in Redbud Park, during which the Marlow Lions Club offered "arts and crafts, food, music and fireworks." Pearl thoroughly enjoyed the entire experience, just as she had enjoyed many other activities after leaving the legislature. But she missed serving in the legislature and decided to seek, once again, to serve as a representative from Pickens District.[27]

Temporary Retirement

Chapter Twelve
▼▼▼

ONE MORE TERM

W hile enjoying life in Marlow, Pearl continued to follow Chickasaw political affairs, developing a growing affinity for Governor
Anoatubby. She especially appreciated his efforts to expand various tribal
businesses to generate revenue and to promote both enhanced educational
opportunities and improved health care for Chickasaw citizens. For a period after his election as governor, Anoatubby had enjoyed a "honeymoon"
period with the legislature. However, over the ensuing three years, the
legislature became divided into factions that generally either supported
or opposed the governor on various issues. This problem was exacerbated
when David Stout suffered a heart attack and died. Stout had defeated
Pearl by a narrow margin in 1987 and had become chairperson of the legislature and an effective leader. He was so highly regarded that the new
legislative building was named in his honor after his death.[1]

So contentious were the legislative factions that, with Stout's seat
vacant, the legislators often split six to six when voting on resolutions or
enactments. Harold Hensley of Ardmore, with whom Pearl earlier had
clashed over travel expenses, served as chairperson pro tempore, following Stout's death. During the May 1991 meeting of the legislature, Hensley, a former supporter of the executive department who now was a leader
of the opposition, got into a dispute with legislators over the propriety of

*Pearl was honored, along with twenty-five other Indian women, for being an
elected official in a tribal government. Among officials of the Chickasaw Nation
who were with her and four other Chickasaw women that day was Pearl's dear
friend Gary Childers. (Courtesy Pearl Scott Collection)*

▼▼▼
183

a particular resolution, which resulted in four of the legislators walking out of the meeting, leaving the body without a quorum. Hensley then indicated that the remaining legislators could wait for the four to return or "we can walk too. I prefer to walk. I've got a funeral to attend." He also noted that the upcoming legislative elections might result in his not returning to the legislature, a remark that drew applause from members of the audience in attendance. Hensley departed along with three of his supporters. The first four legislators to depart soon returned, and one of them made a speech regarding the deadlock in the legislature.[2]

It was against this backdrop of controversy that Pearl decided to seek election to the legislature, representing the Pickens District. She specifically sought the Pickens District, Seat 1 position. The incumbent seeking re-election was Harold Hensley. Two other candidates, Ella Ross and Tommy Keel, filed for the same position,. Ross was a full-blood Chickasaw and a graduate of Chilocco Indian School. Keel was a graduate of Tishomingo High School, an employee of Maxwell Construction Company at Madill, a Vietnam war veteran, and an active leader in the Veterans of Foreign Wars organization.[3]

In the material on her life and qualifications published in the 1991 election issue of *The Chickasaw Times*, Pearl reviewed her family history and her community activities, especially noting that she had been voted by the city of Marlow as its Homecoming '90 Queen. She also reviewed her record of service to the Chickasaw people since 1972 and indicated that she had earned forty-two hours of college credit in courses dealing with subjects such as mental, physical, and environmental health. She also stressed the need for representation of the western portion of the Chickasaw Nation in the legislature. Not said was that she now enjoyed the support of the increasingly popular Governor Anoatubby, who was running for re-election in 1991.[4]

When the votes were counted in the general election, Pearl had received 35 percent of the votes, followed by Keel with 29 percent, Ross with 20 percent, and Hensley with 16 percent. Consequently, a runoff election between Pearl and Keel was conducted. Pearl won handily with 59 percent of the vote to Keel's 41 percent. Anoatubby and his running mate, David E. Brown, had garnered 77 percent of the vote. Hensley's outspoken leadership of the legislative faction that had opposed the executive department on many issues likely played a major role in his defeat in the general election, while Pearl's support of Anoatubby, although not as visible as Hensley's opposition had been, certainly was a mark in her favor, as was her significant experience in serving the Chickasaw people.[5]

Pearl and other newly elected officials of the Chickasaw Nation took their oaths of office during special ceremonies on the morning of October 1 in the Chickasaw Community Center at Ada. That evening at Sulphur, Pearl was among special guests at an inaugural celebration honoring Governor Anoatubby. Regarding her position in the legislature, Pearl commented, "It is a tremendous responsibility. . . . People generally do not realize the problems we must deal with and the large amounts of money we must handle for our people." Pearl was "proud and happy to again be able to serve, but I know it will be a busy three years."[6]

Pearl's status as a Chickasaw leader was evident when some American Indians began protesting the use of Indian names, dress, and chants to support athletic teams. This was heightened when fans of the Atlanta Braves major league baseball team began "chanting in unison and waving styrofoam tomahawks." This action, televised nationally on numerous occasions, sparked controversy and some protests. The local newspaper approached the leading Choctaw and Chickasaw residents of the community, Harvey York and Pearl, to obtain their views on the subject. Pearl indicated that to her the use of Indian names for team mascots was an honor. "The names do not offend me," Pearl said, "because I think it brings notoriety to Indian people." However, she did oppose the use of Indian dances and chants, finding them offensive "because most of the people doing them do not know the language or the proper way to do the dances. Most people feel Indians are merely hopping around during their dances, but there are specific steps involved." Moreover, she thought that spectators should not be attempting to chant like Indians because they "simply don't know what they are doing."[7]

On October 18, 1991, during Pearl's first legislative meeting of her new term, she had the opportunity to cast a deciding vote in support of Governor Anoatubby and her friend Gary Childers. A resolution was presented to approve Governor Anoatubby's appointments of Lynn Worcester and Childers to the Chickasaw Tax Commission. During the discussion, one legislator indicated that he thought a legislator should serve on the commission, and another voiced opposition to tribal employees filling these positions. A vote was taken, the resolution passed by a seven to six vote, with Pearl voting with the majority.[8]

Pearl again demonstrated her support of Governor Anoatubby during the December 20 meeting of the legislature. At issue was a resolution to approve the tribe's application to the United States Department of Energy for a grant to conduct a feasibility study on the possible establishment of an "above-ground, Monitored Retrievable Storage (MRS) facility for the temporary storage of waste products." Strongly recommended by the governor, if approved, the grant would consist of $100,000 to provide for the study, which would include travel expenses for legislators and other tribal officials to visit existing MRS facilities in other parts of the United States. The conduct of the study would not obligate the tribe to allow the establishment of such a facility, but if one were to be constructed, it was argued, "the potential exists to provide literally hundreds of jobs and a significant income to the tribe through its operation" of such a facility. After some discussion, seven legislators, including Pearl, voted "yes" for the resolution, while five voted "no," and one abstained from voting. Anoatubby later determined that there was fairly widespread opposition to even doing the study, much less building such a facility. As a result, the grant application was never submitted.[9]

Although somewhat distracted in late 1991 and early 1992 by the illness and subsequent death of her sister Opaletta, Pearl managed not to miss any legislative meetings during that period. In March of 1992, she was invited to the state capitol to be honored as an "elected woman official in Oklahoma Tribal Government in observance of Women's History Month." Pearl was among twenty-six women invited representing nine tribes. Five of the women were Chickasaws. The affair was hosted by Senator Enoch Kelly Haney, women members of the Oklahoma State Senate, and the Oklahoma Indian Affairs Commission. After a ceremony in the Blue Room, the women were introduced in the Senate chamber. Pearl appreciated the recognition and enjoyed meeting and visiting with the women from other tribes.[10]

Pearl remained a staunch supporter of the governor throughout her three-year term in the legislature. Throughout this period, the legislature was attempting to define its prerogatives and authority, leading to frequent clashes with the executive department.

When Anoatubby vetoed legislative enactments, Pearl would vote against subsequent legislative votes to override those vetoes, even when the majority favored the override. In September of 1992, for example, Pearl was one of only three legislators who voted to sustain Anoatubby's veto of the Legislative Reform Act of 1992. Under the Chickasaw Constitution, when the legislature passed an enactment or a resolution over the governor's veto, the governor had the option of petitioning the Chickasaw tribal court to rule whether the bill or resolution was constitutional. In the case of the Legislative Reform Act of 1992, the bill was declared unconstitutional along the grounds that Anoatubby cited in vetoing the legislation.[11]

Pearl had enjoyed many of her activities and her family during the years that followed her leaving the Chickasaw Tribal Legislature in 1987. By 1991, however, she missed the more direct involvement in Chickasaw affairs she had enjoyed previously, and she was ready once again to stand for election to a legislative seat. This portrait photograph of Pearl was taken in 1993.

Pearl did enjoy a break from the conflict when she attended the Annual Meeting of the Chickasaw Nation, held in conjunction with the annual Chickasaw Festival in Tishomingo on October 3. She wrote a long article for the *Marlow Review*, detailing the events of the meeting and festival. Pearl also was selected to be a delegate to represent the Chickasaw legislature at an Indian Heritage Festival at Huntsville, Alabama, on October 17. The newly formed Chickasaw Nation Dance Troupe also traveled to Alabama to perform during the event.[12]

Despite the political turmoil, Pearl kept her focus on helping people in her part of the Chickasaw Nation. She was especially pleased with the opening in early March 1993 of a Chickasaw Nation Smoke Shop just south of Marlow on Highway 81. Described in the press as the "idea of Chickasaw Legislator Pearl Scott," the facility was only the fourth smoke shop opened by the tribe, and it was the first one not to be located along I-

35. The former office/game room of the Dunk-N-Slide amusement park was remodeled to create the smoke shop. Moreover, Pearl already was pushing for the smoke shop operation to be expanded in the future to include a trading post and a bingo facility.[13]

Ironically, just about the time Pearl was succeeding in getting a smoke shop for the Marlow area, she had to quit smoking. She previously had suffered some respiratory difficulties which she attributed to asthma. This influenced her choice of a household pet. Beginning in the late 1980s, she acquired the first of several Chihuahuas. By the early 1990s, the health problem began to grow more serious and reflected the early stages of emphysema. Like many people her age, Pearl had begun smoking in the early 1940s, and by the time cigarettes became identified as a health risk, she was addicted to them. At one point Pearl switched to Doral menthol cigarettes, probably with the hope that they would be less harmful to her lungs than "regular" smokes. Fellow legislator Robert Stephens used to joke that when he died he was going to wait at the Pearly Gates smoking cigarettes until Pearl eventually joined him there for a smoke.[14]

Smoking was an integral part of Pearl's regimen for relaxing at home. Arnetta's granddaughter Arne re-

Robert Stephens was one of Pearl's colleagues in the Tribal Legislature. Both were smokers and they enjoyed smoking and chatting prior to the legislative sessions being called to order and during breaks. Stephens once joked that when he died, he would smoke a cigarette outside the "Pearly Gates" and wait for Pearl to join him for a smoke before passing on into heaven. (Courtesy Chickasaw Nation Archives)

membered in the 1980s that Pearl had placed by her easy chair a TV tray that always had crossword puzzles, cigarettes, and asthma inhalers on it. There she could watch television with her dog in her lap, smoke, and look at fish swimming in one of the aquariums she had in her living room for her enjoyment. Often she would "stay up real late and watch westerns." As a child, Arne thought Pearl was a "wild woman!"[15]

Quitting smoking was especially difficult for Pearl, but she accomplished the feat. At times, however, the desire for a smoke was almost overwhelming. She would "just get hungry" for a cigarette. When that happened, she remembered, "I'd go down to the smoke shop—I kind of had to watch over it anyway—and I'd smell that smoke and I'd be satisfied."[16]

Pearl also organized and hosted a meeting and dinner at the High Chaparral restaurant in Marlow, featuring Governor Anoatubby and Lieutenant Governor Brown as special guests. Others in attendance were Mevelyn Kirkpatrick, Chickasaw legislator; Charles Blackwell, Chickasaw Nation ambassador to the federal government; Larry Lawler, state senator; Wayne Holden, mayor of Duncan; Ray McCarter, Marlow superintendent of schools; Willie Kirkpatrick, Johnston County commissioner; Cricket Holland, president of the Marlow Chamber of Commerce; and Thurman Lowery, reporter for the *Marlow Review*. Anoatubby told the group that such meetings were held throughout the Chickasaw Nation as "get acquainted" functions. The reporter noted that Anoatubby paid tribute to Pearl by observing that "although Marlow was on the outer fringes of the nation, the fact that Pearl Scott was a member of their legislature made it [Marlow] even more important than it might otherwise be."[17]

Pearl also took time to get involved in efforts to prevent drug and alcohol abuse and to help those who already were afflicted. This, of course, had been part of her work as a community health representative. With long-time friend Harvey York and brother, George, Jr., Pearl attended the "kickoff" of the Chickasaw Nation's "Red Ribbon Drug and Alcohol Awareness Week," staged at the Chickasaw Nation's Alcohol and Drug Treatment Center at Kullihoma, near Ada. As part of the effort, the Stephens County Community and Family Education Association provided 5,000 red ribbons to be distributed to elementary students in the area. Harvey York and Pearl represented the Chickasaw Nation in presenting

Pearl, the fifth person from the right on the front row, posed with members of the 1993 Chickasaw Tribal Legislature for this official photograph. They were joined by Pearl's friend, Governor Bill Anoatubby, second from the left on the front row. (Courtesy The Chickasaw Times)

red ribbons to Marlow High School Principal Mickey Hoy for Marlow secondary school students. The red ribbons were designed to be a national symbol for "community action, substance-abuse prevention, and drug-free, healthy lifestyles for youth. . . ." Wearing them was to signify that the wearer was committed to remain free of drug and alcohol abuse.[18]

In the legislative elections of 1993, two of Anoatubby's harshest critics were defeated, and a third declined to stand for re-election. Moreover, an old political opponent of Anoatubby's, whom Pearl had defeated in 1991, ran for a different seat and was defeated 768 to 334. As a result, although political conflicts certainly were not ended, the legislature beginning in October of 1993 was much more disposed to work in harmony with the governor. Consequently, legislative sessions were generally less contentious than they had been in the previous two years.[19]

Pearl was especially proud of one particular accomplishment in 1994. She long had been aware that many elderly or disabled Indians throughout the Chickasaw Nation had difficulty obtaining transportation to receive medical treatment. Consequently, she brought the matter before the legislature and advocated the establishment of a transportation program to meet this need. As a result, the Chickasaw Nation purchased several vans and placed one of them in the Stephens County area.[20]

The members of the 1994 Chickasaw Tribal legislature. Pearl is second from the left on the front row. This was the final group of legislators with whom Pearl would work as an elected official of the Chickasaw Nation. (Courtesy Chickasaw Nation Archives)

Rainelle Rhonc was hired as an area transportation driver, and Pearl was proud of the fifteen-passenger Dodge Ram 350. It was to be used to transport "any elderly Native American person, regardless of tribe, who possesses a CDIB (certificate of degree of Indian blood) card and who requires a ride to and from doctor's offices, medical facilities, nutrition centers and senior citizen sites." In the evenings and on weekends, the van would be used to transport young participants in the district Chickasaw youth council to various activities. A special dinner, organized by Pearl and featuring Governor Anoatubby as the keynote speaker, was held in Marlow on August 23 to explain the new transportation program and other Chickasaw programs.[21]

Pearl decided that, at age seventy-eight, she wanted to "serve one more term to finish my work; then I will step down and feel that my work is finished." Consequently, she filed to run for re-election to fill Seat 1 of the Pickens District in the legislature. In her "personal message" in the election issue of *The Chickasaw Times*, she noted that there was much work to do in developing needed facilities in the western area of the

Pearl received a special plaque from the Chickasaw Tribal Legislature during a special reception honoring her for her years of service as a legislator and her "lifelong dedication to the Chickasaw People." (Courtesy The Chickasaw Times)

Chickasaw Nation. She noted with pride the bus to transport elderly and youth to appropriate functions and mentioned that she sometimes took youngsters in her car to activities in Sulphur or Ada when the bus in not available. She also pointed out that during her years in the legislature, she had served on seven standing committees and various *ad hoc* committees.[22]

Pearl's opponent was Linda Briggs of Marietta, an active community leader who previously had served as treasurer for the City of Marietta. Like Pearl, Briggs was one-quarter Chickasaw. At the time of the election, she was serving as a member of the Marietta School Board and as a director of the Love County Chamber of Commerce. Briggs ran a positive campaign, emphasizing the need for enhanced health care for all Chickasaws, care of the elderly, and educational opportunities for Chickasaws of all ages. She noted that the legislature had been moving in a "positive, productive direction" and that she would continue "to contribute my time, energy and administrative and organizational skills to increase the momentum."[23]

When the votes were tallied, Briggs had received 59 per cent of the votes to Pearl's 41 percent. Perhaps Pearl's age and the beginnings of some health problems played a role in her loss. She had outlived many of her long-time friends and supporters, and voters who did not know her personally may have believed that a younger, energetic person such as Briggs likely would be more effective. At any rate, Pearl accepted her loss gracefully.[24]

Pearl's many years of service to the Chickasaw Nation were recognized in several ways. Following the September 1994 legislative meeting, a reception was held to honor Pearl, during which she was presented a special plaque commemorating her work on behalf of the people of the Pickens District. Governor Anoatubby also hosted an appreciation dinner for Pearl on the evening of September 22, 1994, at the Chickasaw Motor Inn at Sulphur. During the program that evening, Anoatubby took the opportunity to praise Pearl for almost twenty-three years of dedicated work on behalf of the Chickasaw people. He also presented several gifts to Pearl as an expression of his appreciation for her service.[25]

Eleven years later, Anoatubby would remember Pearl as having been an especially effective advocate in the legislature for the Marlow area. Pearl was "instrumental in seeing things happen in her area and she would stay on a particular mission until it was accomplished." "If she felt we needed to get something done," Anoatubby said, "she'd be sure to let us know." Harbour Whitaker, publisher of the *Marlow Review*, observed that Pearl had been a "driving force" in the Chickasaw Nation and that she "always was bringing us press releases, making sure that the western

Pearl and Governor Bill Anoatubby posed for this photograph on the grounds of the Chickasaw Nation's headquarters in Ada. Although Pearl was not reelected to the legislature in 1994, Anoatubby knew that it was important to retain her involvement in tribal affairs. A recognized leader in her community, Pearl would continue to serve her people as the Governor's Liaison for the Marlow area. (Courtesy Pearl Scott Collection)

perimeter of the Chickasaw Nation was fully represented."[26]

Pearl's career as a legislator had come to an end, but her service to the Chickasaw Nation was not over. Anoatubby realized that Pearl was an invaluable contact for the western portion of the Chickasaw Nation. Moreover, her status in the Marlow area, her years of working with Chickasaws and other Indian people, and her devotion to the continued progress of the Chickasaw Nation meant that she could be an effective liaison between the governor and the Chickasaw people in her area. Thus, Pearl was hired to serve in that capacity, which she did for the remainder of her life. In March 2005 Anoatubby observed that Pearl continued "to be a go getter . . . someone you can count on to know what is going on in the community and to let you know what she believes and what she thinks we should be doing." Gary Childers noted that same month that Pearl had recently suggested that the Chickasaw Nation consider opening a grocery store at Marlow.[27]

▼▼▼

Although Pearl would never again hold elective office, she remained in frequent contact with "Governor Bill" and others in the executive department of the Chickasaw Nation, such as long-time friend Gary Childers. She also remained as active in the community as her health would permit. As 1994 came to an end, Pearl could not have anticipated that the new year would have some significant, and welcome, surprises in store for her.

Chapter Thirteen
▼▼▼

AN HONORED ELDER

I f Pearl thought that she might get bored by not having responsibilities as a legislator, she quickly realized that she had been mistaken. Although she no longer held an elective office, she had been a leader among the Indian people for decades, and she found that many people were comfortable talking to her and relying on her to represent them. Her status as a liaison officer simply formalized the natural tendency for people to call her when they had a concern or a problem. For the next ten years, Pearl regularly would pass on to Governor Anoatubby information regarding problems and needs of the Chickasaw people in the Marlow area. As late as 2005, Anoatubby noted that "we hear from her regularly. She will have ideas. Other people have needs and she will let us know what they are. . . ."[1]

For Pearl, serving as a community liaison officer for Governor Anoatubby was both an honor and a job she took seriously. It represented an opportunity to continue helping people. The added income certainly was helpful, but she would have performed the job without pay or title, because she loved the contact with the people and with Governor Anoatubby. In Pearl's view, "Governor Bill" was both a "good governor" and a "good man." She appreciated the fact that Anoatubby was not "blustering;" instead, he was "quiet" and "smart." When thinking of someone in a position of responsibility and

Just before she was inducted into the Oklahoma Aviation and Space Hall of Fame, Pearl posed beside a photograph of her in an aviator's outfit in front of the Curtiss Robin monoplane in which she made history. (Courtesy Pearl Scott Collection)

authority, "you've never seen anybody so nice. . . ," Pearl observed. Her relationship with Anoatubby played a major role in the quality of Pearl's life during her final decade of service to her people.[2]

In 1995 Pearl would celebrate her birthday in December in a special way, but that would simply cap what would prove to be a year of pleasant surprises. One of them would involve her experiences with Wiley Post and would lead to a significant honor for Pearl. KWTV, Channel 9 in Oklahoma City, on August 15 aired an interview with Bob Kemper, an aviation historian who had participated in the special event memorializing the sixtieth anniversary of the plane crash that killed Wiley Post and Will Rogers.   A reporter for The *Daily `Oklahoman* used the interview with Kemper as a source for a story on the memorial event. Kemper was quoted in the article as saying that the only two people who had ever flown the *Winnie Mae* were Wiley Post and his chief mechanic. Kemper had not heard of Pearl and her experiences with Post, but that soon would change.[3]

During the late 1980s and well into the 1990s, Pearl befriended a neighborhood boy who went by the nickname "Boomer." Pearl would have Boomer do various chores around her house and paid him for the work. She helped him save his money and came to treat him like a son. Boomer, in turn, loved Pearl and appreciated the important role she played in his life. In this photo, Boomer was a ninth grade student at age fifteen in 1996. (Courtesy Pearl Scott Collection)

About two weeks later, Kemper received a letter with a Marlow return address that had been forwarded to him by an editor at the newspaper. He was stunned by the first sentence of the letter that began, "I too flew the Winnie Mae." The letter was from Pearl, and Kemper found it to be a "lengthy, fascinating letter." In the letter Pearl explained her relationship to Post and explained how she came to fly the *Winnie Mae*. "She gave a description of the airplane, even down to the color of the upholstery in the interior," Kemper recalled. He quickly contacted Pearl and arranged to see her in Marlow to interview her.[4]

Kemper and his wife, Sarah, took cameras and went to see Pearl the next weekend. It was a surprising but delightful meeting for the Kempers. When they arrived at Pearl's home, they found a "short, feisty, beautiful woman." What struck Kemper "most was when I walked into her living room, next to her easy chair, on the end table, was a model of the *Winnie Mae*. That just stunned me." Kemper had "never met an elderly lady who had a model of the *Winnie Mae* on her end table!" The Kempers stayed with Pearl for about three hours, having a detailed conversation about her aviation exploits, during which they also learned about her Chickasaw background. She showed them scrapbooks with articles and photos. By the time the Kempers left Pearl's home, they were completely charmed.[5]

As an aviation historian, Kemper found Pearl's story to be especially compelling, both for her unique association with Wiley Post and for its illustration of a unique and short-lived period in aviation history. Only for a brief period in history could a one-eyed, ex-convict have become arguably the "World's Greatest Aviator," teach a pre-teen girl how to fly, and have her flying extensively on her own at age thirteen. Moreover, she was such a natural flyer that Post trusted her to fly his beloved *Winnie Mae*. Kemper wrote some articles on Pearl for aviation magazines, but he wanted to do something more significant and permanent in recognition of Pearl "than a magazine that would get dumped in thirty or sixty days."[6]

Consequently, he visited with the director of the Oklahoma Air and Space Museum at the Kirkpatrick Center in Oklahoma City, related Pearl's story to him, "and he was just as stunned" as Kemper. Thus encouraged, Kemper formally nominated Pearl for induction into the Oklahoma Aviation and Space Hall of Fame. The nomination materials were duplicated and submitted to the museum's directors and members of their Hall of Fame selection committee. Those individuals were "just as surprised" as Kemper and the museum director. Pearl was selected for induction that same year, with the ceremony scheduled for the evening of November 2.[7]

Pearl was shocked, overwhelmed emotionally, and proud when she received the news. "Guess what I did," Pearl intimated, "I cried." To be recognized by aviation historians and fellow aviators pleased her, and her family and friends were thrilled. For his part, Kemper was delighted that his nomination had been so well received, "because it really gave this woman the recognition she deserved for being a unique person in a unique time having had experiences that will never be duplicated again

Never at a loss for words, Pearl is shown expressing her appreciation for her inclusion in the Chickasaw Nation Hall of Fame. The induction ceremony took place on the evening of October 5, 1995, on the campus of Murray State College at Tishomingo. (Courtesy Pearl Scott Collection)

by anyone." Pearl's streak of happy surprises for 1995 did not end with this announcement, however.[8]

Not long after learning that she would be inducted into the Oklahoma Aviation and Space Hall of Fame, Pearl was informed that she had been selected for entry into the Chickasaw Nation Hall of Fame. Pearl was especially honored to be recognized by the Chickasaw Nation for a lifetime of achievements as an aviator, a mother, a community leader, and a servant for the Chickasaw people. The Chickasaw Nation Hall of Fame dinner and induction ceremony was scheduled for the evening of October 5, 1995, in the ballroom on the campus of Murray State College at Tishomingo.[9]

Articles in newspapers such as the *Marlow Review*, the *Duncan Banner*, The *Daily Oklahoman*, and *The Chickasaw Times* carried stories about Pearl being selected for the two halls of fame. Pearl enjoyed seeing and hearing from her family and friends about headlines such as "That daring young woman in her flying machine," "Grandmother still flying high," and "Double honors for Pearl Scott." In one of the stories, she was quoted as saying that, "I am still black and blue from pinching myself to

Following her induction into the Chickasaw Nation Hall of Fame, Pearl was congratulated by friends, family, and admirers. Here she is shaking hands with longtime friend Gary Childers. In the background between Childers and Pearl is Lt. Governor David Brown. To the right of Pearl is her daughter, Louise Thompson, Governor Bill Anoatubby, and her brother, George Carter, Jr.

make sure this is all real."[10]

During the induction program on October 5, Pearl was lauded by Governor Anoatubby, who found it "difficult to say anything about Pearl in such a short time, simply because it is hard to focus on any single aspect of her life that is extraordinary in comparison to the rest of her life." He then briefly reviewed her aviation and Chickasaw Nation careers. Anoatubby presented her a wooden plaque bearing a lithographed likeness of her with text recognizing her as a member of the Chickasaw Nation Hall of Fame, while her brother George, Jr., and her children, grandchildren, and great grandchildren watched, beaming with pride. In her acceptance remarks, Pearl observed that she had begun "working for the tribe in 1972" and that "I haven't stopped yet and I don't intend to now."[11]

In the printed program for the evening, beside Pearl's name and photograph, the following text was printed: "A spirited woman born ahead of her time, Pearl is the epitome of independence and equality—traits evident today in our unconquered and unconquerable nation." Also in-

Preparing to travel from Marlow to Oklahoma City for Pearl's induction into the Oklahoma Aviation and Space Hall of Fame were, left to right: Craig Thompson, LaRue Williamson Armstrong, George Carter, Jr., Billy Guy Thompson, Teresa Scott Fuller, Louise Carter Thompson, Pearl, Bill Scott, Georgia Thompson Smith, and Billy Roy Thompson. (Courtesy Marlow Chamber of Commerce)

ducted posthumously that evening was David R. Stout, who had narrowly defeated Pearl in her bid to be re-elected to the legislature in 1987. Pearl was deeply honored by Anoatubby's remarks and by her induction into the Chickasaw Nation Hall of Fame.[12]

Soon after the excitement of her first hall of fame induction began to recede, it was time to prepare for the next honor. The Oklahoma Aviation and Space Hall of Fame dinner and induction ceremony was scheduled for the evening of November 2, 1995, at the Kirkpatrick Center in Oklahoma City. Others slated for induction that same evening included Jay Gentry, who had trained over four thousand Army Air Corps pilots during World War II; Roger Hardesty, an aviation entrepreneur and president of the United States Aviation Museum, Inc.; James Jabara, America's first jet fighter ace who downed fourteen enemy fighters during the Korean War; and Benjamin King, a fighter ace in World War II who also served in Korea and Vietnam. When Pearl reviewed the names of previous inductees, she was especially humbled: "It is such an honor to be in the Aviation Hall of Fame with Will Rogers, Wiley Post, Oklahoma astronauts, World War aces and pioneers of aviation. . . ."[13]

When the evening of the induction arrived, Pearl was thrilled to have

At her table during the dinner preceding the 1995 Oklahoma Aviation and Space Hall of Fame Induction Ceremony, Pearl posed for this photo with Carter and Nita Scott's daughter Teresa and Pearl's daughter Louise. Pearl thoroughly enjoyed every aspect of the elegant event. (Courtesy Pearl Scott Collection)

with her daughter Louise, son-in-law Bill Thompson, her son Bill, numerous grandchildren, her brother George, Jr., and various other relatives in attendance. Numerous friends also were present, including Penn Rabb, who was dressed in his formal military dress uniform. Pearl, who considered Penn to be one of "My Boys," commented on how handsome he looked. Governor Bill Anoatubby and other representatives of the Chickasaw Nation were present. During the course of the evening, Governor Anoatubby spoke, as did Oklahoma Governor Frank Keating. When it was Pearl's turn to be inducted, she was honored by the showing of a video on her life, followed by a presentation by her grandson Captain Craig Thompson, an airline pilot.[14]

Watching Pearl with interest was Bob Kemper. He noted that the audience was stunned when they saw Pearl's video and learned about her remarkable accomplishments, but "none of them were more stunned than Pearl." She knew it was going to happen, but she still seemed surprised when it actually occurred. Pearl, Kemper observed, "was ebullient. She was just overflowing not just with emotion, not just the grandeur, but the

▼▼▼

whole scope of the thing." Pearl looked "more radiant than any bride," Kemper noted. "She was just glowing and taken aback by all the attention and all the dignitaries that were there."[15]

The evening was a wonderful event for Pearl's family. Her granddaughter Beverly Scott remembered that Pearl was, "So tiny; she looked so beautiful." Her daughter Louise had purchased a beautiful new dress for Pearl to wear that evening and "she looked real pretty." During the reception before the dinner and induction ceremony, Beverly noticed Pearl fidgeting and standing behind one of the smaller airplanes on exhibit in the reception area. Thinking Pearl might need some reassurance, Beverly asked her if she was ready and if she had her "notes all set." Pearl responded, "Well, I didn't write down notes. I don't need notes." Among the crowd was the Commander of NORAD, "generals crawling all over the place, an astronaut" and other dignitaries, but Pearl was confident and ready to respond to her induction.[16]

When Pearl was introduced, she walked confidently to the podium and, Kemper remembered, "wowed them all." Her remarks were "ad-libbed off the top of her head and it was perfect." Kemper was "thrilled to death too. I literally had tears streaming down my face; I was so thrilled for her." Beverly noted that Pearl seemed comfortable in front of the crowd of approximately four hundred people, many of them prominent individuals. Pearl "held them enthralled for thirty or forty minutes . . . talking about when there were no highways in the sky and all you had was a stick and the world was your oyster. . . ."[17]

Pearl was proud to have her story told to such a distinguished audience. But she was quick to point out that her induction was "a tribute to my parents . . . for having the faith and believing in me." Her aviation exploits would have been impossible without their remarkable trust in Pearl and her abilities. They were indeed proud of what Pearl had accomplished, but they could not have anticipated that one day she would receive such a significant recognition.[18]

Pearl received an outpouring of telephone calls, cards, letters, and flowers from people congratulating her on her induction into both halls of fame. She thanked as many as possible personally, and she also placed a "Thank You" notice in *The Marlow Times* to thank all who had expressed

Craig Thompson offered the microphone to Pearl for her response following his introduction of her during the Oklahoma Aviation and Space Hall of Fame In-duction Ceremony. In the background is Gerry Bonds, who served as co-master of ceremonies for the event. (Courtesy Pearl Scott Papers)

their congratulations to her in so many different ways. The publicity resulting from her inductions also caused Pearl to be invited to a join the National OX5 Aviation Pioneers Organization, Oklahoma Wing. Pearl had enjoyed a wonderful year, but a birthday surprise was yet to come.[19]

Not long after her induction into the Oklahoma Aviation and Space Hall of Fame, Pearl began a month-long trip with Louise and her hus-band, Bill, to visit Carter, his wife Nita, grandchildren, and great grand-children. One of the planned stops was Gulfport, Mississippi, where her grandson Craig Thompson resided. Craig and two of his pilot friends, Captain Marten Smith and Captain Lamar Switzer (both would call Pearl "Grandma,") had arranged a surprise in honor of Pearl's eightieth birthday on December 9. They took Pearl, Louise, and Bill up in Switzer's nine-passenger King Air turbo-prop aircraft to see the Gulf of Mexico, the floating casinos, and other sights. Prior to takeoff, Pearl was offered the co-pilot's seat next to Smith, who was flying the plane, ostensibly to afford her a better view.[20]

Following a prearranged plan, Smith took the plane above 9,000 feet,

Back on the ground following Pearl's flight on her eightieth birthday, December 9, 1995, during which Pearl was thrilled to pilot this King Air airplane. Participating in the special occasions were, left to right: Bill Thompson; Louise Thompson; and airline pilots Craig Thompson, Marten Smith, and Lamar Switzer. Smith and Switzer were friends of Craig's, and Switzer was the owner of the airplane. (Courtesy Pearl Scott Papers)

contacted the tower, "explained" that he had a "special lady with him with quite a history in aviation as evidenced by her recent induction into a hall of fame associated with it," and then requested permission to turn the controls over to Pearl. "They told him to let that little lady do anything she wants to up there," Pearl recalled. After giving Pearl a quick review of the various instruments and gauges, Smith surrendered control of the aircraft to "the birthday girl." At age eighty, Pearl was thrilled to be flying such a magnificent airplane. Being above the clouds, Pearl was obliged to "fly blind," using the instruments, which she did for about an hour, eventually returning control to Smith who landed the King Air.[21]

Flying this sophisticated airplane gave Pearl's psyche a significant

boost. Her confidence had declined due to the decrease of "one-on-one contacts she had enjoyed while working" and because of health problems since she had left the legislature the previous year. "For awhile, I had kind of lost my self confidence," Pearl admitted. But, as she controlled the King Air, she thought, "Here I am, flying a three million dollar plane, and all their (the passengers) lives are in my hands—and that gave me my confidence back." Once again, Pearl believed she could "do anything I set my mind to anymore." I enjoyed it—every minute of it," Pearl exclaimed, "and I am looking forward to the next time." Unfortunately, there would be no next time, as Pearl's declining health would not allow that to happen again. Yet, she always cherished the wonderful memory of her eightieth birthday surprise.[22]

Chapter Fourteen

MORE HONORS AND ACTIVITIES

T he next two years were quiet ones for Pearl, as she settled in at home with her Chihuahua, Bambi, and enjoyed visiting with friends and family members. She had been told by a doctor that a Chihuahua would be good for her respiratory condition. Already interested in a obtaining a pet, she had obtained a Chihuahua several years earlier. After having several Chihuahuas, by the time of her eightieth birthday, she had Bambi, who proved to be a wonderful companion for her. At home, Pearl spent a great deal of time in her "easy chair" with Bambi nestled in her lap. When her children jokingly told her that she "thought more of her dogs than she did of her own kids," Pearl would respond wryly that the dogs had the virtue of not talking back to her. Over time, Pearl and Bambi became virtually inseparable.[1]

Pearl never lost her sense of humor. At some point she had acquired a large, circular bed that featured a big, red, curved headboard. She also kept a "brilliant red" bedspread on it. She liked the bed and kept it, even though it pretty much filled her bedroom. Since the bed had been a "bugaboo" for her son Bill for years, one day he exclaimed, "Mama, get rid of that bed and get you a nice, comfortable queen size if you need it. Besides that, it looks like

State Representative Ray McCarter, left, arranged for Pearl to be honored by the Oklahoma House of Representatives on November 11, 2002. She was flanked by McCarter, a citizen of the Chickasaw Nation, and Chickasaw Governor Bill Anoatubby. McCarter and Anoatubby had lifted Pearl up on a stand behind the podium so she could be elevated sufficiently high to be seen. (Courtesy Marlow Chamber of Commerce)

Pearl was hailed as a "Pioneer" in a special edition of Oklahoma Today *magazine that focused on Oklahoma's rich aviation heritage. The issue featured a story on Wiley Post and an overview of aviation history in Oklahoma. Pearl attended a special press conference held at Wiley Post Airport in Bethany, Oklahoma, to announce the issue. She posed for this photograph, which included, left to right: Joan Henderson, publisher of* Oklahoma Today: *Pearl, Oklahoma Governor Frank Keating: and Louisa McCune, editor-in-chief of the magazine. (Courtesy Pearl Scott Collection)*

it came out of a French whore house!" Without hesitation, Pearl looked him in the eye and replied, "How would you know?" As a joke, Carter gave his mother a red pillow shaped like a woman's breasts. Pearl placed the red pillow on her red, round bed and kept both items for the remainder of her life.[2]

If Pearl had begun to believe by 1998 that she had received the last of her honors for her aviation exploits, she was mistaken. The July/August 1998 issue of *Oklahoma Today* magazine was a special "Air and Space" issue featuring Wiley Post on the cover and a story on his life and accomplishment. Other Oklahoma aviators were featured, including Pearl. A full page of the magazine was devoted to Pearl, who was listed as "The Pioneer." The page featured a wonderful contemporary photograph of Pearl in a late-1920s vintage flight jacket with scarf, leather head gear, and goggles high on her forehead, ready to be pulled down over her eyes for action. Brief text on the page recounted her connection to Wiley Post and her role in aviation history.[3]

Pearl was both surprised and pleased to be honored by *Oklahoma Today:* "I feel so honored and lucky to be the one that was picked out of the many . . . in the Oklahoma Air and Space Museum Hall of Fame as the 'Pioneer' for the . . . magazine." While much of her original aviation gear had been destroyed in the house fire years earlier, Pearl told a reporter that she still had her log book and permit from those days.

Bambi Scott, Pearl's faithful companion during the final decade of her life, is seen here relaxing in a chair on Pearl's front porch. (Courtesy Marlow Chamber of Commerce)

Pearl attended a press conference held by *Oklahoma Today* at Wiley Post Airport in Bethany on July 6 to promote the special issue. There she proudly posed for a photograph with Oklahoma Governor Frank Keating, *Oklahoma Today's* Publisher Joan Henderson, and Editor-In-Chief Louisa McCune, which was published in *The Marlow Review.*[4]

Being featured in *Oklahoma Today* caused Pearl to receive some additional recognition. She was featured in a major story in *The Lawton Constitution* newspaper on July 28, 1998, in which her aviation career and resultant honors were reviewed. Pearl enjoyed retelling her stories of Wiley, her flying in air circuses, and giving people shows with her aerobatics. She also credited Post with being the "biggest influence in my life. If it wasn't for him I would have given up and I wouldn't have all of this," Pearl said, pointing toward a wall covered with plaques and certificates. Pearl also revealed that she recently had been included in a new book on the life of Wiley Post, had been interviewed for a television documentary on Post, and had been invited to be a guest at meetings of various organizations interested in aviation history, including the Confederate Air Force, and the Association of '99's.[5]

▼▼▼

Pearl's round of activities continued when she was invited to attend ceremonies in Oklahoma City marking the centennial of Wiley Post's birth on November 22, 1998. Organized by the Wiley Post Centennial Committee, the celebration began at 1:30 p.m. with the formal dedication of a special Wiley Post monument at his grave in Memorial Park Cemetery. The imposing granite monument included etchings of a portrait of Post, a depiction of Post in his pressure suit, the *Winnie Mae*, and a flattened globe of the world. Post was proclaimed "Father of Modern Aviation," and text recounted his principal exploits. An oil portrait of Post by noted artist Mike Wimmer was unveiled at 4 p.m. on the fourth floor of the state capitol building, where it was to be permanently displayed.[6]

Pearl was honored to attend a special celebration honoring the centennial of Wiley Post's birth in Oklahoma City on November 22, 1998. There she was delighted to see the new monument at Post's gravesite and enjoyed the festivities of the day with her son Bill Scott, left, and daughter and son-in-law Louise and Bill Thompson. (Courtesy Pearl Scott Papers)

Pearl soon received yet another pleasant surprise as a result of her historical connection to Wiley Post. While Pearl was celebrating her eighty-fifth birthday on December 9, 1998, the space shuttle *Endeavour* was orbiting Earth with, among other objects, two hundred commemorative Wiley Post Centennial Celebration decals on board. The shuttle had been launched on December 4, and it landed at Kennedy Space Center on December 15. The decals were returned to Melissa Colvin at the Oklahoma Air and Space Museum, who had worked with the Wiley Post Centennial Committee on the project. In turn, the decals were forwarded to the committee. One of the decals, along with a certificate explaining its significance, was sent to Pearl by Cheryl Neal of the committee. Pearl "had no idea about it" but she was "so proud of this." The "space-flown" decal joined Pearl's collection of artifacts and memorabilia that stimulated pleasant memories of Wiley, flying, and youth.[7]

Pearl was visited by Rodger Harris, head of the Oral History Archives at the Oklahoma Historical Society, in March of 1999. Harris was a native of Marlow, and he knew of Pearl's family and her general background. The interview was to be transcribed and placed in the archives of the society for use by historians in the future. The session provided Pearl the opportunity to relive her life from childhood to that moment, and she never tired of telling about her family, her first car, her aviation experiences, her children, and her working for the Chickasaw Nation.[8]

Pearl celebrated her eighty-fifth birthday at home with a cake presented to her by Beverly Yvette Carter, the daughter of George, Jr. The camera caught Pearl just as she blew out the one large candle on her cake. On the back of the photo, Pearl wrote, "Happy 85ᵗʰ birthday to me—Ha! Ha! Doesn't Bev look like Arnetta?" (Courtesy Bill Scott)

During the course of the conversation, Pearl confirmed that she was still active in the Chickasaw Nation as a governor's office liaison: "Governor Bill told me I'm him over here." And she was proud of what the Chickasaw Nation had provided for the Marlow area, including the bus, the smoke shop, and an outpatient clinic she had helped obtain. "Now I have another project in mind that I got to talk to the governor about," she exclaimed. At the end of the interview, she pointed out that she was proud of her aviation career and her "Indian nation" career. But her "most important" career was motherhood, "And I am proud of my kids."[9]

Pearl was honored again by the Chickasaw Nation in September of 1999, when she was named grand marshal for the Chickasaw Festival and Annual Meeting parade that was to be held at Tishomingo on October 2. In addition, "a docu-drama highlighting Pearl Carter Scott's extraor-

Pearl was named grand marshall for the Chickasaw Nation Festival Parade, which was held in Tishomingo on October 2, 1999. Taking a break during the various festivities were, left to right: Pearl's sons Carter and Bill, Pearl, and Chickasaw Governor Bill Anoatubby. (Courtesy Marlow Chamber of Commerce)

dinary life" was scheduled for presentation on the evening of September 30 in the Fletcher Auditorium at Murray State College. The presentation was a major production featuring actors portraying Pearl, George, Sr., young Pearl, young Lucy, Governor M. E. Trapp, United States Senator Thomas P. Gore, and Wiley Post. Pearl's dog, Bambi, was played by herself. In addition to the actors, videos were shown as integral parts of the presentation. The play included four scenes, two each written by Lona Barrack and Jeannie Barbour, followed by guest tributes to Pearl by Debbe Ridley, Jack Graves, and D. B. Green, all from Marlow; former Governor Overton James; and Governor Bill Anoatubby.[10]

Being selected by the Chickasaw Nation for these honors was especially meaningful to Pearl, "I feel very honored to be picked as one" who "has made a success and done so much in my life, being a Chickasaw Indian." She was amazed that "they have taken a lot of videos of different people [talking] about me. They even went into my old home on 2nd Street where I was raised. . . ." Pearl also observed that she had been "fortunate to have lived such a wonderful life, and I am proud of my af-

In addition to being honored as grand marshall of the Chickasaw Nation Festival Parade on October 2, 1999, that evening at Murray State College she and many other festival participants were treated to a docudrama honoring Pearl. Seated with Pearl on the front row to view the performance were, left to right: George Carter, Jr.; Bill Scott; and Guy Smith, Pearl's great grandson. (Courtesy Pearl Scott Collection)

filiation with my tribe. I cannot thank the members of the tribe enough for this tremendous honor." Pearl mentioned that she had been working for the tribe since 1972, and "I haven't stopped yet and I don't intend to stop now." Finally, she concluded that "God's been good to me. It's been a wonderful life."[11]

Sheila J. Robinson of *The Duncan Banner*, one of the journalists who wrote about the docudrama, must have remained interested in Pearl, for she interviewed Pearl for two additional stories, both of which appeared in *The Duncan Banner* on January 2, 2000. The first story was on Pearl's father, and the second was on Pearl and her relationship with Wiley Post. Pearl never tired of telling stories of her youth, George, Sr., and Wiley and she enjoyed being interviewed.[12]

Pearl's pace of activities slowed down significantly in 2000 and 2001. Her breathing difficulties became more pronounced at times, and her strength seemed to decline. She spent more time at home with Bambi and family and friends. However, she did have the opportunity to meet

Following the docudrama honoring Pearl, she received a gift, flowers, and expressions of appreciation for her role in the history of aviation and for her service to the Chickasaw Nation from Governor Bill Anoatubby, left, and Lt. Governor Jefferson Keel. (Courtesy The Chickasaw Times)

Russian cosmonauts Colonel Alexander Volkov and Dr. Alexander Martynov. The cosmonauts were honored at a special reception at Ada, hosted by East Central University, the Oklahoma Space and Aeronautics Commission, and the Chickasaw Nation. The highly decorated Volkov had flown in space three times, had been a test pilot, and had commanded the Mir Space Station. Martynov was the author of 120 scientific articles and six books dedicated to spacecraft motion control in planetary atmospheres. Pearl told the cosmonauts about her connection with Wiley Post and his invention of the pressure suit, and the Russians gave Pearl an autographed copy of the book *An A-Z of Cosmonautics*. For Pearl, "It was a thrill to have the opportunity to meet those men."[13]

Pearl was excited to receive an invitation to attend the 2001 Will Rogers/Wiley Post Fly-In at the birthplace ranch of Rogers near Oologah, Oklahoma. The annual event was sponsored by the Will Rogers Memorial at Claremore to honor the memory of Rogers, who was an influential advocate of aviation, and his friend Wiley Post. Pearl was thrilled with the prospect of mingling with the many pilots who would be there with their vintage airplanes and making a speech to an audience of aviation enthusiasts. All three of Pearl's children traveled to Marlow to accompany her to Oologah for the event, but the morning she was to make the trip, she woke with "breathing problems" and was hospitalized in Duncan.[14]

To a reporter who telephoned her, Pearl commented from her hospital bed, "Isn't that an awful thing. . . . You can hardly keep from crying, but I know that wouldn't do

In October 2000 Pearl met Russian cosmonauts Colonel Alexander Volkov, left, and Dr. Alexander Martynov at a reception held in their honor at East Central University. Pearl took the opportunity to remind them that her friend Wiley Post invented the pressure suit, which paved the way for humans to function in space. (Courtesy Pearl Scott Collection)

my body any good. I push myself. I'm eighty-six and I still think I'm sixteen." Michelle Lefebvre-Carter, executive director of the Will Rogers Memorial Museums, had sent her a book on the 1929 Powder Puff Derby by a lady who had participated in that event. The author was going to be at the fly-in, and Pearl had planned on getting her book autographed. Moreover, she had been told that there would be "a lot of old fliers there" that she might have known and with whom she would enjoy visiting. "That's what gets me—I wanted to be there so bad." Pearl also noted that she was expected to speak at the event and she hated to let the organizers down by not being there. Pearl soon went home from the hospital, determined to remain as active as possible and hoping to attend the fly-in honoring Will and Wiley in 2002. Circumstances, primarily her physical condition, would prevent her from attending the fly-in for the next two years. [15]

State Representative Ray McCarter of Marlow decided early in 2002 to honor Pearl for her lifetime of achievements. He arranged for Pearl to appear before the Oklahoma House of Representatives on February 11 to receive a special resolution signed by himself, Senator Sam Helton, and House Speaker Larry Adair. The resolution praised Pearl for her unique role in the history of aviation and her work on behalf of the Chickasaw Nation. Moreover, the resolution, authored by McCarter, noted that the legislative body took great pride in "recognizing those who have excelled in life, career, and through great adversity."[16]

Pearl was honored at the beginning of the business day for the House of Representatives. The lawmakers had a heavy agenda ahead of them and were eager to begin the day's work. Chickasaw Governor Bill Anoatubby and Representative McCarter joined Pearl at the podium. Anoatubby spoke briefly, observing that Pearl had been "a leader all her life. . . . From her pioneering efforts in aviation to her work with the Chickasaw Nation, she has displayed the courage, strength of character and indomitable spirit that is an inspiration to everyone who knows her." McCarter then presented Pearl to the lawmakers, noting that "Pearl is indeed a treasure to this great state and its people."[17]

McCarter offered the microphone to Pearl in the event that she would like to make some brief remarks, the norm for such situations being three to five minutes. She indeed wanted to address the assemblage, so Anoatubby and McCarter lifted Pearl up to the extension at the podium, where she could barely see over the microphone. Pearl began telling her aviation story, mesmerizing the representatives with amazing but true adventures. Forty-five minutes later, she "wound her talk down with a sigh," much to the relief of Speaker Adair, who was by this time eager to get underway with the House's business. As Anoatubby and McCarter moved to help Pearl down from the podium, "she leaned forward, took the microphone in her right hand, and proudly pronounced" that she would like to tell the representatives about "her life growing up in Marlow." And she proceeded to do so! After about fifteen minutes, the Speaker had enough, and Anoatubby and McCarter "lifted her from the podium with her still talking, let her enjoy her standing ovation by the House members, and adjourned to the House Lounge for pictures." Later that day, McCarter penned a letter to Pearl in which he observed, "You were just fabulous. Everyone was spellbound by your recollections."[18]

Also present at the capitol that day was Assistant Fire Chief Jon Hanson, the media spokesperson for Oklahoma City's Fire Department during the rescue and recovery operations after the bombing of the Alfred

On the fifty-eighth anniversary of D-Day, Pearl and her family staged a surprise party at her house to honor her brother, George, Jr., for his service during World War II and the Korean War. It was held in the shade of her carport. George, shown here in front of a table displaying various gifts, was "tricked" into attending the party by his nephew Dan Williamson. Note the photo of Bill Scott mounted on a broom with a sign indicated "Bill was here." Bill and other family members who were unable to attend telephoned George to express their love and gratitude for his service to his country. (Courtesy Pearl Scott Collection)

P. Murrah Federal Building in 1995. Hanson became a celebrity who represented the brave fire fighters and others who risked their lives in the operation. Pearl was honored when Hanson asked to have a photograph made of him with Pearl.[19]

Being honored by the Oklahoma House of Representatives certainly was a great honor for Pearl, and a few months later she had the opportunity to help honor her brother, George, Jr. In recognition of George's heroism during World War II and the Korean War, Pearl and her family organized a surprise party at Pearl's home on June 6 to honor him. Coordinated by Louise, the gathering took place under the roof of Pearl's carport.[20]

George's nephew Dan Williamson of Duncan was enlisted to get George to the party without letting him know about it in advance. Dan invited George to go with him for some barbeque, an invitation which ordinarily would have been quite tempting to George. However, George declined, indicating that he did not feel "too well." Dan then countered with an offer to go get a milkshake and George agreed. Instead of going to a drive-in restaurant, however, Dan took George to Pearl's home, where the family was assembled. Waiting for George and Dan were Pearl; Louise and her husband Bill Thompson; nephews Art and Bob Williamson; nieces Wanda Kizer, LaRue Armstrong, and Arletta Savage; great-nephew Mike Lightner and his wife Becky; and great-niece Kris Ball. In addition, family members who were unable to be present but who

With Bambi at her feet, Pearl was in good spirits, waiting with her daughter Louise to get the party honoring George, Jr., started. (Courtesy Pearl Scott Collection)

phoned George during the party included his daughter Beverly Martel, grand-daughter Leslie Ross, nephews Bill and Carter Scott, and great-niece Teresa Fuller.[21]

Pearl's carport was decorated in red, white, and blue. Floral arrangements in patriotic colors, along with small United States flags, provided the appropriate ambiance for the celebration, which also included a cake decorated to match the patriotic theme of the occasion. Bill and Louise had framed George's discharge certificates and other mementos, and Louise had arranged and framed all of his military medals and ribbons. Bill's son Brad, while on vacation in 2000, had gathered some sand and stones from the spot on Omaha Beach where, as near as Brad could determine, George went ashore on D-Day. For the tribute celebration, Bill combined the stones, the sand, and two photos to create a framed collage. All of these items served as focal points of the family celebration and were presented to George.[22]

▼▼▼

On the back of the collage that Bill Scott put together for George, he expressed in writing the sentiments of the family:

> For our hero, George W. Carter, Jr., who laid his life on the line on D-Day and thereafter throughout World War Two to ensure we and our country's freedoms would be protected forever.
>
> This is but a small token compared to all our love for you, as our love for our "Uncle Junior" is immeasurable.
>
> The shingles (small stones) and golden sand from Omaha Beach were collected by Brad Scott (a nephew) in the summer of 2000 for you as a reminder that you will never be forgotten for your bravery by our country, your friends, and most of all, your family.
>
> The picture of you saving your friend was copied from Steven Ambrose's documentary, "D-Day." The smaller picture was lifted from a photograph dated March 1951.
>
> On behalf of your sister, daughter, grandkids and all levels of nieces and nephews, we present this small token with out heart-felt love and devotion.

George was completely surprised and deeply moved by this demonstration of love and respect on the part of his family. Pearl provided information on the gathering as well as a photo of George to the *Marlow Review* for a feature story which appeared on June 20.[23]

Pearl planned to attend the Will Rogers/Wiley Post Fly-In at the Will Rogers Birthplace near Oologah on August 15, and again the planners were excited by the prospect of having her there. When asked by a local reporter about how she would be traveling to the fly-in, Pearl observed that it would be by car, not airplane, noting with a chuckle that she did not "get around as much as I used to." When asked about Post, Pearl responded, "Oh, my, he's the best. He's the best. I don't think anyone will ever equal him." Unfortunately, Pearl once again had to cancel her plans to attend because she was not physically up to making the trip.[24]

Soon thereafter Pearl received a letter from the Lyndon B. Johnson Space Center in Houston. It was an invitation to attend the launch on November 2 and landing of the Space Shuttle *Endeavour*. The letter was signed by each of the astronauts and cosmonauts who would be involved in the mission. Pearl's name had been placed on the official invitation list by one of the astronauts, and Pearl was absolutely thrilled by the prospect of seeing the launch and landing. When asked about her upcoming adventure, Pearl commented, "I would have liked to have flown on the shuttle. That would have completed the aviation part of my life."[25]

Pearl's invitation came as the result of her having acquired a new admirer, Commander John B. Herrington, United States Navy, who would serve as mission specialist 2 on Shuttle Mission STS-113. Herrington was a native of Wetumka, Oklahoma, and a graduate of the University of Colorado at Colorado Springs. He held a master of science degree in aeronautical engineering from the U. S. Naval Postgraduate School, and had

Governor Bill Anoatubby and Pearl took a break while touring NASA facilities in Florida to pose for this photograph on November 7, 2002. They were in Florida along with a large contingent from the Chickasaw Nation to honor Commander John Herrington, a Chickasaw, on the occasion of his being a member of the crew of the shuttle Endeavour, which was scheduled to be launched on November 9. Herrington was slated to become the first American Indian to fly in space. Unfortunately, the launch was postponed and the Chickasaws returned home on November 9. (Courtesy The Chickasaw Times)

learned about Pearl and her pioneering aviation exploits. He was impressed by her youthful courage, by the fact that she was the first Chickasaw aviator, and by her subsequent contributions to the Chickasaw Nation. This was especially meaningful to Herrington, for he, too, was a citizen of the Chickasaw Nation. And he soon was to become the first American Indian to fly in space.[26]

Herrington's maternal great-grandmother was a full-blood Chickasaw, making Herrington one-eighth Chickasaw. Although he was not raised in an Indian environment, his mother made certain that he was a registered member of the tribe. He also believed that he had some Choctaw ancestry in his father's family but could not document it. The astronaut noted that "I take tremendous pride in who I am, where I came from." He observed that whenever he had the opportunity to be with Indian people, he felt a strong sense of kinship. Herrington's venture into space would be celebrated by Native Americans from throughout the United States, not just Chickasaws.[27]

Before traveling to Florida for the shuttle launch in November, Pearl was able to attend the annual meeting of the Chickasaw Nation and ride in the parade with Charles Blackwell on Saturday, October 6. Blackwell was the Chickasaw Nation's ambassador to the government of the United States, and Pearl was honored to ride with him. After the annual meeting and parade, Pearl returned home to gather her strength and make arrangements for her trip to Florida.[28]

The shuttle launch was scheduled for November 9 and Pearl was determined to see it in person and to participate in the related festivities. This would take some effort because she still was suffering from recurrent breathing problems. An entourage of approximately two hundred Chickasaws, including Governor Anoatubby, planned to travel to the Kennedy Space Center (KSC) in three buses and by plane. Pearl, however, devised a different plan. On November 6, she departed Marlow by car, driven by nephew, Dan Williamson of Duncan. They were bound for Florence, Alabama, the home of Pearl's daughter, Louise. Pearl's son Bill met her at Louise's home as well. From there, Dan, Louise, Bill, and Pearl departed for Cocoa Beach, Florida, and the Kennedy Space Center (KSC), arriving there Friday evening, November 8.[29]

Before departing Marlow, Pearl had worked with American Medi-Serv in Duncan to arrange with a similar company in the Cocoa Beach area to have a supply of oxygen waiting for her when she arrived with her family at the Oceanfront Best Western Motel The oxygen was supplied in a stationary canister with a fifty-foot range and in harness-type canisters. Pearl was well prepared for possible breathing problems that might occur.[30]

▼▼▼

On Saturday morning, a committee of personnel from the KSC and the Johnson Space Center officially welcomed the Chickasaws to Florida with a reception. Participating in the reception were Herrington's parents, an Osage/Cherokee employee of NASA, a color guard from the Seminole Nation of Florida, and "the Native American Drum Corps." Following the reception, all two hundred Chickasaw guests were taken on a tour of KSC. A part of the tour featured a simulated space station replicating the *Endeavour's* destination. Seeing these sights sent Pearl's imagination soaring. That evening the visitors also enjoyed a special buffet dinner, with a program featuring American Indian music and dancing.[31]

During the dinner program, William F. Readdy, associate director for space flight, expressed appreciation for the outstanding group of Chickasaws who had made the trip to Florida in Herrington's honor. Readdy then stated that Herrington "had sent a special message to one person, a little lady who he wanted to thank and who had been his inspiration." Readdy then asked Pearl to stand. The audience, guests, and NASA personnel alike rose and gave Pearl, the aviator who had inspired an astronaut, a rousing ovation. Pearl later commented, "You couldn't ask for anyone to be any better than those NASA people were to me."[32]

Early Sunday morning the Chickasaw contingent was transported by bus to the elegant Peabody Hotel in Orlando, Florida, where they enjoyed breakfast followed by a symposium on "Linking Education to Employment." Governor Anoatubby and a host of other distinguished speakers were featured. After the symposium, the group had a luncheon at the hotel, a bus ride back to Cocoa Beach, and then free time before the evening festivities. Pearl used the time to rest since she was beginning to have breathing difficulties, even with the availability of oxygen.[33]

Sunday evening the visiting Chickasaws, NASA personnel, members of other American Indian tribes, and additional NASA visitors gathered at the Rocket Garden, the area of the KSC that featured displays of the various rockets used throughout NASA's history, including the gigantic Saturn V that had been employed to transport astronauts to the moon. In those extraordinary surroundings, a reception honoring Commander Herrington was held. The Chickasaw Dance Troupe performed two dances, and the Chickasaw Princesses performed "The Lord's Prayer." Cree

Indian recording artist Buffy Sainte-Marie sang "America the Beautiful," and a Chickasaw elder prayed for the astronauts' safety during the mission.[34]

Following the entertainment, the reception continued with a buffet featuring American Indian food and a mission briefing by an astronaut. Then the visitors boarded buses and were transported to the Banana Beach viewing area to witness what promised to be a spectacular shuttle launch sometime between 1 a.m. to 3:30 a.m. on Monday morning. Pearl's increasing excitement was matched only by her increasing difficulties with breathing. As it happened, a phenomenon known as "red tide" was adding to Pearl's respiratory problems. Red tide is caused by the rapid bloom of certain types of microscopic algae in coastal waters. Airborne toxins generated by red tide can significantly impact people with existing respiratory conditions, such as that suffered by Pearl. Fortunately for Pearl, a physician from the Carl Albert Indian Health Facility at Ada had made the trip, and she stayed close to Pearl to monitor her condition.[35]

Anticipating the experience of a lifetime, Pearl and the others at Banana Beach were destined to be disappointed. Not long after their arrival at the viewing site, NASA announced that the launch had been postponed due to an oxygen leak. By this time, Pearl was tired and, ironically, needing oxygen because she was working hard to breathe. She recalled, "They hustled me on to our room and oxygen as quickly as possible." Governor Anoatubby spoke for the frustrated Chickasaw contingent when he observed that "the safety of Commander Herrington and the other astronauts must always be the top priority. . . . Plus, we could not have asked for a better experience. . . . It was a wonderful opportunity and historic for Native America."[36]

Pearl's group departed Florida the next morning, and after spending the night at Louise's home, Pearl and her nephew departed for Marlow the next morning, arriving home that evening. Early the following morning Pearl received a call from Chickasaw Nation Headquarters informing Pearl that they were sending a media crew to interview her for a special video production on her life. That crew arrived the next day and interviewed Pearl extensively. They also talked with others in Marlow, visited the local museum, and taped photographs that would help illustrate various phases of Pearl's life.[37]

Following this whirlwind of activity, Pearl was exhausted, and her breathing problems had not improved since her encounter with the red tide. She finally went to the doctor who immediately admitted her into the hospital at Duncan on Saturday, November 16. Pearl had contracted pneumonia. This caused Pearl considerable distress, because she had been invited to be the guest of honor at a Chickasaw Nation event at the McSwain Theater in Ada on Friday, November 22, to view the re-

Just out of the hospital after a bout with pneumonia, Pearl attended the Chickasaw Nation's "Countdown to Endeavour" event at the McSwain Theater in Ada. The purpose of the event was to watch the launch of Endeavour on closed circuit television and to honor Pearl. Although the launch was postponed to the next day, Pearl had a wonderful time. Here she is visiting with astronaut Paul Richards, who traveled to Ada to attend the event and to honor Pearl. (Courtesy Pearl Scott Collection)

scheduled launch of Herrington's shuttle mission. To her relief, Pearl was released from the hospital on the day before the gathering in Ada, and she was grateful to the doctors and staff at the hospital who "got me feeling well enough to go" to the event in Ada.[38]

Billed "Countdown to *Endeavor*," the event at the McSwain Theater featured music, a question-and-answer session with an astronaut, performances by the Chickasaw Princesses and the Chickasaw Nation Dance Troupe, and a NASA film titled "History of Space." Pearl had been pleased when she arrived to find a poster-sized reproduction of the page about her that had been printed in the special aviation and space issue of *Oklahoma Today*. She was even more surprised, however, when the highlight of the evening proved to be the first showing of the video production "Pearl Scott: Pioneer Aviatrix" that had been quickly but effectively produced by the Chickasaw Nation. Unknown to Pearl, the video was being transmitted to NASA at the same time it was being shown in

Pearl proudly displayed the model of Endeavour that was given to her by Commander John Herrington, who told Pearl that her life story had inspired him in his quest to fly in space. Behind Pearl is a phtotgraph in poster form of her at ate eighty-two in an aviator's outfit. The photo was used to honor her as an aviation pioneer in Oklahoma Today magazine. Pearl commented on various occasions that she wished she had been able to go to the moon. (Courtesy The Marlow Review)

the theater. At the conclusion of the video, Pearl was "swamped. I'm telling you, little kids from about ten or twelve-years old—everybody wanted my autograph and wanted a picture of me."[39]

When news came that the launch again had been postponed, this time due to inclement weather at an emergency landing site in Spain, Pearl and the audience went home disappointed but having enjoyed a wonderful evening. Herrington and his comrades were successfully launched into space the following day and went on to complete a highly successful mission. From her home in Marlow, Pearl followed the news of the mission closely, was proud of Herrington's spacewalk, and rejoiced when he and the other members of the crew completed their mission safely.[40]

Chapter Fifteen
▼▼▼

WINDING DOWN

T he hectic pace of activities slowed for Pearl in 2003. She continued both to represent Governor Anoatubby as a liaison officer for the Marlow area and to express her ideas for potential projects to him and to his special assistant, Gary Childers. She also continued to enjoy friends and relatives as often as possible. And in the spring of 2003, she was able to enjoy watching her son Bill receive a special honor.

The Lawton Constitution newspaper had chosen its All-Area Football Team for the 1952-53 season, and Bill was honored by being selected to that team. His old friend Penn Rabb saw the news in the paper and contacted Bill to inform him of the honor. This good news was followed by a formal invitation to the event, scheduled for the evening of April 28, 2003, in the Great Plains Coliseum Annex in Lawton. Bill decided to return to Oklahoma with his son Bryan to visit his mother and to attend the banquet that was held to recognize the honorees in Lawton. Bill invited Bryan, Pearl, and Penn to attend with him, and Pearl had a wonderful time, beaming with pride when Bill was recognized that evening. As it happened, Bill had traveled the farthest of those who attended. During the course of the evening, Pearl leaned over to Bryan and, with a big

Pearl still was able to get out of the house and visit people in 2003. This photo of her was taken in May of that year as she came to downtown Marlow to observe the filming of a documentary on the history of country music. The segment filmed in Marlow dealt with music played in association with medicine shows that traveled the nation early in the twentieth century. Pearl remembered such shows coming to Marlow and enjoyed visiting about them with the movie's producer. (Courtesy The Marlow Review)

▼▼▼

Pearl was proud when her son Bill was named to the Lawton Constitution's All-Area Football Team for the 1952-53 school year. On August 28, 2003, she attended the banquet honoring the athletes with Bill, his son Bryan, and Bill's friend Penn Rabb. Here Bill posed for a photo in front of the newspaper's promotional display for the event.

smile, whispered "Honey, it feels so good to sit down here and not to stand up there to give a speech!"[1]

In late May, Pearl and others in the Marlow community enjoyed watching a small movie production company at work in their community. Billy Teel of Oklahoma City, head of Speedway Records and the Country Roots Foundation, was in town to film a segment of "Country Roots," a movie detailing the influence of medicine shows along the Chisholm Trail and showing how they contributed to the development of country music in America. Marlow was located on the western edge of the Chisholm Trail, and medicine shows frequented the community through the 1920s. [2]

Pearl was an interested observer because she remembered medicine shows from her youth, even recalling a distant relative who operated such a show spending the night occasionally with the Carter family. Teel was excited to have the opportunity to meet and visit with Pearl about her remembrances of the medicine shows that came to town. Often the shows used a musician such as a banjo, guitar, or fiddle player to draw crowds so

Pearl was thrilled to ride with Commander John Herrington in the Chickasaw Nation's Annual Meeting Parade on October 4, 2003. Herrington had indicated that Pearl's youthful, pioneering exploits in aviation inspired him, and Pearl was pleased to think that she had motivated an astronaut, especially a Chickasaw. (Courtesy Marlow Chamber of Commerce)

the proprietor could pitch his products. Pearl related her memories of the music that accompanied the shows that came to Marlow, and Teel was "thankful" that he "got an opportunity to sit down and talk with Pearl. She is truly a great lady and a wealth of historic information."[3]

On Saturday, October 4, Pearl was thrilled to participate in the Chickasaw Nation Annual Meeting parade, riding with her friend Commander John Herrington. Pearl was pleased to have him in Oklahoma, where he could be seen and honored by Chickasaws and other American Indians, as well as by the general public. Herrington was happy to participate in the parade and to see Pearl again. The symbolism of the first Chickasaw aviator and the first Chickasaw astronaut riding together was a powerful reminder of the advances in aviation technology that had been made in just over seventy years from Pearl's Curtiss Robin to Herrington's Space Shuttle *Endeavour*.[4]

Later in October, Pearl was honored to accept an invitation from Bob Kemper to serve on the board of directors of a newly formed non-profit organization The Curtiss-Wright Wiley Post Hangar, Inc. This organization was created to reconstruct the original Curtiss-Wright Hangar. First located at the northwest corner of May Avenue and Britton Road in Oklahoma City, the hangar was to be relocated at the Wiley Post airport, a suburb in northwest Oklahoma City. Wiley Post had used the Curtiss-Wright hangar to store the *Winnie Mae,* and there maintenance was performed on the aircraft. The hangar was disassembled in the 1990s and put into storage with the hope of reconstructing it in an appropriate location. Pearl was excited about the goals of the organization, commenting that in Oklahoma "we are too quick to tear down our own history," but her health made it impossible for her to attend many meetings. Nevertheless, Kemper noted that Pearl "had a direct impact on what we were doing and I was in communication with her."[5]

As Pearl approached her eighty-eighth birthday, she must have believed that she would never visit NASA again or receive yet another significant honor for her role in aviation history. If that was the case, she was mistaken. On Thursday, November 6, 2003, the Native American Intertribal Council at the Kennedy Space Center hosted a special program at the Cocoa Village Civic Center titled "Remember the Journey: Strengthen the Circle." The program was a tribute to Pearl's astronaut friend Commander John B. Herrington. Keynote speakers for the program were Governor Bill Anoatubby and Herrington.[6]

Pearl was among eighteen distinguished American Indians whose photos and biographies were published in the special printed program for the event. Among those individuals with whom Pearl was listed were World War II hero Ira Hayes, legendary athlete Jim Thorpe, revered Sioux leader Sitting Bull, famed Nez Perce Chief Joseph, renowned Seminole Chief Osceola, Apache War Chief Geronimo, and highly respected Cherokee Chief Wilma Mankiller. Anoatubby took the opportunity to praise Pearl publicly yet another time, noting that "she has displayed the courage, strength of character and indomitable spirit that is an inspiration to everyone who knows her." Pearl also received a replica of the Space Shuttle *Endeavour,* autographed by Herrington, and it immediately became one of her most prized possessions. She told a reporter for the *Marlow Review* that she hoped to be able to invite Herrington to Marlow in the near future.[7]

Pearl returned from Florida to devastating news. Her faithful companion Bambi had died in her absence. For a number of years, Bambi had been by Pearl's side or at her feet on a daily basis. Pearl had taken her everywhere possible, even having a special safety seat in her car for Bambi so she could look out of the car's windows while belted into her seat. Bambi had contracted diabetes and had the beginnings of kidney failure, so Pearl had been taking special care of her in line with the recommendations of her veterinarian.[8]

Pearl had boarded Bambi with the veterinarian while she was in Florida, knowing that Bambi would receive good care. While Pearl understood that Bambi's health was declining, her death hit Pearl hard. Pearl's cheerful, optimistic outlook on life, which

Pearl returned from a trip to NASA in Florida in November of 2003 to find that her beloved Bambi had died. Pearl's health was deteriorating, and losing her faithful companion was disheartening. This photo from 1999 shows Bambi in her usual spot by Pearl in her easy chair. (Courtesy Pearl Scott Collection)

she had maintained despite her own health problems, was dealt a serious blow. For years, Pearl had visited frequently with her friend Gary Childers about Chickasaw-related matters as well as personal concerns. On numerous occasions in the months following Bambi's death, she broke down and "sobbed" when talking about Bambi and how lonely she was without her faithful friend. Pearl's resolve to overcome her own physical problems was shaken, and, Childers believed, she never completely regained her former zest for life. Bambi's remains were cremated, and Pearl kept her ashes.[9]

Pearl's health was tenuous as she celebrated her eighty-eighth birthday. Her breathing difficulties placed increasing strain on her heart, and she was losing weight. Her mental capacity had not diminished, however. Although somewhat demoralized by the loss of Bambi, in the presence of others she

▼▼▼

Despite her health problems, Pearl was determined to attend the 2004 Annual Will Rogers/Wiley Post Fly-In at the Will Rogers birthplace ranch near Oolagah in northeastern Oklahoma. The event would feature antique aircraft and their pilots from all parts of the United States. Michelle Lefebvre-Carter and the staff of the Will Rogers Memorial Museums made Pearl a special guest of honor, and she addressed the assembled aviators and other participants while sitting in a wheel chair with a huge smile on her face. Later, Lefebvre-Carter presented Pearl a beautifully decorated cake featuring an image of Pearl standing in front of her Curtiss Robin monoplane. Pearl refused to let anyone cut the cake and took it home intact. (Courtesy Will Rogers Memorial Museums)

retained her sense of humor, her easy smile, and her bright eyes. And she retained her determination to be of service to the Chickasaw people. She continued to work effectively as a liaison officer for Governor Anoatubby. As late as March of 2005, Gary Childers, special assistant to Governor Anoatubby, observed that "Every time something is wrong or somebody needs something over on that side of the nation, they call Pearl. And Pearl will take care of it." She continued to be the "number one advocate" for the Marlow area, periodically calling Childers with new ideas for projects and programs.[10]

In addition to her ongoing work for the Chickasaw Nation, Pearl was determined to attend the 2004 Will Rogers/Wiley Post Fly-In. Perhaps she sensed it would be her last opportunity to do so. She knew the travel would be challenging physically, but she wanted to see the vintage airplanes and visit with fellow pilots and aviation buffs. And she was able to do that as a special guest. Although she was frail and used a wheel chair to get around, she was in a great mood. Using a microphone and public address system, she spoke to the assembled crowd from her wheelchair with a smile on her face and a twinkle in her eye. Michelle Lefebvre-Carter, executive director of the Will Rogers Memorial Museums that sponsored the fly-in, presented Pearl with a framed sketch of the last flight of Rogers and Post and a cake with Pearl's picture on it. Pearl was delighted with the artwork and the cake, refusing to allow anyone to cut it so she could take it home intact. Lefebvre-Carter did everything possible to make Pearl feel both welcome and honored, and Pearl had a wonderful time.[11]

Pearl's euphoria over participating in the fly-in was short lived. Her youngest child, Carter Roy, who still resided in Alabama, had been diagnosed with cancer in early 2003. Told that he had approximately six months to live, Carter, with the determination that had characterized him as a bull rider in his youth, fought hard to defeat the disease. He lived eighteen months after receiving the diagnosis, three times longer that expected. His illness hung over Pearl like a dark cloud. She knew the odds were against him, but she maintained hope that he could continue to defy death indefinitely.[12]

About a month before he died in October of 2004, Carter told Pearl by telephone that he had left something for her in the bathroom of her house and for her to go find it when they completed their conversation. Pearl did so and found hanging on a wall in the bathroom a printed poem with a picture of a beautiful rose on an attractive plaque. The poem was titled "Don't Quit." Carter knew that his impending death would devastate his fragile mother, and he hoped the words of the poem would remind her of her personal motto, "Never Give Up," and would help her through her inevitable grief. The final four lines of the poem drove home its message:

> So stick to the fight when
> you're hardest hit,
> It's when things seem worse,
> that you must not quit.[13]

In his final days, Carter seemed ready to die. As a small child, he had received a small, white *Bible* from his Sunday school teacher at the First Methodist Church in Marlow. He had put his name in it and was proud of it. When he got married and was traveling extensively with his work, he asked Pearl to keep the little *Bible* for him. Every few years, he would ask Pearl if she still had his *Bible*, and she would assure him that she indeed had it. Not long before his death, he told his minister that he was "ready to go and meet God. All I have to do is get my little *Bible* and go." The fact that he wanted his *Bible* was related to Pearl, so she sent it to him. He had it with him when he died.[14]

Pearl's religious convictions provided some comfort in that she knew she would see Carter, her parents, Wiley, Roy Scott, and other relatives and friends again after her own death. Nonetheless, the loss of Carter was devastating and seemed to impact Pearl physically. Her appetite increasingly declined until it seemed that she was subsisting on virtually nothing. Already frail, she continued to loose weight. When she commented that "No parent should ever outlive one of their children," the pain in her voice and in her eyes was evident. Several months later in February of 2005, Pearl could sit with Bill and Louise, reminisce about Carter, and chuckle about some of his antics and misadventures as a child. But the pain of his loss endured.[15]

Pearl received her last great honor in that same month. Renowned Chickasaw artist Mike Larsen earlier had proposed to the Chickasaw Nation a special project that would allow him to paint the portraits of twenty-four Chickasaw Elders. The project was approved and Larsen, assisted by his wife Martha, began the project with Pearl as his first subject. The Larsens spent two hours with Pearl and fortunately caught her on an "up" day, although they realized that she was quite tired by the end of the session. They interviewed Pearl, and Martha took numerous photographs from which Larsen would paint her portrait. Pearl talked happily about her life and struck Martha Larsen as a "visionary and a very accomplished person." While Pearl had known many notables such as Wiley Post, Will Rogers, and John Herrington, her pride came from her Chickasaw heritage and her family. "We left feeling as though we had walked through time and gotten a peak at history," Martha Larsen wrote.

Pearl was dealt a devastating blow by the death of her youngest child, Carter, shown here in front of his home in Alabama with his wife, Nita. (Courtesy Pearl Scott Collection)

Mike Larsen appropriately titled Pearl's portrait "Wiley, My Daddy & Me."[16]

In late February, Pearl was asked what her American Indian heritage had meant to her, and she replied, "It has meant everything." Acknowledging that she was "only half" Indian, one-fourth Chickasaw and one-fourth Choctaw, she asserted, "I'm Indian." Although she had been "raised white," Pearl knew many Indian families in her youth and throughout her years of marriage and motherhood. But what bonded her to her Chickasaw heritage were her training and experiences as a community health representative and as a tribal legislator. Pearl's life was greatly enriched by the fact that she discovered and embraced the Chickasaw Nation and its people.[17]

As vital and strong as Pearl's mind remained, her body was weak and failing. Her heart began to fail, and her respiratory difficulties became more acute. In early March she was taken to Integris Baptist Hospital in Oklahoma City and placed in the intensive care unit. Nurse Shirley deJarnette had been told about Pearl's aviation background, and that knowledge proved useful during her first encounter with Pearl. Nurse deJarnette quickly determined that her patient was a "very sweet little lady." As they conversed, it quickly became apparent that Pearl was confused; "she couldn't tell me where she was . . . and was actually trying to get out of the bed." As soon as deJarnette mentioned Wiley Post, however, Pearl laid back in the bed and began telling the nurse about her blind father, Wiley Post, and the joys of flying by the seat of your pants.[18]

Nurse deJarnette and her coworkers were amazed by Pearl's stories. When asked how she had the nerve to actually fly an airplane at such a young age, Pearl replied, "Well, it was just fun." The famed heart transplant pioneer Dr. Nazih Zuhdi

The last significant honor Pearl received was being included in a group of twenty-four Chickasaw elders to be depicted by renowned Chickasaw artist Mike Larsen. Pearl was the first of the elders to have her portrait painted by Larsen. Here the artist is shown visiting with Pearl in her home in preparation for the project. (Photo Courtesy Martha Larsen)

called every day to remind deJarnette that the ICU staff was taking care of "a famous lady." While the nurses and physicians looked upon Pearl as a celebrity, she never acted the part. "You would never know by looking at her or talking to her, because she never called attention to her status or exploits," deJarnette recalled. The nurses would have to "pull her stories out of her," but then "her eyes would light up and she would have a big ol' smile on her when she talked about stuff like that."[19]

Immediately deJarnette noted that Pearl was on oxygen, and the nurse "was praying to God" it would not become necessary to put her on a ventilator. This did not happen because Pearl gave clear instructions that the physicians were not to take extraordinary measures to extend her life. On Sunday, March 27, Pearl "out of the blue" told deJarnette that she "wasn't going to be in this world much longer." The nurse, noting that her condition seemed to be stable, asked, "Why do you say that?" Pearl replied, "I don't know but I am ready to go and I'm not afraid. I've had a good life; I have nothing to complain about." "And then," deJarnette remembered, the next day "she was gone." Not hooked up to machines, Pearl died peacefully, secure in her religious faith. It was, as deJarnette observed, "a dignified death for a dignified lady."[20]

In Pearl's effects was "My Humble Prayer" by Katheryn Eckles, printed in Pearl's own hand. This prayer also was among a variety of other prayers Pearl had clipped from newspapers or magazines. This particular prayer must have held special meaning to Pearl for her to have hand printed it in large script, presumably for easier reading. It read:

> Father, grant me the wisdom
> and the strength and grace to bear
> the daily adversities
> that momentarily causes despair.
> Give me patience and understanding
> to do the things I should,
> and throughout my daily conduct,
> help me do some good.
> Let me not show resentment
> for what other people do,
> but give me the prowess
> to see their point of view.
> When worldly things upset me,
> or sorrows cross my path,
> help me to look behind the clouds,
> and perceive the aftermath.
> Above all, let me recognize
> the urgent needs of others near,
> that I may cooperate in some way,
> until their sun may reappear.
> And always, throughout my life,
> anytime and anywhere,
> let me ever feel thy nearness,
> by the simplicity of prayer.

Also among the clippings of prayers was the following untitled maxim that she had printed: "When you get to the end of your rope, tie a knot in it and hang on." This, of course, was simply another way of expressing the motto she learned from the examples of her father and Wiley Post—"Never Give Up!"[21]

Pearl's funeral was held on Friday, April 1, 2005, at 2 p. m. at the First Methodist Church of Marlow, where her mother had taken her to church as a child, where she had taken her children, and where she had remained a member throughout her life. Officiating was the Reverend Terry Koehn. Louise's son Bill Thompson played a major role in the service as did Chickasaw Governor Bill Anoatubby. It was appropriate for Anoatubby to play a prominent part in the proceedings, for shortly before her death, Pearl observed, "There have been three people that I look up to. That's my daddy, Wiley Post, and Governor Bill. . . . I believed everything they'd say." Many individuals offered stories about Pearl, most of which brought smiles to the faces of the mourners. While it was a sad day for her family and friends, they were reminded of many happy memories of the "feisty" little lady who made aviation history, faithfully served her people, and embraced motherhood with every ounce of energy she could muster.[22]

Anoatubby was particularly eloquent in speaking about Pearl, observing that she "was truly a legend in the history of Oklahoma, the world of aviation and in the Chickasaw Nation." Moreover, he continued, "The legacy she leaves us is one of hope for better days, love for all things and all people and determination to make contributions to the greater good." "She will be missed," he said, "but she will be remembered for all her works. No one will fill Pearl's shoes. . . that would be impossible. Her memory lives on in all that she has done."[23]

In addition to her brother, George, Jr., Pearl had remained proud of her three children, ten grandchildren, seventeen great-grandchildren, two great-great grandchildren, and various other nephews and nieces. Six of her grandchildren--Billy R. Thompson, Guy Scott Thompson, Craig Thompson, Bryan Scott, Bradley Scott, and Carl Scott--served as her pallbearers. Honorary pallbearers included Commander John Herrington, Governor Bill Anoatubby, Governor Overton James, Gary Childers, Representative Ray McCarter, Senator Sam Helton, Harbour Whitaker, Jack

Pearl died peacefully on Monday, March 28, 2005, secure in her religious faith and the knowledge that she had led a full, useful life. Her grave marker in the Marlow cemetery appropriately features the Seal of the Chickasaw Nation and an airplane propeller. (Courtesy Pearl Scott Papers)

Graves, Bill Renfrow, Penn Rabb, Bob Williamson, Dan Williamson, Art Williamson, Bob Hill, Kenny Gilmore, and D. B. Green.[24]

A brief graveside service was held after her funeral, and Pearl was buried in the Marlow Cemetery near George, Sr., Lucy, Opaletta, and Arnetta. Bill and Louise had made arrangements for Bambi's ashes to be placed at Pearl's feet. This was done and Pearl and Bambi were buried together. Pearl had indeed gone from riches to rags to riches in her long, remarkable life. The riches she found in the love of her family, the leadership of the Chickasaw Nation, and the Indian people she helped were more meaningful to her than monetary wealth ever could have been. She long will be remembered in the annals of aviation history and the Chickasaw Nation.[25]

ENDNOTES

▼▼▼

A Note on Sources

Many of the documents that the author used in researching this biography are located either in the Pearl Scott Papers or in the Pearl Scott Collection. The Pearl Scott Papers consist of original documents and photographs in the possession of Pearl Scott's son, Bill Scott, who resides in Boyce Virginia. In this Bibliography, that collection is referred to as PSP.

The Pearl Scott Collection consists of documents and photographs gathered by the author and donated to the Chickasaw Nation Archives, presently housed in the Minko Building, located in the Chickasaw Nation's headquarters complex in Ada, Oklahoma. It is anticipated that this collection will be moved to The Center for the Study of Chickasaw History and Culture in Sulphur, Oklahoma, when that facility becomes operational in 2007 or 2008. This collection is referred to as PSC.

Chapter One

[1] Pearl Scott, "Personal Journal," Pearl Scott Papers, Billy J. Scott, Boyce, Virginia. Pearl Scott Papers hereinafter cited as PSP.

[2] Pearl Scott, "Genealogical Records," PSP.

[3] Ibid.; Joseph Carter Brooks, Email to Paul F. Lambert, August 9, 2005, Pearl Scott Collection, Chickasaw Nation Archives, Ada, Oklahoma. Pearl Scott Collection hereinafter Pearl Scott Collection cited as PSC.

[4] Scott, "Genealogical Records"; Brooks, Email to Paul Lambert, August 9, 2005; U. S. Bureau of the Census, "Twelfth Census of the United States," Schedule No. 1—Population, 1900, Choctaw Nation, Indian Territory.

[5] Scott, "Genealogical Records"; *Marlow Review,* "Ill Only 1 Day: George Carter Died Wednesday," Undated Newspaper Cliping, PSP; Brooks, "Genealogical Information."

[6] Scott, "Personal Journal"; Pearl Scott, "Memories of Marlow... From Then to Now," *Marlow Review,* May 17, 1990, Newspaper Clipping, PSC; Pearl Scott, Interview with Rodger Harris, March 4, 1999, Marlow, Oklahoma, Oral History Collections, Oklahoma Historical Society, Oklahoma City, Oklahoma. A copy of the transcript may be found in PSC.

⁷ Scott, "Personal Journal"; Scott, "Memories of Marlow," June 21, 1990; "Professor Emil Trebing," website for Arkansas School for the Blind, Little Rock, Arkansas, www.arkansasschoofortheblind.org.history.htm.

⁸ Scott, "Memories of Marlow," May 17, 1990; Scott, "Personal Journal"; Scott, Interview with Harris.

⁹ Scott, "Genealogical Records"; Scott, Interview with Harris; Scott, "Memories of Marlow," May 17, 1990.

¹⁰ Scott, "Memories of Marlow," May 17, 1990; Scott, "Personal Journal"; Scott, Interview with Harris"; Pearl Scott, Interview with Paul F. Lambert, February 23, 2005, Marlow, Oklahoma, PSC.

¹¹ Scott, "Genealogical Records."

¹² Scott, "Personal Journal"; Scott, Interview with Harris; Brooks, Email to Lambert, August 9, 2005.

¹³ Wikipedia, a free encyclopedia, "Durant Motors, " Internet Website, http://en.wikipedia.org/wiki/Oakland_Motor_Car; Brooks, Email to Lambert, August 9, 2005.

¹⁴ Scott, "Personal Journal"; Scott, Interview with Harris.

¹⁵ Jack and Betty Graves, Interview with Paul F. Lambert, March 3, 2005, Marlow, Oklahoma, PSC; Scott, "Personal Journal."

¹⁶ Scott, "Personal Journal"; Jack and Betty Graves, Interview with Lambert.

¹⁷ Scott, Interview with Harris; Scott, "Personal Journal."

¹⁸ Scott, "Personal Journal"; Brooks, Email to Lambert, August 9, 2005

¹⁹ Scott, "Personal Journal."

²⁰ Ibid.; Scott, "Memories of Marlow," June 21, 1990; Lonnie Patterson, Interview with Paul F. Lambert, March 3, 2005, Marlow, Oklahoma, PSC.

²¹ Scott, "Memories of Marlow," June 21, 1990.

²² Ibid.; Pearl Scott, Interview with Lambert, February 23, 2005.

²³ Jack and Betty Graves, Interview with Lambert; Pearl Scott, Interview with Lambert, February 23, 2005; Scott, "Personal Journal."

²⁴ Jack and Betty Graves, Interview with Lambert; Pearl Scott, Interview with Lambert, February 23, 2005; Scott, "Personal Journal."

²⁵ Pearl Scott, "Detailed Drawing of Childhood Home," PSP.

²⁶ Scott, "Personal Journal."

²⁷ Ibid.

²⁸ Jack and Betty Graves, Interview with Lambert; Scott, "Memories of Marlow, June 21, 1990; Scott, "Personal Journal."

²⁹ Scott, "Personal Journal"; Scott, "Memories of Marlow, June 21, 1990.

³⁰ Scott, "Personal Journal"; Scott, "Memories of Marlow, June 21, 1990.

³¹ Bill J. Scott, Interview with Paul F. Lambert, April 4, 2005, Marlow, Oklahoma, PSC.

³² Scott, "Personal Journal;" Scott, "Memories of Marlow, May 17, 1990; Paul F. Lambert, Conversation with Debbe Ridley, September 2, 2005, Marlow, Oklahoma.

³³ Scott, "Personal Journal."

▼▼▼

[34] Scott, "Memories of Marlow," June 21, 1990.

[35] Scott, "Personal Journal."

Chapter 2

[1] Scott, "Personal Journal;"; Pearl Scott, Interview with Lambert, February 23, 2005.

[2] Scott, "Personal Journal"; *Marlow Review*, "Willie Wilson is Buried Here," October 24, 1929, Newspaper Clipping, PSP.

[3] Kaye Arthur, "Fitting Tribute to a Courageous War Hero," *Marlow Review*, June 20, 2002, 1B; George Carter, Jr., Beverly Carter, and Kathy Martel, Interview with Paul F. Lambert, April 4, 2005, Marlow, Oklahoma, PSC. Hereinafter cited as George Carter, Jr., Interview with Lambert.

[4] Scott, "Memories of Marlow," May 17, 1990; George Carter, Jr., Interview with Lambert.

[5] George Carter, Jr., Interview with Lambert.

[6] Ibid.

[7] Scott, "Personal Journal."

[8] Ibid.

[9] Ibid.; Scott, "Memories of Marlow," June 7, 1990.

[10] Art and Bob Williamson, Interview with Paul F. Lambert, June 14, 2005, Oklahoma City, Oklahoma City, Oklahoma, PSC.

[11] Scott, "Personal Journal"; Scott, "Memories of Marlow," June 21, 1990; Pearl Scott, Interview with Lambert.

[12] Scott, "Personal Journal"; Scott, Interview with Harris.

[13] Scott, "Personal Journal"; Scott, "Memories of Marlow," May 17, 1990.

[14] Scott, "Memories of Marlow," June 7, 1990.

[15] Scott, "Personal Journal."

[16] Scott, "Memories of Marlow," June 7, 1990; Bill J. Scott, Email to Paul F. Lambert, June 12, 2005, PSC.

[17] Scott, "Memories of Marlow," June 21, 1990; Scott, "Personal Journal."

[18] Scott, "Personal Journal"; Pearl Scott, Interview with Lambert, February 23, 2005.

[19] Scott, "Personal Journal"; Scott, Interview with Harris.

[20] Scott, "Personal Journal"; Pearl Scott, Interview with Lambert, February 23, 2005.

[21] Scott, "Personal Journal."

[22] Scott, Interview with Harris; Scott, "Personal Journal."

[23] Scott, Interview with Harris; Scott, "Personal Journal"; Scott, "Memories of Marlow," June 7, 1990.

[24] Scott, Interview with Harris.

[25] Ibid.

[26] Ibid.

[27] Scott, "Memories of Marlow," May 17, 1990. Scott, "Personal Journal."

Endnotes

[28] Pearl Scott, Interview with Lambert, February 23, 2005; Scott, "Memories of Marlow," 17, 1990; Scott, "Personal Journal."

[29] Scott, "Personal Journal"; Scott, "Memories of Marlow," May 17, 1990.

[30] Scott, "Personal Journal."

[31] Scott, "Personal Journal."; Scott, "Memories of Marlow," May 24, 1990; Pearl Scott, Interview with Harris.

[32] Scott, "Personal Journal."; Scott, "Memories of Marlow," May 17, 1990.

[33] Scott, "Memories of Marlow," May 17, 2005; Scott, "Personal Journal."

[34] Scott, "Memories of Marlow," May 17, 2005; *Marlow Review,* "Marlow Pioneer to relive History," May 29, 2003, P.1.

[35] Scott, "Personal Journal."

[36] Scott, "Memories of Marlow," May 17, 1990

[37] Scott, "Personal Journal."

[38] Ibid.

[39] Pearl Scott, Interview with Lambert, February 23, 2005.

[40] Scott, "Personal Journal."

[41] Scott, "Personal Journal."; Scott, "Memories of Marlow," June 21, 1990.

[42] Scott, "Personal Journal"; Scott, "Memories of Marlow" June 21, 1990.

[43] Scott, "Personal Journal"; Scott, "Memories of Marlow" June 21, 1990.

[44] Scott, "Personal Journal"; Scott, "Memories of Marlow" June 21, 1990.

[45] Bill J. Scott, Email to Lambert, June 12, 2005, PSC,

[46] Scott, "Personal Journal"; Scott, "Memories of Marlow," June 21, 1990.

[47] Scott, "Personal Journal."

[48] Ibid.; Scott, "Memories of Marlow," May 17, 2005.

[49] Scott, "Personal Journal."; Scott, "Memories of Marlow," May 17, 2005.

[50] Scott, "Personal Journal."

Chapter 3

[1] Scott, "Personal Journal."

[2] Ibid.

[3] Ibid.; Scott, "Memories of Marlow," May 17, 1990; Pearl Scott, Interview with Harris.

[4] Pearl Scott, Interview with Lambert, February 23, 2005.

[5] Scott, "Personal Journal."

[6] Scott, "Memories of Marlow," May 17, 1990; Pearl Scott, Interview with Lambert, February, 23, 2005; Scott, Interview with Harris.

[7] Scott, "Memories of Marlow," May 17, 1990; Pearl Scott, Interview with Lambert, February, 23, 2005; Scott, Interview with Harris.

[8] Scott, "Personal Journal."

[9] Ibid.

[10] Ibid.; Scott, Interview with Harris.

[11] Scott, Interview with Harris; Scott, "Personal Journal."

[12] Scott, "Personal Journal"; Pearl Scott, Interview with Lambert, February 23, 2005.

[13] ClassicCars.com, "William C. Durant, 1861-1947," www.classicar.com/articles/william-durant.

[14] George Carter, Jr., Interview with Lambert.

[15] Scott, Interview with Harris; Pearl Scott, Interview with Lambert, February 23, 2005.

[16] Scott, Interview with Harris; Scott, "Personal Journal."

[17] Scott, "Memories of Marlow," May 17, 1990; Scott, "Personal Journal"; Scott, Interview with Harris.

[18] Scott, "Memories of Marlow"; May 17, 1990; Scott, "Personal Journal."

[19] Bob Burke, *From Oklahoma to Eternity: The Life of Wiley Post and the Winnie Mae* (Oklahoma Heritage Association, Oklahoma City, Oklahoma, 1998), 25-26.

[20] Burke, *Wiley Post*, 30-36.

[21] Burke, *Wiley Post*, passim.

[22] Scott, "Personal Journal," Scott, "Memories of Marlow," May 17, 1990; Mort Karman, "Flying High," *Duncan Banner*, September 30, 2002, 5A; Scott, Interview with Harris; Pearl Scott, Interview with Lambert, February 23, 2005.

[23] Scott, "Personal Journal"; Scott, "Memories of Marlow," May 17, 1990; Karman, "Flying High"; Scott, Interview with Harris.

[24] Scott, "Personal Journal"; Scott, Interview with Harris; Burke, *Wiley Post*, 39.

[25] Scott, Interview with Harris; Pearl Scott, Interview with Lambert, February 23, 2005.

[26] Ibid.; Burke, *Wiley Post*, 155-164.

[27] Scott, Interview with Harris; Pearl Scott, Interview with Lambert, February 23, 2005.

[28] Scott, Interview with Harris; Pearl Scott, Interview with Lambert, February 23, 2005.

[29] Scott, Interview with Harris; Pearl Scott, Interview with Lambert, February 23, 2005; Scott, "Personal Journal."

[30] Scott, Interview with Lambert, February 23, 2005; *Marlow Review*, "Air Port Plans Call for First Class Project,"October 8, 1929, Newspaper Clipping, PSP.

[31] Scott, Interview with Lambert, February 23, 2005; *Marlow Review*, "Air Port Plans Call for First Class Project."

[32] Scott, Interview with Harris; Scott, "Personal Journal"; Karman, "Flying High."

[33] Pilotfriend.com, "Curtiss Robin," www.pilotfriend.com/Century-of-flight/racing/aircraft; Robert L. Osborn, "The Curtiss 'Robin'," *Aviation*, May 21, 1928. Reproduced in www.airminded.net; Logbook for Pearl Carter's Curtiss Robin Airplane, PSP.

[34] National Museum of the United States Air Force, "Curtiss OX-5 Engine," www.wpafb.af.mil/museum/engines/eng15.htm; Bob Richardson, "The OX-5 Pioneers," *Hangar Flying*, PSP.

[35] Holcomb's Aerodrome, "Curtiss OX-5 Robin Specifications," www.airminded.net/curtrob/curtrob.html.

Endnotes

[36] *Southwest Aviator*, "Alexander Eaglerock Biplane," www.swaviator.com/html/is-sueAM00/eaglerock AM00.html, online version of *Southwest Aviator* magazine; Pearl Scott, Interview with Lambert, February 23, 2005; Scott, "Personal Journal."

Chapter 4

[1] Scott, Interview with Harris; Scott, "Personal Journal."

[2] Scott, Interview with Harris; Scott, "Personal Journal."

[3] Scott, Interview with Harris; Scott, "Personal Journal."; Pearl Scott, Interview with Lambert, February 23, 2005.

[4] Bill Porter, "Wiley Post's Student Still Loves to Fly," Unidentified newspaper clipping, PSP; Scott, "Personal Journal."

[5] Scott, "Personal Journal"; Eula Pearl Carter, Student Pilot's Permit, PSP.

[6] Scott, "Personal Journal"; Eula Pearl Carter, Student Pilot's Permit, PSP.

[7] Scott, "Personal Journal."

[8] Scott, "Memories of Marlow," May 24, 1990; Scott, "Personal Journal."

[9] Scott, "Personal Journal."

[10] Scott, "Memories of Marlow," June 21, 1990; George Carter, Jr., Interview with Lambert.

[11] Scott, Interview with Harris; Pearl Scott, Interview with Lambert, February 23, 2005; Scott, "Memories of Marlow," May 24, 2005.

[12] Scott, Interview with Harris.

[13] Burke, *Wiley Post*, 106-108, 165-166.

[14] Pearl Scott, Interview with Lambert, February 23, 2005; Scott, "Memories of Marlow," May 24. 1990; Scott, "Personal Journal."

[15] Pearl Scott, Interview with Lambert, February 23, 2005; Scott, "Personal Journal"; Bob Kemper, Email to Paul Lambert, May 1, 2005, PSC.

[16] Pearl Scott, Interview with Lambert, February 23, 2005; Scott, "Personal Journal"; Scott, "Memories of Marlow," May 24, 1990; Pat Reeder, "It's a wonderful life," *Claremore Daily Progress*, August 4, 2004, 1.

[17] Bob Kemper, Interview with Paul F. Lambert, April 6, 2005, Oklahoma City, Oklahoma, PSC; Kemper, Email to Lambert, May 1, 2005, PSC.

[18] Scott, "Personal Journal."

[19] Scott, "Memories of Marlow," May 24, 1990.

[20] *Marlow Review*, "Easter Surprise," Undated Newspaper Clipping, PSC; *Marlow Review*, "Flying Circus During Fourth of July Stunts," 1929, Undated Newspaper Clipping, PSP; *Marlow Review*, "No One Claims Airplane Ride," April 4, 1929, Newspaper Clipping, PSP.

[21] *Marlow Review*, "Flight Made To Ada," Undated Newspaper Clipping, PSP.

[22] Pearl Scott, Interview with Lambert, February 23, 2005; Scott, "Personal Journal."

[23] Pearl Scott, Interview with Lambert, February 23, 2005; Scott, "Personal Journal."

[24] *Marlow Review*, "And the Speed Cops Couldn't Do Anything," Undated Press Clipping, PSP.

[25] Unidentified Newspaper Clipping, "Man In Oklahoma Pilots Own Plane Though Sightless," PSP.

[26] *Marlow Review*, "Takes Plane To Game," Undated Newspaper Clipping, PSP.

[27] Pearl Scott, "History of the Marlow School Band," *Marlow Review*, Undated Newspaper Clipping, PSP.

[28] Ibid.

[29] Ibid.; Scott, Interview with Harris.

[30] Scott, "Personal Journal"; PS, "Memories of Marlow," May 17, 1990.

[31] Scott, "Memories of Marlow," May 17, 1990.

[32] Scott, Interview with Harris.

[33] Unidentified newspaper clipping, PSP.

Chapter 5

[1] Scott, "Personal Journal"; Scott, Interview with Harris.

[2] Scott, "Personal Journal"; Scott, Interview with Harris.

[3] Scott, "Personal Journal"; Beverly Louise Scott, Interview with Paul F. Lambert, April 1, 2005, Marlow, Oklahoma, PSC.

[4] Scott, "Personal Journal"; Scott, Interview with Harris; Pearl Scott, Interview with Lambert, February 23, 2005.

[5] Scott, "Memories of Marlow," May 24, 1990.

[6] Scott, "Personal Journal."

[7] Ibid.

[8] Bill Scott, Email to Paul F. Lambert, August 5, 2005, PSC.

[9] *Marlow Review*, "Made Flying Trip to Wilson Last Sunday," Undated Newspaper Clipping, PSP; *Marlow Review*, "Will Fly to Dallas," Undated Newspaper Clipping, PSP.

[10] Scott, Interview with Harris.

[11] English Department, University of Illinois, Urbana-Champaign, "About the Dust Bowl," www.english.uiuc.edu/maps/depression/dustbowl.htm.

[12] Ibid.; Scott, "Personal Journal."

[13] Scott, "Personal Journal."

[14] Ibid.; Scott, "Memories of Marlow," May 17, 1990.

[15] Scott, "Personal Journal."; Scott, "Memories of Marlow," May 17, 1990; Pearl Scott, Interview with Paul F. Lambert, January 31, 2005, Marlow, Oklahoma, PSC.

[16] Scott, "Personal Journal"; Scott, "Memories of Marlow," May 17, 1990.

[17] Scott, "Personal Journal"; Scott, "Memories of Marlow," May 17, 1990.

[18] Scott, "Personal Journal"; Scott, "Memories of Marlow," May 17, 1990.

[19] Louise Scott Thompson, Bill Scott, and Pearl Scott, Interview with Paul F. Lambert, January 31, 2005, Marlow, Oklahoma, PSC.

[20] Thompson, Scott, and Scott, Interview with Lambert; Scott, "Personal Journal."

[21] Thompson, Scott, and Scott, Interview with Lambert.

Endnotes

[22] Scott, "Personal Journal"; Scott, Interview with Harris; Kemper, Email to Lambert, May 9, 2005, PSC.

[23] Roy P. Stewart, "Country Boy," *The Oklahoma Cowman*, January 1985, 8.

[24] Scott, "Personal Journal"; Scott, Interview with Harris; Pearl Scott, Interview with Lambert, February 23, 2005.

[25] Burke, *Wiley Post*, 197-205.

[26] Ibid., 205-209.

[27] Pearl Scott, Interview with Lambert, February 23, 2005.

[28] Scott, "Personal Journal."

[29] Ibid.

[30] Ibid.

[31] *Marlow Rewiew'* "Ill Only 1 Day"; Scott, "Personal Journal."

[32] *Marlow Rewiew'* "Ill Only 1 Day.

[33] Scott, "Personal Journal."

[34] Ibid.

[35] Ibid.; Pearl Scott, Interview with Lambert, February 23,2005.

[36] State of Oklahoma, Stephens County, "Probate Filing," In the Matter of G. W. Carter, deceased, February 25, 1937.

[37] Scott, "Memories of Marlow," May 17, 1990; Scott, "Personal Journal."

[38] State of Oklahoma, Estate Tax Division, "Order Exempting Estate From Payment of Estate and Inheritance Taxes," Estate of G. W. Carter, deceased, Probate No. 1776; State of Oklahoma, Stephens County, State of Oklahoma, Stephens County, "Final Decree," In the Matter of the Estate of G. W. Carter, Deceased, Probate No. 1776; State of Oklahoma, Stephens County, "Final Account of Administrator or Executor For Distribution and Discharge," Probate No. 1776.

[39] *Lucy Hodges v. Roy Hodges*, "Divorce Petition," In the District Court of Stephens County, Oklahoma, No. 13111, October 14, 1940.

[40] 65 Okla. Cr. 277, 85 P.2d 443, Hodges v. State, Case No. A-9401, December 16, 1938.

[41] 66 Oklahoma. Cr. 422, 92 P.2d 590, Hodges v State, Case No. A-9401, July 7, 1939.

[42] Lucy Hodges vs. Roy Hodges, "Divorce Petition," In the District Court of Stephens County, No. 13111, October 14, 1940.

[43] Ibid.

[44] Bill Scott, Email to Lambert, August 5, 2005, PSC.

[45] Ibid.; Bill Scott, email to Lambert, June 17, 2005, PSC.

Chapter 6

[1] Scott, "Memories of Marlow," June 7, 1990; Pearl Scott, Interview with Lambert, February 23, 2005.

[2] Scott, "Memories of Marlow," June 7, 1990.

[3] Ibid.

[4] Scott, "Memories of Marlow," June 21, 1990.

▼▼▼

[5] George Carter, Jr., Interview with Lambert.

[6] Ibid.

[7] Paul F. Rabb, Interview with Lambert, March 23, 2005, Oklahoma City, Oklahoma, PSC; Jack and Betty Graves, Interview with Lambert.

[8] Billy J. Scott, "Reflections on Pearl," Unpublished Notes, PSP.

[9] Thompson, Scott, and Scott, Interview with Lambert, January 31, 2005; Thompson, Scott, and Scott, Interview with Lambert, February 1, 2005.

[10] Thompson, Scott, and Scott, Interview with Lambert, January 31, 2005.

[11] Ibid.; Rabb, Interview with Lambert.

[12] Thompson, Scott, and Scott, Interview with Lambert, January 31, 2005; Rabb, Interview with Lambert.

[13] Thompson, Scott, and Scott, Interview with Lambert, January 31, 2005.

[14] Ibid.

[15] Bill Scott, "Reflections on Pearl."

[16] Ibid.; Scott, "Memories of Marlow," June 21, 1990.

[17] Thompson, Scott, and Scott, Interview with Lambert, January 31, 2005; Thompson, Scott, and Scott, Interview with Lambert, February 1, 2005.

[18] Thompson, Scott, and Scott, Interview with Lambert, January 31, 2005; Thompson, Scott, and Scott, Interview with Lambert, February 1, 2005.

[19] Thompson, Scott, and Scott, Interview with Lambert, February 1, 2005.

[20] Ibid.

[21] Ibid.; Bill Scott, Email to Lambert, May 4, 2005, PSC.

[22] Bill Scott, Email to Lambert, May 4, 2005, PSC.

[23] Thompson, Scott, and Scott, Interview with Lambert, February 1, 2005.

[24] Ibid.

[25] Ibid.

[26] Bill Scott, Email to Lambert, May 4, 2005, PSC; Bill Scott, Email to Paul Lambert, May 12, 2005, PSC.

[27] Thompson, Scott, and Scott, Interview with Lambert, February 1, 2005.

[28] Ibid.

[29] Ibid.

[30] Ibid.

[31] Ibid.

[32] Ibid.

[33] Jack and Betty Graves, Interview with Lambert; Thompson, Scott, and Scott, Interview with Lambert, February 1, 2005.

[34] Jack and Betty Graves, Interview with Lambert; Thompson, Scott, and Scott, Interview with Lambert, February 1, 2005.

Endnotes

[35] Ibid.; Scott, "Memories of Marlow," June 7, 1990.

[36] Scott, "Memories of Marlow," June 7, 1990.

[37] Thompson, Scott, and Scott, Interview with Lambert, January 31, 2005.

Chaper 7

[1] Thompson, Scott, and Scott, Interview with Lambert, February 1, 2005.

[2] George Carter, Jr., Interview with Lambert; George Carter, Jr., Letter to Bryan and Brad Scott, September 24, 1983, PSP; Arthur, "Fitting Tribute."

[3] Keith Long, "George Carter Recalls Omaha Landing," *Marlow Review*, Undated Newspaper Clipping, PSP; George Carter, Jr., Letter to Bryan and Brad Scott.

[4] Long, "George Carter Recalls"; George Carter, Jr., Letter to Bryan and Brad Scott.

[5] Long, "George Carter Recalls"; George Carter, Jr., Letter to Bryan and Brad Scott.

[6] Ibid.; Bill Scott, Email to Lambert, June 12, 2005, PSC.

[7] Long, "George Carter Recalls"; George Carter, Jr., Letter to Bryan and Brad Scott; Arthur, "Fitting Tribute"; George Carter, Jr., Interview with Lambert.

[8] Long, "George Carter Recalls."

[9] Ibid.; Letter from George Carter, Jr., to Bryan and Brad Scott; Arthur, "Fitting Tribute."

[10] Thompson, Scott, and Scott, Interview with Lambert, January 31, 2005; Rabb, Interview with Lambert.

[11] Thompson, Scott, and Scott, Interview with Lambert, January 31, 2005.

[12] Ibid.

[13] Rabb, Interview with Lambert; Thompson, Scott, and Scott, Interview with Lambert, January 31, 2005; *Marlow Review*, "Local Couple Betrothal Told," Undated Newspaper Clipping, PSP.

[14] Thompson, Scott, and Scott, Interview with Lambert, January 31, 2005.

[15] Ibid.; Rabb, Interview with Lambert.

[16] Penn Rabb, *Tomahawk and Peace Pipe: The 179th Infantry Regiment*, (Oklahoma Heritage Association, Oklahoma City, Oklahoma, 2000), 67; Thompson, Scott, and Scott, Interview with Lambert, January 31, 2005; Rabb, Interview with Lambert; Pearl Scott, Interview with Lambert, February, 23, 2005.

[17] Thompson, Scott, and Scott, Interview with Lambert, January 31, 2005; Scott, "Memories of Marlow," May 24, 1990.

[18] Department of Defense, "Form 214, Honorable Discharge Papers for George Carter, Jr.," February 27, 1952, PSP; War Department, "Form 53, Enlisted Records and Report of Separation for George Carter, Jr.," No Date, PSC; George Carter, Jr., Interview with Lambert.

[19] George Carter, Jr., Interview with Lambert; *Boston Globe*, "Hill 303 Massacre," June 25, 1999, A2, Reproduced on the Kortegaard Engineering website www.rt66.com/~korteng/SmallArms/hill303.htm.

[20] George Carter, Jr., Interview with Lambert.

[21] Ibid.; Long, "George Carter Recalls" Arthur, "Fitting Tribute."

[22] George Carter, Jr., Interview with Lambert.

[23] Ibid.

[24] Ibid.; Arthur, "Fitting Tribute"; _____ Rogers, Adjutant General, Department of the Army, Letter to George Carter, Jr., December 8, 1950, PSP; *Oklahoma City Times*, "State War Heroes Are Decorated in Fort Sill Ceremony," Undated Press Clipping, PSP.

[25] George Carter, Jr., Interview with Lambert; Arthur, "Fitting Tribute."

[26] Rabb, Interview with Lambert; Bill Scott, Email to Lambert, May 10, 2005, PSP.

[27] Rabb, Interview with Lambert; Bill Scott, Email to Lambert, May 10, 2005, PSP.

[28] Rabb, *Tomahawk and Piece Pipe*, 87.

[29] Ibid, 103-104; Bill Scott, Email to Lambert, May 10, 2005.

[30] Rabb, *Tomahawk and Piece Pipe*, 87; Bill Scott, Email to Lambert, May 10, 2005.

[31] Rabb, *Tomahawk and Peace Pipe*, 104-105.

[32] Ibid, 105-107.

[33] Ibid, 134-135.

[34] Thompson, Scott, and Scott, Interview with Lambert, January 31, 2005.

[35] Rabb, *Tomahawk and Peace pipe*, 189.

[36] Bill Scott, Email to Lambert, May 17, 2005, PSP.

[37] Ibid.

[38] Ibid.

[39] Thompson, Scott, and Scott, Interview with Lambert, January 31, 2005; Rabb, Interview with Lambert.

Chapter 8

[1] Thompson, Scott, and Scott, Interview with Lambert, January 31, 05.

[2] Ibid.; *Marlow Review*, "Pickett's Summer Camp," July 17, 2003, 4.

[3] Thompson, Scott, and Scott, Interview with Lambert, January 31, 2005; *Marlow Review*, "Pickett's Summer Camp."

[4] Thompson, Scott, and Scott, Interview with Lambert, January 31, 2005; *Marlow Review*, "Pickett's Summer Camp."

[5] Thompson, Scott, and Scott, Interview with Lambert, January 31, 2005; *Marlow Review*, "Library Donation by Scott is Tribute to City, Mother," August 1, 1991, Undated Press Clipping, PSP.

[6] Bill Scott, "Reflections on Pearl."

[7] Thompson, Scott, and Scott, Interview with Lambert, January 31, 2005; *Marlow Review* "Library Donation by Scott is Tribute to City, Mother."

[8] Thompson, Scott, and Scott, Interview with Lambert, February 1, 2005.

[9] Bill Scott, Email to Lambert, August, 5, 2005, PSP.

[10] Beverly Louise Scott and Louise Thompson, Interview with Paul F. Lambert, April 1, 2005, PSC. Hereinafter cited as Scott and Thompson, Interview with Lambert.

Endnotes

[11] Thompson, Scott, and Scott, Interview with Lambert, February 1, 2005.

[12] Ibid.

[13] Scott, "Personal Journal."; Thompson, Scott, and Scott, Interview with Lambert, January 31, 2005; Scott, "Memories of Marlow," June 21, 1990.

[14] Pearl Scott, Interview with Lambert, February 23, 2005; Thompson, Scott, and Scott, Interview with Lambert, January 31, 2005; Pearl Scott, Interview with Lambert, February, 1, 2005.

[15] Pearl Scott, Interview with Lambert, February 1, 2005.

[16] Ibid.; Pearl Scott, Interview with Lambert, February 23, 2005; Bill Scott, Email to Lambert, May 17, 2005, PSP.

[17] Thompson, Scott, and Scott, Interview with Lambert, February 1, 2005.

[18] Rabb, Interview with Lambert.

[19] Scott, "Personal Journal"; George Carter, Jr., Interview with Lambert.

[20] Scott, "Personal Journal."

[21] Ibid.

[22] Ibid.

[23] Scott and Thompson, Interview with Lambert.

[24] Pearl Scott, Undated Letter to Bill Scott, PSP.

[25] Ibid.

[26] Thompson, Scott, and Scott, Interview with Lambert, January 31, 2005; George Carter, Jr., Interview with Lambert.

[27] Thompson, Scott, and Scott, Interview with Lambert, January 31, 2005; George Carter, Jr., Interview with Lambert.

[28] Pearl Scott, Interview with Lambert, February 23, 2005; Scott, "Personal Journal."

[29] Scott, "Personal Journal."

[30] Bill Foster, "Wiley Post's Student Still Loves to Fly," Unidentified Newspaper Clipping, PSP; *Oklahoma City Times*, "Grandmother Definitely Has Head in the Clouds," November 8, 1979, 1D.

[31] Scott, "Personal Journal"; *Oklahoma City Times,* "Grandmother Definitely has Head in the Clouds."

Chapter 9

[1] Scott and Thompson, Interview with Lambert.

[2] *Eula Pearl Kizarr v. A. J. Kizarr*, Petition for Divorce No. JFD-72-242, In the District Court of Stephens County, Oklahoma, August 15, 1972, PSC.

[3] Richard Green, "A Political History of the Chickasaw Nation," Unpublished Manuscript, Chapter 7, 1, CNA.

[4] Ibid., Chapter 7, 1-2.

[5] Ibid., Chapter 7, 2; Pat Woods, Interview with Paul F. Lambert, Ada, Oklahoma, March 7, 2005, PSC.

[6] Woods, Interview with Lambert; Scott, Interview with Harris; Scott, "Personal Journal."

[7] Scott, Interview with Harris; Printed Program, "Community Health Representative Graduation Ceremony," Desert Willow Training Center, November 21, 1972, PSP.

[8] Scott, Interview with Harris.

[9] Ibid.

[10] Printed Program, "Community Health Representative Graduation Ceremony," PSP

[11] "List of Work Shops Attended by Pearl Scott Kizarr," PSP; Pearl Scott, Interview with Lambert, February 23, 2005; "Pearl Kizarr C.H.R. Attends Seminar at Eastern Okla. State," *Marlow Review*, Undated Press Clipping, PSP.

[12] Bill J. Anoatubby, Interview with Paul F. Lambert, March 7, 2005, Ada, Oklahoma, PSC; Gary Childers, Interview with Paul F. Lambert, March 7, 2005, Ada, Oklahoma, PSC; Pearl Scott, Interview with Lambert, February 23, 2005.

[13] Pearl Scott, Interview with Lambert, February 23, 2005.

[14] Scott and Thompson, Interview with Lambert; Pearl Scott, Interview with Lambert, February 23, 2005.

[15] Pearl Scott, Interview with Lambert, February 23, 2005.

[16] Scott and Thompson, Interview with Lambert.

[17] Anoatubby, Interview with Lambert.; Scott and Thompson, Interview with Lambert; Childers, Interview with Lambert.

[18] Scott, "Personal Journal"; George Carter, Jr., Interview with Lambert; Scott and Thompson, Interview with Lambert.

[19] Anoatubby, Interview with Lambert; *Marlow Review*, "Free Vaccination for Dogs With Indian Owners," July 22, 1976, Newspaper Clipping, PSP.

[20] Pearl Scott, Interview with Lambert, February 23, 2005.

[21] Woods, Interview with Lambert; Pearl Scott, Interview with Lambert, February, 23, 2005.

[22] Ibid.; Scott, Interview with Harris.; Pearl Scott, "List of Chickasaw Activities," PSP.

[23] Undated Newspaper Advertisement, *Marlow Review*, PSP.

[24] *Duncan Banner*, "Chickasaw Center Clothing Room Hours Set Friday," January 27, 1977, Newspaper Clipping, PSP.

[25] *Marlow Review*, "Letter to the People!" January 27, 1977, Newspaper Clipping, PSP.

[26] *Duncan Banner*, "Hospital Transportation Set for Indians," January 30, 1977, Newspaper Clipping, PSP.

[27] Scott, "Memories of Marlow," May 24, 1990.

[28] *Marlow Review*, "Rubbing Elbows with Mr. Speaker," February 17, 2000, 1B.

[29] *Duncan Banner*, "Group Retraces Historic 'Trail of Tears'," July 9, 1978, Undated Newspaper Clipping, PSP; Undated Newspaper Clipping, "Pearl Kizarr Makes 1978 'Trail of Tears' Tour," PSP.

[30] *Duncan Banner*; "Group Retraces Historic 'Trail of Tears'," Undated Newspaper Clipping, "Pearl Kizarr Makes 1978 'Trail of Tears' Tour," PSP.

[31] *Duncan Banner*; "Group Retraces Historic 'Trail of Tears'," Undated Newspaper Clip-

ping, "Pearl Kizarr Makes 1978 'Trail of Tears' Tour," PSP.

[32] *Duncan Banner;* "Group Retraces Historic 'Trail of Tears'," Undated Newspaper Clipping, "Pearl Kizarr Makes 1978 'Trail of Tears' Tour," PSP.

[33] *Marlow Review*, "'Flying Grandmother' Mrs. Kizarr Earns Honor," December 21, 1978, Newspaper Clipping, PSP.

[34] *Duncan Banner*, "Pearl Kizarr Named Nutrition Specialist," October 29, 1978, Newspaper Clipping, PSP.

[35] Ibid.

[36] Kenneth Neill, "The Lost Tribe," M*emphis Magazine*, December 1979, 57-58.

[37] Ibid.

[38] Scott and Thompson, Interview with Lambert.

[39] Ibid.; George Carter, Jr., Interview with Lambert.

[40] *Eula Pearl Kizarr v. A. J. Kizarr*, Petition for Divorce No. JFD-79-498, In the District Court of Stephens County, Oklahoma, December 18, 1979; *Eula Pearl Kizarr v. A. J. Kizarr*, Decree of Divorce, In the District Court of Stephens County, Oklahoma, January 7, 1980, PSC.

[41] *Chickasaw Times*, "Pearl Kizarr Retires as Health Employee," Undated Newspaper Clipping, PSP; Overton James, Letter to Pearl Scott, May 5, 1980, PSP; Anoatubby, Interview with Lambert; Woods, Interview with Lambert; Bill J. Anoatubby, Email to Lambert, July 17, 2005, PSC.

[42] D. B. Green, Interview with Paul F. Lambert, March 3, 2005, Marlow, Oklahoma, PSC.

[43] *Chickasaw Times,* "Pearl Kizarr Retires as Health Employee."

Chapter 10

[1] Scott, Interview with Harris.

[2] Green, "Political History," *Passim.*

[3] Ibid., Part IV, 7-18; Richard Green, Email to Lambert, June 6, 2005, PSC.

[4] Richard Green, Email to Lambert. June 6, 2005, PSC; *Chickasaw Times*, "The Chickasaw Nation. . . Sovereign and Progressive," Undated Newspaper Clipping, PSC.

[5] Pearl Scott, Interview with Lambert, February 23, 2005; Anoatubby, Interview with Lambert; *Chickasaw Times*, "Overton James," October 1983, 6; *Chickasaw Times*, "Bill Anoatubby," October 1983, 6.

[6] *Chickasaw Times*, "Pearl Kizarr Scott," October 1983, 9.

[7] Pearl Scott, "Letter to Pickens District Voters," *Marlow Review*, Undated Newspaper Clipping, PSP.

[8] Gary Childers, "Democracy in the Chickasaw Nation: Post-statehood Elections, 1907-2003," Unpublished Manuscript, Chickasaw Nation Archives, 6.

[9] *Chickasaw Times*, "T. S. Colbert," October, 1983, 10.

[10] *Marlow Review*, "Thank You," October 13, 1983, 3; Scott, "Letter to Pickens County Voters."

[11] Overton James and Bill Anoatubby, "Open Letter to Chickasaw Voters," PSP.

[12] *Marlow Review*, "Marlow Native Vying for Chickasaw Seat," November 3, 1983, Newspaper Clipping, PSP.

[13] *Marlow Review*, "Scott Wins Chickasaw Council Seat, November 17, 1983, Undated Newspaper Clipping, PSP; Overton "Buck" Cheadle, Letter to Pearl Scott, November 7, 1983, PSP.

[14] Pearl Scott, Interview with Lambert, February 23, 2005; Childers, Interview with Lambert.

[15] Scott and Thompson, Interview with Lambert; Childers, Interview with Lambert.

[16] Official Minutes of the Chickasaw Tribal Legislature, November 1983, Chickasaw Nation Headquarters. Hereinafter cited as Official Minutes.

[17] Ibid.; Official Minutes, 1983-1985.

[18] Official Minutes, November 18, 1983.

[19] Ibid.; Robert Stephens, quoted in Green, "Political History," Part V, Chapter 1, 6.

[20] *Marlow Review*, "Southwest Choctaws To Meet Tuesday," December 1, 1983, Newspaper Clipping, PSP; Lebanon Senior Citizens Center, "Community Meeting Notice," March 14, 1984, PSP.

[21] Official Minutes, September 21, 1984; *Chickasaw Times*, "Tribal Court Petition Received," Undated Newspaper Clipping, PSP; Childers, Interview with Lambert.

[22] George E. Haddaway, Letter to Pearl Scott, February 29, 1984, PSP.

[23] Official Minutes, August 23, 1985.

[24] Green, "Political History," Part V, Chapter 3, 7-8.

[25] Overton James, "Good News Not Often Presented," *Chickasaw Times*, May 1984, 3.

[26] Official Minutes, July 19, 1984.

[27] Ibid.

[28] Ibid., November 18, 1984.

[29] Ibid., September 21, 1984; *Chickasaw Times*, "Tribal Court Petition Received," October 1984, 6; Official Minutes, November 18, 1984.

[30] *Chickasaw Times*, "Gov. James Denies Charges," March 1985, 2; Green, "Political History, Part V, Chapter I, 9.

[31] Green, "Political History," Part V, Chapter 1, 8-17.

[32] Ibid., Part V, Chapter 1, 17-19 and Chapter IV, 1-3.

[33] Ibid., Part. V, Chapter. 4, 12; *Chickasaw Times*, "Legislature Elects Officers," November 1985, 2; "Annual Meeting Held at Byng," *Chickasaw Times*, Undated Newspaper Clipping, PSP.

[34] *Marlow Review*, "Chickasaw Meeting Attended by Scott," October 10, 1985, Newspaper Clipping, PSP; *Marlow Review*, "Scott Attends Inter-Tribal Meetings," October 31, 1985, Newspaper Clipping, PSP.

[35] Green, "Political History," Part V, Chapter 4, 15-17, Chapter 5, 1.

[36] Ibid., Part V, Chapter 3, 1.

[37] Ibid., Part V, Chapter 3, 4-5; Official Minutes, January 1985.

Endnotes

[38] Green, "Political History," Part V, Chapter 3, 5-7; *Chickasaw Times*, "Tribal Court Rules Act 'Null and Void'," July 1986, 2; Official Minutes, February 1986.

[39] Green, "Policital History," Part V, Chapter 3, 7-8; Kim Alyce Marks, "Death of Tribal Paper Draws Fire," *The Sunday Oklahoman*, September 28, 1986, Section A, 16; Official Minutes, August 15, 1986.

[40] Official Minutes, August 28, 1986.

[41] *Chickasaw Times*, "Dear Readers," August-September 1986, 12.

[42] Marks, "Death of Tribal Paper Draws Fire"; "Chickasaw Legislators Present the Facts," PSP.

[43] *Chickasaw Times*, "Excerpt from Chickasaw Times Bill. . . ," January 1987, 4; Green, "Political History," Part V, Chapter 3, 10-11.

[44] Overton James, "Report to Chickasaw Tribal Legislature," Official Minutes, January 16, 1987; Bill J. Anoatubby, "Lt. Governor's Overview Report to the Tribal Legislature," Official Minutes, January 16, 1987; Bill Anoatubby, "New Year Brings a Welcome Friend," *Chickasaw Times*, January 1987, 3.

[45] Official Minutes, March 20, 1987.

[46] Ibid.

[47] Ibid., May 15, 1987; Billy Mussett, "Legislator Accuses Colleagues of Abusing Travel Claims," *Ada Evening News*, Undated Press Clipping, PSP.

[48] Official Minutes, June 19, 1987.

[49] Ibid.

[50] Billy Mussett, "Travel Claims Defended; Salary Levels Tabled," Ada Evening News, July 19, 1987, 3A; Official Minutes, July 17, 1987.

[51] Official Minutes, August 21, 1987.

[52] Green, "Political History," Part V, Chapter 4, 5-7.

[53] Ibid., Part V, Chapter 4, 6-7; Pearl Scott, Interview with Lambert, February 23, 2005.

[54] Pearl Scott, Interview with Lambert, February 23, 2005; Chickasaw Times, "Candidates for Pickens District Legislator Seat No. 2," Election Special, 1987, 8.

[55] *Chickasaw Times,* "Candidates for the Pickens District Legislator Seat No. 2," Election Special 1987, 8, 10.

[56] Ibid.

[57] Pearl Scott Campaign Brochure, "My Dear Chickasaw Friends," PSP.

[58] *Marlow Review*, "Scott seeking Re-election to Chickasaw Legislature," May 7, 1987, Newspaper Clipping, PSP.

[59] Childers, "Democracy in the Chickasaw Nation," 9.

[60] Ibid., Official Minutes, October 1, 1987.

Chapter 11

[1] Joseph C. Brooks, Email to Lambert, June 17, 2005, PSC; Joseph C. Brooks, Telephone Conversation with Lambert, June 10, 2005; *Chickasaw Times*, "Obituary for Arnetta Brooks," March 1988, 10.

[2] Joseph C. Brooks, Email to Lambert, June 10, 2005, PSC; Joseph C. Brooks, Email to Lambert, June 17, 2005, PSC; Joseph C. Brooks, Telephone Conversation with Lambert, June 10, 2005.

[3] Joseph C. Brooks, Email to Lambert, June 10, 2005, PSC; Joseph C. Brooks, Email to Lambert, June 17, 2005, PSC; Joseph C. Brooks, Telephone Conversation with Lambert, June 10, 2005.

[4] Joseph C. Brooks, Email to Lambert, June 10, 2005, PSC; Joseph C. Brooks, Email to Lambert, June 17, 2005, PSC; Joseph C. Brooks, Telephone Conversation with Lambert, June 10, 2005; Billy J. Scott, "Notes on Arnetta Brooks," PSP.

[5] Joseph C. Brooks, Email to Lambert, June 10, 2005, PSC; Joseph C. Brooks, Email to Lambert, June 17, 2005, PSC; Joseph C. Brooks, Telephone Conversation with Lambert, June 10, 2005; Billy J. Scott, "Notes on Arnetta Brooks," PSP.

[6] Joseph C. Brooks, Email to Lambert, June 10, 2005, PSC; Joseph C. Brooks, Email to Lambert, June 17, 2005, PSC; Joseph C. Brooks, Telephone Conversation with Lambert, June 10, 2005; Billy J. Scott, "Notes on Arnetta Brooks," PSP; Elizabeth Arnetta Brooks-O'Neal, Email to Lambert, August 1, 2005.

[7] Billy J. Scott, "Notes on Arnetta Brooks"; Joseph C. Brooks, Email to Lambert, June 17, 2005, PSC.

[8] Art and Bob Williamson, Interview with Lambert.

[9] Art and Bob Williamson, Interview with Lambert; Scott, "Personal Journal."

[10] Art and Bob Williamson, Interview with Lambert.

[11] Ibid.

[12] Ibid.

[13] Ibid.

[14] Ibid.

[15] Ibid.

[16] Ibid.

[17] Ibid.; *Chickasaw Times*, "Obituary for Opaletta Carter Williamson," February/March, 1992, 19.

[18] Pearl Scott, Interview with Lambert, February 23, 2005.

[19] Anoatubby, Interview with Lambert; Pearl Scott, Interview with Lambert, February 23, 2005; Green, "Political History," Part V, Chapter 3, 19.

[20] Billy J. Scott, Email to Lambert, June 10, 2005, PSC.

[21] Cody Bannister, "Marlow Pilot Headed to NASA," *Duncan Banner*, October, 26, 1989, Newspaper Clipping, PSP; Unidentified Newspaper Clipping, "Mrs. Scott to Attend Wiley Post Anniversary," PSP.

[22] Scott, "Memories of Marlow," May 17, 1990, May 24, 1990, June 7, 1990, and June 21, 1990.

[23] Pearl Scott, Letter to Unknown Recepient, June 9, 1990, PSP.

[24] Ibid.

[25] Mitch Meador, "Marlow Celebration Ends with a Bang," *Lawton Constitution*, July 5, 1990, 5A.; *Duncan Banner,* "Homecoming Royalty," July 3, 1990, Newspaper Clipping, PSP.

▼▼▼

Endnotes

[26] Meador, "Marlow celebration."

[27] Ibid.

Chapter 12

[1] Marsha Miller, "Chickasaws Stage Walkout, Sessions Remain Deadlocked," *Ada Evening News*, May 17, 1991, 1.

[2] Ibid.

[3] *Chickasaw Times*, "Candidates for Pickens District – Seat 1," Election Issue, 1991, 6, 9.

[4] Ibid.; Childers, "Democracy in the Chickasaw Nation."

[5] Childes, "Democracy in the Chickasaw Nation"; *Chickasaw Times*, "Legislative Run-off Races," August/September, 1991, 2.

[6] *Marlow Review*, "Scott Wins Tribal Seat," Undated Newpaper Clipping, PSP.

[7] *Marlow Review*, "Marlow Indians Puzzled by Flap: Tomahawk Chop Axed," October 1991, Newspaper Clipping, PSP.

[8] "Official Minutes," October 1991.

[9] "Official Minutes," December 1991.

[10] Enoch Kelly Haney, Letter to Pearl Scott, March 16, 1992, PSP; *Marlow Review*, "Pearl Scott to be Honored," Undated Newspaper Clipping, PSP; *Chickasaw Times*, "Indian Women Tribal Officials Honored By State Senate." April 1992, 1.

[11] Official Minutes," September 1992.

[12] Pearl Scott, "Chickasaws Return to Historic Capitol," *Marlow Review*, October 15, 1992, 9B.

[13] *Marlow Review*, "Chickasaw Smoke Shop Opens" February 25, 2003, Newpaper Clipping, PSP; Glen Seeber, "Business Briefcase," *Duncan Banner*, February 28, 1993, Newspaper Clipping, PSP.

[14] Childers, Interview with Lambert.

[15] Elizabeth Arnetta Brooks-O'Neil, Email to Lambert, August 1, 2005, PSP.

[16] George Carter, Jr., Interview with Lambert; Childers, Interview with Lambert; Elizabeth Arnetta Brooks-O'Neil, Email to Lambert, August 1, 2005, PSC.

[17] Thurman Lowery, "Chickasaws Come to Marlow," *Marlow Review*, July 1, 1993, 12.

[18] *Marlow Review*, "FCE, Chickasaws help with Red Ribbon Week, October 18, 1993, 12.

[19] Green, "Political History," Part V, Chapter 7, 18.

[20] *Marlow Review*, "Chickasaw Van to Transport Ailing, Elderly, Youth," August 18, 1994, 8C.

[21] Ibid.

[22] *Chickasaw Times*, "Pickens District: Scott, Briggs Contest Seat 1," Election Issue, 1994, 4.

[23] Ibid.

[24] *Chickasaw Times*, "Tribal Election Results Announced," September 1994, 3.

[25] *Chickasaw Times*, "Legislative Report," October 1994, 2; Chickasaw Nation, Invitation to Appreciation Dinner for Pearl Scott, PSP; "Photo Caption," *Chickasaw Times*, October 1994, 6.

▼▼▼

[26] Anoatubby, Interview with Lambert; Harbour Whitaker, Interview with Paul F. Lambert, Marlow, Oklahoma, March 3, 2005, PSC.

[27] Ibid.; Childers, Interview with Lambert.

Chapter 13

[1] Anoatubby, Interview with Lambert.

[2] Scott, Interview with Harris.

[3] Kemper, Interview with Lambert.

[4] Ibid.; Bob Kemper, Email to Lambert, June 27, 2005, PSC.

[5] Kemper, Interview with Lambert.

[6] Ibid.

[7] Ibid.

[8] Ibid.; Kaye Arthur, "That Daring Young Woman in Her Flying Machine," *Marlow Review*, November 16, 1995, 12B.

[9] Chickasaw Nation, "Printed Program, Chickasaw Nation Second Annual Hall of Fame Banquet," PSP; Chickasaw Nation, "Invitation, Chickasaw Nation Second Annual Hall of Fame Banquet," PSP; *Marlow Review*, "Double Honors for Pearl Scott," October 26, 1995, 1, 3.

[10] *Marlow Review,* "Double Honors for Pearl Scott." Heidi Brandes, "Grandmother Still Flying High," *Duncan Banner*, Undated Newspaper Clipping, PSP; Arthur, "That Daring Young Woman in Her Flying Machine"; *Daily Oklahoman*, "Aviation Hall Sets Induction," Undated Newspaper Clipping, PSP.

[11] *Chickasaw Times*, "Chickasaw Nation Inducts Two into Hall of Fame," October 1995, Newspaper Clipping, PSP.

[12] Chickasaw Nation. "Printed Program, Chickasaw Nation Second Annual Hall of Fame Banquet," PSP.

[13] Oklahoma Aviation and Space Museum, "Printed Program, Oklahoma Aviation and Space Hall of Fame and Clarence E. Page Awards," November 2, 1995, PSP; Arthur, "That Daring Young Woman in her Flying Machine."

[14] Arthur, "That Daring Young Woman in Her Flying Machine"; Billy J. Scott, Email to Lambert, August 5, 2005, PSP.

[15] Kemper, Interview with Lambert.

[16] Ibid.

[17] Ibid.; Scott and Thompson, Interview with Lambert.

[18] Arthur, "That Daring Young Woman in Her Flying Machine."

[19] *Marlow Times*, "Thank You," Undated Press Clipping. PSP.

[20] Kaye Arthur, "Pearl Given Unique Birthday Gift," *Marlow Review*, February 15, 1996, 4B.

[21] Ibid.

[22] Ibid.

Chapter 14

[1] Scott, Interview with Harris; Scott and Thompson, Interview with Lambert; Gary Childers, Email to Lambert, August 8, 2005, PSC.

[2] Lambert, Interview with Billy J. Scott; Elizabeth Arnetta Brooks-O'Neil, Email to Lambert, August 1, 2005, PSC.

[3] *Marlow Review*, "Pioneer Aviatrix—Pearl Carter-Scott," July 2, 1998, 6B.

[4] Ibid; *Marlow Review*, "Oklahoma Today Honor Aviators," July 16, 1998, 12.

[5] *Lawton Constitution*, "Pioneer Aviatrix Flew with Post," July 28, 1998, 1B.

[6] Wiley Post Commission, "Wiley Post Centennial Celebration Invitation," PSP.

[7] Abigail A. Cassell, Letter to Melissa Colvin, January 14, 1999, PSP; Cheryl M. Neal, Letter to Pearl Scott, no date, PSP; Certificate of Authenticity for Wiley Post Centennial Celebration decal, PSP; Sheilla J. Robinson ,"NASA Honors Marlow Aviatrix," *Duncan Banner*, Undated Newspaper Clipping, PSP.

[8] Scott, Interview with Harris.

[9] Ibid.

[10] Chickasaw Nation, "Printed Program, 'Pearl . . . a docu-drama highlighting Pearl Carter Scott's extraordinary life' . . .," Murray State College, September 30, 1999, PSP; Sheila Jackson, "Docudrama Honors Life of Scott," *Duncan Banner*, September 6, 1999, 1; *Marlow Review*, "Marlow's Pearl is a Chickasaw Gem," September 9, 1999, 2B.

[11] Sheila Jackson, "Docudrama honors life of Scott"; *Marlow Review*, "Marlow's Pearl is a Chickasaw Gem"; Chickasaw Nation Press Office, "The 1999 Chickasaw Festival and Annual Meeting Parade Names Pearl Scott As Grand Marshall," Press Release, September 10, 1992, PSP.

[12] Sheila J. Robinson, "Blindness no obstacle for George W. Carter," *Duncan Banner*, January 2002, PSP; Sheila J. Robinson, "Post Helped Teach Youngest Pilot to Fly," *Duncan Banner*, January 2, 2002, PSP.

[13] *Marlow Review*, "Marlow's Own Air Ambassador Meets Russian Space Experts," October 26, 2000, 8B; East Central State University, "Printed Program, Reception for Russian Cosmonauts," PSP.

[14] Mac Bentley, "Breathing Difficulties Ground Marlow Aviator," *Daily Oklahoman,* Undated Newspaper Clipping, PSP.

[15] Ibid.

[16] Oklahoma House of Representatives, The State of Oklahoma, "Citation Honoring Eula Pearl Scott," February 11, 2002, PSP; Ray McCarter, "Recollection of Honoring Pearl Carter," PSP.

[17] McCarter, "Recollection of Honoring Pearl Carter"; Dusk Monetathchi, "Chickasaw aviatrix honored by Oklahoma legislature," *Chickasaw Times*, March 2002, 1.

[18] McCarter, "Recollection of Honoring Pearl Carter"; Ray McCarter, Letter to Pearl Scott, February 11, 2002, PSP.

[19] Photograph in PSP with note by Pearl on reverse.

[20] Arthur, "Fitting Tribute."

[21] Ibid.

[22] Ibid.

[23] Ibid.

[24] "Scott remembers Wiley Post," *Oologah Lake Leader*, August 8, 2002, 3; *Claremore Progress*, "Wiley Student Coming Aug. 15," Undated Newspaper Clipping, PSP.

[25] Crew of STS-113, NASA, Letter to Pearl Scott, August 12, 2002, PSP.

[26] Mort Karman, "Out to Launch," *Duncan Banner*, November 2, 2002, 1A; Biographical Data Sheet for John Bennett Herrington, NASA, PSP.

[27] "A Tribe's Pride," *Duncan Banner*, November 10, 2002, 5A.

[28] Gary Childers, Email to Lambert, July 26, 2005, PSC.

[29] *Marlow Review*, "Spark Spurs Pioneer Aviatrix, Astronaut," December 5, 2002, 5B.

[30] Ibid.

[31] Ibid.; *Chickasaw Times*, "Chickasaws Celebrate Mission of Chickasaw Astronaut," December 2002, 3.

[32] *Marlow Review*; "Spark Spurs Pioneer Aviatrix, Astronaut," *Chickasaw Times*, "Chickasaws Celebrate Mission of Chickasaw Astronaut," December 2002, P. 3.

[33] *Marlow Review*, "Spark Spurs Pioneer Aviatrix, Astronaut,"; *Chickasaw Times*, "Chickasaws Celebrate Mission of Chickasaw Astronaut."

[34] *Marlow Review*, "Spark Spurs Pioneer Aviatrix, Astronaut,"; *Chickasaw Times*, "Chickasaws Celebrate Mission of Chickasaw Astronaut."

[35] *Marlow Review*, "Spark Spurs Pioneer Aviatrix, Astronaut,"; *Chickasaw Times*, "Chickasaws Celebrate Mission of Chickasaw Astronaut."

[36] *Marlow Review*, "Spark Spurs Pioneer Aviatrix, Astronaut,";

[37] Ibid.

[38] Ibid.

[39] Ibid.; *Chickasaw Times*, "Chickasaws Celebrate Mission of Chickasaw Astronaut."

[40] *Marlow Review*, "Spark Spurs Pioneer Aviatrix, Astronaut,"; *Chickasaw Times*, "Chickasaws Celebrate Mission of Chickasaw Astronaut."

Chapter 15

[1] Bill Scott, Email to Lambert, August 5, 2005, PSC; Rabb, Interview with Lambert.

[2] *Marlow Review*, "Marlow a hit with film producer," June 5, 2003, 3.

[3] Ibid.; *Marlow Review*, "Country Roots returns to Marlow," August 7, 2003, 4.

[4] Gary Childers, Email to Lambert, July 26, 2005, PSC.

[5] Bob Kemper, Interview with Lambert.

[6] *Marlow Review*, "Pearl Scott Recognized," December 25, 2003, Newspaper Clipping, PSP; Kennedy Space Center, "Remember the Journey: Strengthen the Circle," Printed Program, November 6, 2003, PSP.

[7] *Marlow Review*, "Pearl Scott Recognized,"; Kennedy Space Center, "Remember the Journey."

[8] Gary Childers, Email to Lambert, July 26, 2005, PSC.

[9] Ibid.

[10] Childers, Interview with Lambert.

Endnotes

[11] Pat Reeder, "Record Crowd Participates in Will Rogers Ranch Fly-in," www.willrogers.com/new/articles/august/wrap/wrap/html; Pat Reeder, Email to Lambert, July 26, 2005, PSP.

[12] Thompson, Scott, and Scott, Interview with Lambert, February 1, 2005

[13] Ibid.

[14] Ibid.

[15] Ibid.

[16] Paul Lambert, Conversation with Mike and Martha Larsen, Oklahoma City, Oklahoma, August 25, 2005; Martha Larsen, "Wiley, My Daddy and Me," Unpublished brief description of the Larsens' experience with Pearl.

[17] Pearl Scott, Interview with Lambert, February 23, 2005.

[18] Roy Deering, "Love for Flying Helped Women Make History," *Daily Oklahoman*, March 31, 2005, 9A; Dr. Nazih Zuhdi, Conversation with Paul F. Lambert, Oklahoma City, Oklahoma, August 17, 2005; Shirley deJarnette, Interview with Paul F. Lambert, Oklahoma City, Oklahoma, September 22, 2005, PSC.

[19] deJarnette, Interview with Lambert.

[20] Ibid.

[21] Katheryn Eckles, "My Humble Prayer," hand printed copy by Pearl Scott, PSP.

[22] Callaway-Smith-Cobb Funeral Home, "In loving memory of Eula Pearl (Carter) Scott," Printed program for funeral of Pearl Scott, April 1, 2005, PSC; Pearl Scott, Interview with Lambert, February 23, 2005.

[23] *Chickasaw Times*, "Chickasaw, Aviation Pioneer Pearl Scott Dies in Marlow," April 2005, 1.

[24] *Chickasaw Times*, "Obituary for Eula Pearl Scott," April 2005, 39.

[25] Gary Childers, Email to Lambert, August 1, 2005, PSC; Bill Scott, Conversation with Paul Lambert, August 18, 2005.

INDEX

▼▼▼

▼▼▼

Index